Robert Disch is Assistant Professor
of Humanities at Pratt Institute, Brooklyn, New York.
He has coedited several volumes of essays,
including *Hard Rains: Conflict and Conscience in America*,
and is a director and faculty member of
the Glenrock Community, a communal school
in Jeffersonville, Vermont.

THE ECOLOGICAL CONSCIENCE

Values for Survival

Edited by
Robert Disch

A SPECTRUM BOOK

Prentice-Hall, Inc.
Englewood Cliffs, N.J.

We gratefully acknowledge the permission
of Allen Ginsberg to reprint his poem,
"By Air: Albany—Baltimore,"
which first appeared in Look magazine,
November 4, 1969.

C–13–222828–9

P–13–222810–6

Library of Congress Catalog Card Number 71–130009

Current printing (last number): 10 9 8 7 6 5 4 3

Prentice-Hall International, Inc. (London)
Prentice-Hall of Australia, Pty. Ltd. (Sydney)
Prentice-Hall of Canada, Ltd. (Toronto)
Prentice-Hall of India Private Limited (New Delhi)
Prentice-Hall of Japan, Inc. (Tokyo)

contents

For Mother, Father, and Annie

ALLEN GINSBERG

By Air: Albany–Baltimore

To Poe

Albany   throned in snow
      Hudson ribboned North ice white flats
New England's blue sky horizon'd to Space
      Age eyes: Man rides the Map,
Earth balooned vast-bottomed . . .

It's winter, Poe, upstate New York Scythed
      into mental fields, flat arbors & hairy woods
      scattered in Pubic mounds twittering w/birds—
Nobody foresaw those wormpaths asphalted
      uphill crost bridges to small church towns, chill
      snowfields streaked with metal feces-dust.
Farmland whirlpooled into mechanic Apocalypse
      on Iron Tides!
Maelstrom roar of air-boats to Baltimore!
. . . . Wheels drop in Sunlight, over
      Vast building-hive roofs glittering,
New York's ice agleam
      in a dying world.
            Bump down to ground
Hare Krishna Preserver!

Philadelphia smoking in Gold Sunlight, pink blue
      green Cyanide tanks sitting on hell's floor,
many chimneys Smouldering, city flats virus-linked
      along Delaware bays under horizon-smog—
airplane drifting black vapor-filaments
      above Wilmington——The Iron habitations
      endless from Manhattan to the Capital.
Poe! D'jya prophesy this Smogland, this Inferno,
D'jya Dream Baltimore'd Be Seen From Heaven
by Man Poet's eyes Astounded in the Fire Haze, carbon
      Gas aghast!
Poe! D'jya know yr prophecies' *Red Death*
would pour thru Philly's sky like Sulfurous Dreams?

Walled into Amontillado's Basement! Man
    kind led weeping drunk into the Bomb
    Shelter by Mad Secretaries of Defense!

South! from the Bearded Sleeper's Wink
at History, Hudson polluted & Susquehanna
    Brown under bridges laced with factory smoke—
Proving Grounds by Chesapeake,
                    Ammunition & Artillery
Edgewood & Aberdeen
                    Chemical munitions factories
hid isolate in wooden gardens, Princesses
of Industry (like Movie stars hid private in Magic
    Nauseous Mansions in Old Hollywood)—
Poe! Frankenstein! Shelley thy Prophesy,
What Demiurge assembles Matter-Factories
    to blast the Cacodemonic Planet-Mirror apart
Split atoms & Polarize Consciousness &
    let th'eternal Void leak thru the Pentagon
& cover White House with Eternal Vacuum-Dust!
Bethlehem's miles of Christ-birth Man-apocalypse
    Mechano-movie Refinery along Atlantic,
Shit-brown haze worse & worse over Baltimore
    where Poe's world came to end—Red smoke,
Black water, grey sulphur clouds over Sparrows Point,
    Oceanside flowing with rust, scum tide
        boiling shoreward—

Red white blue Yachts on Baltimore harbor,
    the plane bounds down above gas tanks,
gas stations, smokestacks flaring poison mist,
Superhighways razored through hairy woods,
Down to Earth Man City where Poe
    Died kidnapped by phantoms
    conspiring to win elections
        in the Deathly Gutter of the 19th Century.

THE ECOLOGICAL CONSCIENCE

preface

In selecting material for this collection I have been guided by a set of assumptions, conjectures, and personal opinions that have shaped the point of view of the book and contributed to its organization.

First, I have accepted the widespread belief on the part of many experts that man-made changes in the biosphere threaten the integrity of the life-support system essential for the survival of human life. Because of the massive evidence in favor of this assumption, I have not made a conscientious effort to inventory pollutants or to list the familiar doomsday predictions.

Second, I have made the less secure assumption that the international complexities of the environmental crisis together constitute the most serious problem facing mankind. While it may be reasonably argued that the threat of nuclear warfare, ideological conflict, revolutionary upheaval, or unrestrained militarism all present grave dangers to the survival of the world community, these problems are, at least in theory, within the conscious control of human decision-makers.

The environmental problem, on the other hand, is frequently invisible to the eye; it works slowly, silently, and undramatically; when diagnosed it often requires actions that are in conflict with deeply rooted social and religious values, life styles, and economic systems. In other words, the crisis is potentially lethal because it can only be met through levels of international cooperation unknown to world history.

In addition, the environmental crisis contains dangers other than physical extinction. Assuming that the problem is as serious as the experts insist it is, the political consequences could become as disastrous as the problem itself, especially if the industrialized nations fail to intervene before environmental catastrophe precipitates panic reactions and emergency measures. If the Western nations resort to such convenient methods as warfare, genocide, "acceptable" levels of chronic starvation in the Third World, rigid controls over breeding, mandatory sterilization or abortion, genetic manipulation (e.g. reducing the size of human beings so they will consume less; or genetically engineering populations of amiable robots), the cure will prove worse than the disease. Yet, every one of these "solutions" has either been used in the past, is operative in the present, or has been seriously proposed for the future. Already we see nightmare recommendations that read like passages from *Brave New World* or *1984*; already we have allowed a situation to develop in which 500,000,000 people exist in a state of chronic malnutrition, where 10,000 people starve to death each day, and where billions of dollars of energy and resources are consumed monthly for idiotic and socially useless military adventures.

These morbid possibilities lead to several conjectures about the conditions that will have to obtain if mankind is to avoid physical demise or political nightmare. The most important of these supposes that the industrialized nations will have to undergo a profound change in the values and attitudes they hold toward the nonhuman worlds. These new values, based upon the insights of ecology, must affect the policies and practices of science and technology, of politics and economics. Of crucial importance to human survival is that ecological insights and values be successfully integrated into the development and disposition of civilian and military technologies, regardless of the political and economic consequences for vested interest groups.

In order for the industrialized bourgeois nations to incorporate what Dr. Paul Sears has called the "subversive" insights of ecology, they will be required to make more than incremental adjustments in their social, political, and economic systems. The present structure of American institutions, in particular, cannot absorb the radical implications of ecological knowledge without accepting substantial changes, including the likelihood of governmental controls over the exploitation and allocation of resources, over methods of production and marketing, and over whatever other measures are necessary to the maintenance of an ecologically sound biosphere.

Finally, I have not included a detailed analysis of the ecological implications of population growth because I believe that the present threat to the life-support system demands changes in values, institutions, and societal goals regardless of further pressures brought about by larger populations. As the population increases there is—needless to say—every conceivable reason to expect that the associated environmental problems will intensify; but I believe that if the solutions to those problems are to preclude genocide, totalitarian politics, genetic manipulation, or massive starvation, they will of necessity include many of the ecological values and visions discussed by the contributors to this collection.

While the contents of this anthology were derived from the above considerations, the sequence of the chapters resulted more from editorial convenience than from any belief on my part that changes in values must necessarily precede changes in political and economic institutions, or that the widespread development of an ecological conscience is a prerequisite for a society to change its environmental policies. Nor do I wish to imply that the significance of the extreme views of Fuller, Watts, and Snyder is in any way contingent upon the realization of ecological values within the more tangible realms of politics and technology. As historical evidence endlessly proves, the changes in values that can alter or overthrow the political and economic institutions of a society are often profoundly affected by grandiose visions and utopian speculations. The vital spirit of ecology, in fact, is contained within the awareness of the interrelatedness of all things, including the mutual influences that values, actions, and visions exert on one another.

I

THE ECOLOGICAL CRISIS

Barry Commoner

the ecological facts of life

The ecological facts of life are grim. The survival of all living things—including man—depends on the integrity of the complex web of biological processes which comprise the earth's ecosystem. However, what man is now doing on the earth violates this fundamental requisite of human existence. For modern technologies act on the ecosystem which supports us in ways that threaten its stability; with tragic perversity we have linked much of our productive economy to precisely those features of technology which are ecologically destructive.

These powerful, deeply entrenched relationships have locked us into a self-destructive course. If we are to break out of this suicidal track we must begin by learning the ecological facts of life. If we are to find the road to survival we must discover how to mold the technology to the necessities of nature, and learn how these constraints must temper the economic and social demands on technology. This, I believe, is the momentous task which now confronts mankind . . . .

It is the purpose of this contribution to provide some factual background to the foregoing assertions.

The Origin of the Ecosystem

The global ecosystem in which we now live is the product of several billion years of evolutionary change in the composition of the planet's skin. Following a series of remarkable geochemical events, about two billion years ago there appeared a form of matter, composed of elements common on the earth's surface, but organized in a manner which set it sharply apart from its antecedents—life. Themselves the products of several billion years of slow geochemical processes, the first living things became, in turn, powerful agents of geochemical change.

Background paper prepared for the 13th National Conference of the U. S. National Commission for UNESCO, 1969. Reprinted with the permission of the U. S. National Commission for UNESCO.

To begin with, they depleted the earth's previously accumulated store of the organic products of geochemical evolution, for this was their food. Converting much of this food into carbon dioxide, the earth's early life forms sufficiently increased the carbon dioxide content of the planet's atmosphere to raise the average temperature—through the "greenhouse" effect—to tropical levels. Later there appeared the first photosynthetic organisms, which reconverted carbon dioxide into the organic substances that are essential to all living metabolism. The rapid proliferation of green plants in the tropical temperature of the early earth soon reduced the carbon dioxide concentration of the atmosphere, thereby lowering the earth's temperature and depositing a huge mass of organic carbon which became in time the store of fossil fuels. And with the photosynthetic cleavage of water, the earth for the first time acquired free oxygen in its atmosphere. By shielding the earth's surface from solar ultraviolet radiation (through the concurrent appearance of ozone), this event enabled life to emerge from the protection of an original underwater habitat. With free oxygen available new, more efficient forms of living metabolism became possible and the great evolutionary outburst of proliferating species of plants and animals began to populate the planet. Meanwhile terrestrial plants and microorganisms converted the earth's early rocks into soil and developed within it a remarkably complex ecosystem; a similar system developed in surface waters. Taken together, these ecosystems control the composition of the soil, of surface waters and the air, and consequently regulate the weather.

There is an important lesson here. In the form in which it first appeared, the earth's life system had an inherently fatal fault: The energy it required was derived from the destruction of a nonrenewable resource, the geochemical store of organic matter. The primeval life-system became capable of continued existence only when, in the course of evolution, organisms appeared that converted carbon dioxide and inorganic salts to new organic matter—thus closing the loop and transforming what was a fatally linear process into a circular, self-perpetuating one. Here in its primitive form we see the grand scheme which has since been the basis of the remarkable continuity of life: the reciprocal interdependence of one life process on another.

In the course of further evolution the variety of living things proliferated; new interactions became possible, greatly enriching the network of events. Cycles were built on cycles, forming at last a vast and intricate web, replete with branches, interconnections and alternate pathways; these are the bonds that link together the fate of all the numerous animals, plants, and microorganisms that inhabit the earth. This is the global ecosystem. It is a closed web of physical, chemical and biological processes created by living things, maintained by living things, and through the marvelous reciprocities of biological and geochemical evolution, uniquely essential to the support of living things.

The Basic Properties of the Ecosystem

We know enough about some parts of this vast system to delineate the fundamental properties of the whole. These properties define the requirements of any activity—including human society—which is to function successfully within the ecosystem of the earth.

Because they are fundamentally circular processes and subject to numerous feedback effects ecosystems exhibit nonlinear responses to changes in the intensity of any single factor. Consider, for example, the ecological processes which occur in surface waters, such as lakes and rivers. This is the cycle which links aquatic animals to their organic wastes; these wastes to the oxygen-requiring microorganisms that convert them into inorganic nitrate, phosphate and carbon dioxide; the inorganic nutrients to the algae which photosynthetically reconvert them into organic substances (thereby also adding to the oxygen content of the water and so providing support for the animals and the organisms of decay); and algal organic matter to the chain of animals which feed on it, thus completing the cycle.

Since it is a cyclical system with closed feedback loops, the kinetic properties of this ecosystem are strikingly nonlinear. If the load of organic waste imposed on the system becomes too great, the demand of the bacteria of decay for oxygen may exceed the limited oxygen content of the water. When the oxygen content falls to zero, the bacteria die, the biological cycle breaks down, and organic debris accumulates. A similar nonlinearity is observed in the growth of algae. If the nutrient level of the water becomes so great as to stimulate the rapid growth of algae, the dense algal population cannot be long sustained because of the intrinsic limitations of photosynthetic efficiency. As the thickness of the algal layer in the water increases, the light required for photosynthesis that can reach the lower parts of the algal layer becomes sharply diminished, so that any strong overgrowth of algae very quickly dies back, again releasing organic debris. These are relatively simple examples of the ubiquitous propensity of ecosystems for strongly nonlinear responses, for dramatic overgrowths and equally dramatic collapse.

Because the chemical events that occur in an ecosystem are driven by the metabolism of living things they are subject to the special constraints of biological chemistry. One important characteristic is that the rate of chemical reactions in living cells, being determined by the catalytic action of enzymes, is subject to the considerable specificity of enzymes for their substrates. Another feature is a consequence of the long course of evolutionary selection which has been at work in living things. Living cells are capable of carrying out an enormous variety of particular chemical reactions. What is remarkable, however, is that the number of different biochemical substances which are actually synthesized in living cells is *very much smaller* than the number of substances which could, in theory, be formed—given the types of reactions which can occur. Thus conditions suitable for the separate chemical reactions which give rise to both *dextro* and *levo* amino acids are present in cells —but because of the stereospecificity of the relevant enzyme system only the synthesis of the *levo* forms occurs at an appreciable rate. Because of similar constraints, cells produce many fatty acids with even-numbered carbon chain lengths, but no fatty acids with odd numbers of carbons. Similarly, organic compounds which contain *no* groups are singularly lacking in living things.

Thus, living systems have had a long opportunity to, so to speak, try out the enormous variety of biochemical reactions that *could* take place in the cell. In effect, the biochemical constituents now found in living cells represent the survivors of this evolutionary trial, presumably selected for their compatibility with the essential features of the overall system of cellular metabolism. This situation is analogous to the tendency of genes found in current organisms to be maximally advantageous—i.e., that nearly all mutations to alternative genes are lethal. Therefore in the same sense, we can expect that the entry into an ecosystem of an organic reagent not normally found in living systems is likely to have deleterious effects on some living organisms.

The feedback characteristics of ecosystems result in amplification and intensification processes of considerable magnitude. The fact that in food chains small organisms are eaten by bigger ones and the latter by still bigger ones inevitably results in the concentration of certain environmental constituents in the bodies of the largest organisms at the top of the food chain. Smaller organisms always exhibit much higher metabolic rates than larger ones, so that the amount of their food which is oxidized relative to the amount incorporated into the body of the organism is thereby greater. Consequently, an animal at the top of the food chain depends on the consumption of an enormously greater mass of the bodies of organisms lower down in the food chain. Therefore, any *non*-metabolized material present in the lower organisms of this chain will become concentrated in the body of the top one.

Because of the circularity of ecosystems and their complex branching patterns, the behavior of any given living member of the system is dependent on the behavior of many others. The specific relationships are varied: one organism may provide food for another; one organism may parasitize and kill another; two organisms may cooperate so closely in their livelihood as to become totally dependent on each other. As a result of such relationships, a change in the population of any one organism is likely to have powerful effects on other populations. Because of these numerous interconnections, a singular cause and effect relationship is rare. Instead a given intrusion on an ecosystem is likely to have effects which spread out in an ever-widening circle from its original source, affecting organisms and parts of the environment often very remote from the initial point of intrusion.

The stability of an ecosystem is achieved by a complex network of dynamic equilibria which permits alternative relationships to develop when any particular link in the network becomes inoperative. In a very simple form, this relationship is illustrated by a common farmyard practice. The farmer who wishes to maintain cats in order to control mice will provide for the cats an alternative source of food, in the form of a doorstep dish of milk. Otherwise, the cats might kill so many mice as to run out of food; they would then leave the farm in search of richer fields, if it were not for the milk on the doorstep. There is an increasing body of more sophisticated evidence to support the generalization that the stability of an ecosystem depends closely on its degree of complexity, on the fineness of the ecological web.

The cyclical processes of an ecosystem operate at an overall rate which is determined by the intricate coupling of the numerous separate events that constitute the whole. One result is that the ecosystem web has a kind of natural resonance frequency which may become evident in periodic fluctuation in a particular population of organisms—for example, seven-year locusts. Similarly, an ecosystem seems to be characterized by a specific "relaxation time"—that is, a rate at which it can successfully respond to an external intrusion by means of internal readjustment. Hence, we can expect the system to maintain its integrity only so long as external intrusions impinge on it at a rate which is compatible with the natural time-constant of the cycle as a whole. Thus, an environmental change—for example, in temperature—which develops slowly may permit organisms to adapt or to evolve adaptive forms, and the system as a whole can persist. In contrast, a rapid, cataclysmic environmental change, such as that which trapped the arctic mastodons in fields of ice, can override the system's natural rate of adaptation and destroy it.

Human Intrusions on the Ecosystem

This brief summary gives us a working knowledge of the system that constitutes the environment—a system generated by the evolution of the vast variety of living things on the earth. But among these living things is man, an organism which has learned how to manipulate natural forces with intensities that go far beyond those attainable by any other living thing. For example, human beings expend in bodily energy roughly 1,000 kilowatt hours per year. However, in a highly developed country such as the United States the actual expenditure of energy per capita is between 10,000 and 15,000 kilowatt hours per year. This extension of the impact of human beings on the ecosphere is, of course, a consequence of technology. Prehistoric man withdrew from the atmosphere only the oxygen required for respiration but technological man consumes a far greater amount of oxygen to support fires, power plants and chemical processes. The carbon dioxide produced by technological processes has measurably altered the carbon dioxide concentration of the atmosphere. Technology has had effects on the ecosystem which approach the magnitude of the natural processes themselves. Technology has also introduced into the environment substances wholly new to it such as synthetic pesticides, plastics and man-made radioisotopes.

What we mean by environmental deterioration is the untoward effect of human activities, especially technology, on the quality of the environment and on the stability of the ecological processes which maintain it. Given the previous list of ecosystem properties it is illuminating to determine the degree to which our major technological activities are consistent with them. Such an inquiry reveals that much of our technology is, in its very success as a productive enterprise, a grave threat to the stability of the ecosystem. Some examples follow.

Sewage treatment technology. One of our best developed technologies is sewage treatment, a technique intended to convert the noxious organic materials of human wastes into innocuous materials that could be assimilated into the aquatic ecosystem. This technology reflects an excellent understanding of *part* of the aquatic cycle: that given sufficient oxygen, aquatic microorganisms can convert organic matter to innocuous inorganic products which are readily carried off in surface waters. By domesticating such microorganisms in artificially aerated sewage plants we can indeed convert nearly all of the organic matter of sewage into inorganic products and discharge them to rivers and lakes.

So far, so good; the fatal stress of an overburden of organic matter on the stability of the aquatic cycle is avoided. But given the circularity of the process, it is evident that now a new stress must appear, this time the impact of excessive inorganic nutrients on the growth of algae. And given the nonlinearity involved in the growth of dense algal populations we ought to expect trouble at this point. And indeed the trouble has come—but it has been largely unexpected. Only in the last decade, when the effects of algal overgrowths had already largely destroyed the self-purifying capability of an ecosystem as massive as Lake Erie was the phenomenon recognized as a serious limitation on the technology of sewage treatment. In effect, the modern system of sewage technology has failed in its stated aim of reducing the organic oxygen demand on surface waters because it did not take into account the circularity of the ecological system on which it intruded. Because of this circularity the inorganic products of sewage treatment were themselves reconverted to organic nutrients by the algae, which on their death simply reimposed the oxygen demand that the treatment was supposed to remove on the lakes and rivers. This failure can be attributed, therefore, to a simple violation of a fundamental principle of ecology. The price that we pay for this defect is the nearly catastrophic pollution of our surface waters.

The nitrogen cycle. One of the great fundamental cycles in the ecosystem is that traversed by the element nitrogen. In this cycle the vast store of the element in the nitrogen gas of the air is converted to the organic materials of the soil and water; the latter is in turn transformed ultimately to nitrate, which is in turn the source of organic forms of nitrogen in plants and in the animals that feed on them. Finally, such organic matter is returned to the soil as waste, completing the cycle. The nitrogen cycle of the soil is of enormous importance in agricultural technology, being the basis for the yields of protein and other nitrogenous foods which it produces.

In natural soils nitrates are produced slowly in the soil by the action of microorganisms on humus. Once free in the soil, nitrate is quickly taken up by plant roots and converted to proteins. Most plants ordinarily contain little free nitrate and in an efficient natural soil system nitrate production and removal are so dynamically balanced as to keep the nitrate level of the soil relatively low as well. As a result little of it leaches into surface waters, so that the concentration of nitrate in surface waters is ordinarily only of the order of a few parts per million.

In the United States, as in most advanced countries, the nitrogen cycle has been subjected to major changes arising from new agricultural technology. One important change has been the development of a break in the physical continuity of the nitrogen cycle, especially in the Midwest. Originally, in the Midwest cattle were raised and fattened largely by grazing in pastures, from which they acquired their nutrition and to which they contributed organic wastes which maintained the natural fertility of the soil. As indicated earlier, in such a natural system the nitrogen cycle in the soil operates with low levels of soil nitrate, so that relatively little of the latter leaches into surface waters.

However, in recent years, a major change has taken place: most cattle are removed from the pasture for a considerable period of fattening in confined feedlots. Here, feed is brought to the animals and their wastes become heavily deposited in a local area. The natural rate of conversion of organic waste to humus is limited, so that in a feedlot most of the nitrogenous waste is converted to soluble forms (ammonia and nitrate). This material is rapidly evaporated or leached into ground water beneath the soil, or may run directly into surface waters during rainstorms. This is responsible, in part, for the appearance of high nitrate levels in some rural wells supplied by ground water, and for serious pollution problems due to eutrophication in a number of streams in the Midwest. Where feedlot manure is allowed to reach surface water untreated it imposes a heavy oxygen demand on streams already overloaded by municipal wastes.

A livestock animal produces much more waste than a human being, and the total waste produced by domestic animals in the United States is about ten times that produced by the human population. Much of this waste production is confined to feedlots. For example, in 1966 more than ten million cattle were maintained in feedlots before slaughter, an increase of 66 percent over the preceding eight years. This represents about one-half of the total United States cattle population. Because of the development of feedlot techniques, the United States is confronted with a huge waste disposal problem—which is considerably greater than the human sewage which we are attempting to handle with grossly inadequate treatment.

The physical separation of livestock from the soil is related to an even more complex chain of events, which again leads to severe ecological problems. When, as it has in much of the Midwest, the soil is used for intensive grain production rather than pasturage, the humus content is depleted; generally such soils now contain about one-half the humus present before intensive agriculture was introduced (e.g., ca. 1880). In order to maintain and increase crop productivity, farmers have resorted to increasingly heavy applications of inorganic fertilizer, especially of nitrogen. Since 1945 the annual use of inorganic nitrogen fertilizer in the United States has increased about 14-fold. This has yielded an appreciable increase in crop productivity. However, in a humus-depleted soil, porosity is reduced; as a result plant roots are not adequately aerated and their efficiency in withdrawing nutrient salts from the soil is diminished. In these conditions, the crop may be well nourished by using inorganic fertilizer to maintain a high nitrate level around the roots. However, since efficiency of nutrient uptake is low, a good deal of the nitrate is not taken up by the crop, but leaches into ground water or drains from the fields into lakes and streams. Where streams traverse heavily fertilized farmlands, for example in Illinois, nitrate concentrations in excess of the levels which lead to algal overgrowths have been observed consistently in recent years. Nearly all the streams in Illinois are now polluted by algal overgrowths. When such streams are the source of municipal water supplies—as they are in some Illinois towns —there is a risk of infant methemoglobinemia, due to the conversion of excess nitrate to nitrite in the infant's digestive tract.

We see in the impact of modern agricultural technology on the nitrogen cycle gross violations of a number of basic ecological principles. Feedlot practice breaks the physical continuity of the cycle, transferring organic wastes from large soil areas, where they can be accommodated into the natural cycle, to confined places, or surface waters. Here the heavy, rapid influx of organic matter or if its inorganic degradation products stresses the natural system beyond its capacity to accommodate, and the cycle breaks down, destroying the self-purifying capacity of surface waters and intruding nitrates in toxic amounts into livestock and man. Reflected in this situation is the propensity for the multiplication and spread of ecological perturbations, and the inability of an ecosystem to accommodate a stress which is imposed at a rate which exceeds the system's natural rate of response.

The most serious long-term effect of modern agricultural technology on the nitrogen cycle may be due to its effects on the natural complexity —and therefore stability—of the soil ecosystem. For example, modern agricultural systems have increasingly reduced the use of legumes which, with their associated bacteria, are capable of restoring the organic nitrogen content of the soil through fixation of nitrogen taken from the air. Recent studies, especially of tropical areas, suggest strongly that microbial nitrogen fixation is far more important in maintaining the nitrogen cycle than believed previously. There appear to be numerous bacteria, not only in legumes, but widely associated with many different species of plants that are capable of rapid conversion of air nitrogen into useful soil materials. When this subject has been more fully investigated, it is likely to be found, I believe, that such widespread bacterial nitrogen fixation has been a major factor in maintaining the natural fertility of soil not only in the tropics but in temperate regions as well.

What is particularly alarming is that this natural process of nitrogen fixation is seriously disrupted by inorganic nitrogen fertilizers. It has been known for some time from laboratory experiments that when nitrogen-fixing bacteria are exposed to excessive amounts of nitrate, the process of nitrogen fixation stops. Under these conditions nitrogen-fixing bacteria may not survive, or if they do, may mutate to nonfixing forms. It is probable, therefore, that the widespread use of inorganic nitrogen fertilizer is depleting the natural population of microbial nitrogen-fixers, upon which we would have to rely considerably in any program to restore the natural efficiency of the soil. Here then is an instance in which a new technology—intensive use of inorganic nitrogen fertilizer—cuts important strands in the web of ecosystem processes, thereby impoverishing the structure of the system, laying it open to collapse under the continued stress of the technology, and diminishing the opportunities for recovery.

Synthetic detergents. The story of the nondegradable detergents introduced into the environment during the period 1945–65 is now well known, but the lessons are worth recording here. This technological failure was again the result of a lack of concern with one of the distinctive features of natural biological systems—that their chemical events are governed by the extreme catalytic specificity of enzymes. The nondegradability of these detergents was due to the failure of the enzymes in the bacteria of decay to break down the carbon-carbon bonds in the organic backbone of the detergents, a process which these bacteria readily carry out on natural hydrocarbon chains such as those of fatty acid soaps. The failure can be traced to the fact that the nondegradable detergents possessed a branched carbon skeleton, for it is quite characteristic of degradative enzymes to prefer unbranched chains over branched ones. For fifty years this specificity has been known to biologists and has, in fact, for a long time been employed in starch technology to produce highly branched residual dextrins from partial enzymatic degradation branched starches. Here again is the technological failure of a massive intrusion into the environment which resulted from a lack of concern with one of the fundamental principles of ecology—the extreme specificity of chemical events in natural biological systems.

The nondegradable detergents have now been largely replaced by straight-chain substances which are, therefore, accessible to the action of bacterial enzymes. But this change still fails to make modern detergent technology compatible with the demands of ecology, for the new detergents, like the old ones, contain considerable amounts of polyphosphate. The massive introduction of this material into the surface waters through municipal sewage (the phosphate released to surface waters from this source has increased about 27-fold since 1900) has sharply increased the nutrient available to algae and has, therefore, exacerbated the effect of sewage treatment technology on algal overgrowths. A good deal of the pollution due to algal overgrowths can be traced to phosphate imposed on surface waters by detergents in municipal wastes—again a failure to observe the ecological facts of life.

Insecticides. One important aspect of the biological capital on which agricultural productivity depends is the network of ecological relationships that relate insect pests to the plants on which they feed, and to the other insects and birds that, in turn, prey on the pests. These natural relations serve to keep pest populations in check. Pests which require a particular plant as food are kept in check by their ability to spread onto other plants; the other insects which parasitize and prey upon them exert important biological control over the pest population.

What has happened in attempts to control cotton pests—where the great bulk of synthetic insecticide is used in the United States—shows how we have broken down these natural relations and allowed the normal pest-regulating machinery to get out of hand. Here the massive use of the new insecticides has killed off some of the pests that once attacked cotton. But now the cotton plants are being attacked instead by new insects that were never previously known as pests of cotton. Moreover, the new pests are becoming increasingly resistant to insecticide, through the natural biological process of selection, in the course of inheritance, of resistant types. In the Texas cotton fields, for example, in 1963 it took fifty times as much DDT to control insect pests as it did in 1961. The tobacco budworm, which now attacks cotton, has been found to be nearly immune to methylparathion, the most powerful of the widely used modern insecticides.

In certain important cotton-growing areas the insecticides kill off insect predators and parasites, which are often more sensitive to the insecticide than the pest itself. The result: insecticide-induced outbreaks of pests. Finally, DDT affects liver enzymes which inactivate sex hormones; one result is that DDT causes abnormal shell formations in birds, which is the apparent cause of the sharp decline in the population of certain raptorial species.

If we continue to rely on such broad-spectrum insecticides recovery of the natural forms of control will become increasingly difficult. Where restoration of natural biological control has been successful, it has depended on a natural reservoir of insects which are predatory or parasitic toward the pests; if, through widespread dissemination of insecticides species that make up this natural reservoir are lost, biological control may be difficult to reestablish.

The ecological failures involved in the use of DDT and related insecticides are only too evident: The failure to anticipate that an unnatural substance such as DDT is likely to be incompatible with the evolution-tested system of cellular biochemistry; the failure to take into account the effect of food chains on the accumulation of DDT in the bodies of top carnivores, including man; the failure to appreciate the multiple relationships which regulate the population of a given insect; the failure to anticipate the nonlinear responses which cause massive insect outbreaks.

And again, this is an instance in which a new technology is destructive of the natural biological capital—the biological systems of control —upon which we must depend for stable agricultural productivity.

Some other examples. In further support of the generalization that we consistently fail to take into account basic ecosystem properties in our recent technological developments, certain other examples are worthy of brief note.

A long list of examples can be provided which show that the effects of amplification and biological interactions on substances newly introduced into the ecosphere have been ignored. Apart from the earlier example of DDT these include: the accumulation of iodine 131 in the thyroids of animals and human beings following dissemination of this radioisotope from nuclear explosions and, more recently, from peaceful operation of nuclear reactors; the appearance of toxic levels of mercury, applied to seeds in the form of mercurial fungicides, ultimately in the eggs of hens fed on the grain produced on the plants grown from such seeds. A particularly striking example of such a failure to take into account ecological amplification effects in technological considerations was reported recently by Tamplin, relative to radioactive wastes from nuclear reactors.[1] Starting from the radioactive materials, which according to AEC standards would be allowed to enter a typical river ecosystem during reactor operation, Tamplin has calculated the effects of amplification in the food chain. He shows that, following passage through the food chain, certain radioisotopes released into a river at allowable concentrations can become concentrated in fish at levels which exceed the maximum permissible concentrations if used as human food.

The multiple consequences of environmental intrusions have also been unanticipated by technological planners. Consider a proud example of modern technology, the Aswan High Dam on the Upper Nile River. The dam has already cut down the flow of nutrients to the Mediterranean, reducing the algal population and the productivity of the local fishing industry. At the same time the dam, and its attendant irrigation system, is likely to cause a catastrophic increase of snail-borne schistosomiasis in the Egyptian population. Another example of such "ecological backlash" is the unexpected effect of a campaign to control malaria in remote mountain villages in Sarawak, Malaysia. The insecticides not only killed mosquitoes, but also poisoned cockroaches as well; these were eaten by the village cats, which died. As a result, disease-bearing rodents—primarily controlled by the cats—invaded the villages and serious epidemics resulted. The natural balance was finally restored when the Royal Air Force organized a parachute drop of a force of fresh cats for the villages.

---

[1] [Arthur R. Tamplin, et al., *Prediction of the Maximum Dosage to Man from the Fallout of Nuclear Devices*, V. "Estimation of the Maximum Dose from Internal Emitters in Aquatic Food Supply," UCRL–50163 (Livermore: Lawrence Radiation Laboratory, 1968).]

The Economic Benefits and Ecological Hazards of Technology

The technologies which are responsible for the environmental problems cited above were designed for, and have in fact achieved, important benefits to human welfare: increased food production through the intensive use of inorganic nitrogen fertilizer, and through improved cattle-feeding techniques; improved control of harmful insects through the use of insecticide sprays; improved crop yields due to the use of mercurial fungicides. Most of our major new pollutants are similarly connected to technological benefits. Photochemical smog is a consequence of the development of the efficient and widely used, modern high-compression gasoline engine. Due to their elevated operating temperatures high-compression engines bring about the combination of nitrogen and oxygen in the air. And smog is the result of a complex chain of chemical events triggered by the release of nitrogen oxides. Similarly, nuclear reactors improve our power resources, but at the same time pollute the environment with man-made radioisotopes and with excessive heat.

These pollution problems arise, not out of some minor inadequacies in the new technologies, but because of the very success of these technologies in accomplishing their designed aims. A modern sewage treatment plant causes algal overgrowths and resultant pollution *because* it produces, as it is designed to do, so much plant nutrient in its effluent. Modern, highly concentrated, nitrogen fertilizers result in the drainage of nitrate pollutants into streams and lakes just *because* they succeed in the aim of raising the nutrient level of the soil. The modern high-compression gasoline engine contributes to smog and nitrate pollution *because* it successfully meets its design criterion—the development of a high level of power. Modern synthetic insecticides kill birds, fish, and useful insects just *because* they are successful in being absorbed by insects, and killing them, as they are intended to do.

Moreover, there are usually sound economic reasons for the specific technological design which leads to environmental deterioration. This is particularly evident in the case of the intensive use of inorganic nitrogen fertilizer. Since 1945 the cost of farm labor, land and machinery in the United States has risen about 50–60 percent; but in that time the cost of fertilizer has *declined* about 25 percent. Moreover, intensive use of fertilizer, especially of nitrogen, provides a quick return on the farmer's investment; a fertilizer investment made in the spring is quickly reflected in the return obtained from the crop in the fall. As a result intensive fertilizer use has become crucial to the farmer's economic success. Certain government policies have intensified this effect. For example, the establishment of the Land Bank system has encouraged farmers to grow more crop on less land. This can be accomplished by very intensive use of nitrogen fertilizer, which permits a marked increase in the number of crop plants grown per acre. Similarly, feedlot operations represent a more economically efficient use of agricultural investment than do purely grazing operations.

We can expect, therefore, that efforts to reduce such environmental hazards will compete with the benefits available from the technological process, at least in economic terms. Thus, a nuclear power plant *can* be built in such a way as to reduce the resultant radioactive or thermal pollution. But this increases the cost of plant construction, raises the price of power and reduces the plant's competitive position with respect to other types of power production. Similarly, it would be possible to reduce nitrate pollution from feedlots by requiring the installation of complete (i.e., including tertiary treatment) disposal systems for the resultant wastes, but this would reduce the economy of the feedlot operation, perhaps below that of old-fashioned pasture operation. Organic fertilizers could be reintroduced in place of inorganic nitrogen fertilizer, but since the latter are cheaper to obtain and to spread, crop production costs would rise.

Equally complex relationships encumber most of our major pollution problems. It is now apparent that urban pollution due to photochemical smog cannot be achieved without supplanting present individual use of gasoline-engine transport with electric-powered mass transit systems, or possibly by replacing them with steam-driven vehicles. The first of these actions would require a massive new economic burden on cities which are already unable to meet their social obligations; the second course would mean a serious disruption of one of the mainstays of our economy, the automobile industry. The construction of nuclear power plants is now governed by certain federal standards regarding allowable emission of radioactive wastes. These represent a distinct—if poorly evaluated—health hazard resulting, for example, from the accumulation of iodine 131 in the thyroid. If emission standards are made more rigorous, the added expense might render the nuclear power industry incapable of competing with fossil fuel power plants. This would severely curtail a major federally-financed technological program, and would clearly require a serious political decision.

There is an important generalization to be derived from these observations: Part of the social value of new technological processes—their productivity and economic efficiency—depends on the *avoidance* of a reckoning with the important social costs represented by the ecological hazards which they cause. In effect, the social utility of such new technology is delicately balanced on a scale which can be readily tipped by actions designed to prevent their hazards to the environment. Such a corrective action becomes, thereby, a trigger which can readily set off major economic, social and political sequelae.

In sum, environmental pollution is not to be regarded as an unfortunate, but incidental, by-product of the growth of population, the intensi-fication of production, or of technological progress. It is, rather, an intrinsic feature of the very technology which we have developed to enhance productivity. Our technology is enormously successful in pro-ducing material goods, but too often is disastrously incompatible with the natural environmental systems that support not only human life, but technology itself. Moreover, these technologies are now so massively embedded in our system of industrial and agricultural production that any effort to make them conform to the demands of the environment will involve serious economic dislocations. If, as I believe, environmental pollution is a sign of major incompatibilities between our system of productivity and the environmental system that supports it, then, if we are to survive we must successfully confront these economic obligations, however severe and challenging to our social concepts they may be.

II

THE ECOLOGICAL CONSCIENCE:
VALUES FOR SURVIVAL

The great irony of the environmental crisis is that the workings of natural phenomena—the ecological facts of life—in all their mysterious wonder, are utterly unconcerned with human illusions about man's place in the universe, his power over nature, his destiny, values, mystiques, and taboos. The failure to appreciate the distance encompassed by this ironic gap is one of the reasons that humanity is now approaching the brink of oblivion. If man is to survive this crisis he will do so by developing an ecological psyche, one that will allow him to bridge the gap between his illusions of separateness from and superiority over what he has come to think of as "nature," and to recoginze that he not only is tied to nature, but that he is nature.

An ecological conscience will have many functions to perform in helping mankind achieve a humane world. The obvious—and stupendous—tasks are (1) to place technology in ecological perspective before man is destroyed by the side effects of his own tools; (2) to permit the Western nations to make the sacrifices necessary to equalize the gross inequities between the industrialized and underdeveloped nations without wreaking havoc on the unique and irreplaceable cultural values of the Third World; and (3) to expose the foolishness of reliance on ecologically insane military machines.

Beyond these specific tasks mankind—especially Western mankind— will need the wisdom of ecology to recognize, comprehend, and purge the untenable discrepancies between viable ecosystems and postrenaissance ideas of Homo economicus. The most important of these sanctities involve private property, free enterprise, and gluttonous consumption of resources. The conscience of ecology must teach man that there is no natural right to exterminate a form of life; that one is not entitled to desecrate earth, air, water, or space merely because he happens to own, control, or occupy some portion of it; and that the fact of "legal-

17

ity" in a human court cannot remove ecological crimes from having planetary implications for all mankind.

The development of an ecological conscience will require an unflinching reassessment of past traditions and present practices, both of which are tainted by a blinding Western egocentricity, a mental state that confuses the destruction of the conditions necessary for life with the assertion that man has somehow "conquered nature."

Delusions of this sort are partially the result of historical and religious traditions that, with notable exceptions,[1] have not conceived of human life as an integral, functioning component of natural processes. The very keystone of Western religious belief, the myth of creation in Genesis, confers on man a status apart from the rest of the created world and portrays man as reflecting the image of the creator. Rather than placing human life within creation, Genesis I grants to man the right to dominance over creation, a logical outcome of his anthropomorphic ties to the godhead. According to Professor Lynn White, Jr., in the Judeo-Christian tradition God created the world "explicitly for man's benefit and rule: no item in the physical creation had any purpose save to serve man's purposes. And although man's body is made of clay, he is not simply part of nature: he is made in God's image." [2] Later, Christianity would incorporate Platonic concepts of the separation of the soul from the body, the spirit from the flesh, thus splitting already alienated man from the coherence of his own being.

The tradition of classical humanism, on the other hand, achieved greatness by dissecting the tragic consequences of spiritual blindness and human folly. Yet it too remained persistently indifferent to the consequences of environmental hubris. In Sophocles, for example, the plague on Thebes results from the choices Oedipus makes and not from environmental retribution following arrogance toward nature.

After the close of the Middle Ages when Renaissance humanism was reaching for ways to express its fascination with human power, Machiavelli—the first "modern" thinker—would utilize imagery of building "dykes and barriers" against natural fury. But the concepts that would become associated with the idea of "conquering nature" seldom accounted for the basic facts of ecological revenge: dykes disrupt ecosystems, dams choke rivers with silt, and human and cultural properties are placed in jeopardy when installed on flood plains. Expert in the moral dilemmas and concerns of humanity, the humanism of the West never brought the wisdom of ecology into the mainstream of its tradition.

[1] See Paul Shepard's article in this collection, "Ecology and Man—a Viewpoint."
[2] Lynn White, Jr., "The Historic Roots of Our Ecologic Crisis," *Science,* 155: 1203–7, 1967.

The modern era subsequently inherited religious and humanist concepts that established man's aloofness from nature and permitted a tradition of incongruity to develop between human techniques and the ecological facts of life. It is this tradition, Ian McHarg argues, that has left modern man "obdurately pre-Copernican," entitled to be described as a "planetary disease." Yet McHarg believes that an understanding of this tradition, in conjunction with an awareness that "nature includes an intrinsic value system," could lead to man undertaking a benevolent stewardship of the biosphere, while at last accepting his place in the "process" he is currently bent on destroying.

McHarg's ambivalence about the chances of the pre-Copernican mentality overcoming its historical biases to achieve the values and insights required for survival is amplified by Thomas Merton's sensitive analysis of the chronic American uneasiness toward the wilderness. Between the Puritans' need to hold their community together by seeing in the "wild places" a common enemy and the romantic idealization of the untrammeled, pristine forests imported from Europe in the nineteenth century resides the idea of the puritan/pioneer, whose identity was defined by the paradox that success in his mission meant the end of both the wilderness and the pioneer alike.

The contradictions inherent in the idea of the pioneer reveal the opposed impulses to "master" the continent at any price and for any reason and the opposite feelings of reverence for the wilderness and concern for what its loss would mean to the value of human life. The essayists, poets, naturalists, and artists who took the latter view—Thoreau, George Catlin, Perkins Marsh, Audubon, and John Muir, among others—taught in their different ways of the vital links between man and nature.[3]

In retrospect, there was never a doubt about how the issue would be resolved. In the absence of significant countervailing forces from religious, governmental, or legal institutions, the dynamics of unrestrained capitalism quickly established the victory of economic and cultural vandalism over the ethics of ecology. Before the end of the nineteenth century the native populations were decimated, much of their culture lost forever, the frontier closed, the buffalo all but exterminated, and the values of the naturalists buried under an avalanche of propaganda extolling the virtues of what was erroneously called "progress."

Yet as the essays of Aldo Leopold and Paul Shepard reveal, the insights that the nineteenth-century writers and artists had started to

---

[3] See Leo Marx, *The Machine in the Garden* (New York: Oxford University Press, 1964), for an excellent discussion of ambivalent and conflicting attitudes toward nature in American poetry and fiction.

define were recovered when the concerns of purely scientific ecology inevitably demanded the wider horizons of a "human" ecology, a true set of values for man in the cosmic order. As Paul Shepard indicates, the identity crisis in the Western societies is "not only a social but an ecological problem," a spiritual malaise which could be cured by a recovery of man's true place in the values, processes, and forms of the evolving worlds.

Ian L. McHarg

values, process, and form

It is my proposition that, to all practical purposes, Western man remains obdurately pre-Copernican, believing that he bestrides the earth round which the sun, the galaxy, and the very cosmos revolve. This delusion has fueled our ignorance in time past and is directly responsible for the prodigal destruction of nature and for the encapsulating burrows that are the dysgenic city.

We must see nature and man as an evolutionary process which responds to laws, which exhibits direction, and which is subject to the final test of survival. We must learn that nature includes an intrinsic value system in which the currency is energy and the inventory is matter and its cycles—the oceans and the hydrologic cycle, life-forms and their roles, the cooperative mechanisms which life has developed and, not least, their genetic potential. The measure of success in this process, in terms of the biosphere, is the accumulation of negentropy in physical systems and ecosystems, the evolution of apperception or consciousness, and the extension of symbioses—all of which might well be described as creation.

This can be pictured simply in a comparison between the early earth and the present planet. In the intervening billions of years the earth has been transformed and the major change has been in the increase of order. Think of the turbulence and violence of the early earth, racked by earthquakes and vulcanism, as it evolved toward equilibrium, and of the unrestrained movements of water, the dust storms of unstabilized soils, and the extreme alternations of climate unmodified by a green, meliorative vegetative cover. In this early world physical processes operated toward repose, but in the shallow bays there emerged life and a new kind of ordering was initiated. The atmosphere which

From The Fitness of Man's Environment (Washington, D. C.: The Smithsonian Institution Press, 1968), pp. 209–27. Copyright © 1968 by the Smithsonian Institution. Reprinted by permission of the publisher. Also available in a Harper & Row Torchbook edition.

could sustain life was not the least of the creations of life. Life elaborated in the seas and then colonized the earth, thus increasing the opportunities for life and for evolution. Plants and decomposers created the soils, anchored the surface of the earth, checked the movements of soil particles, modified water processes, meliorated the climate, and ordered the distribution of nutrients. Species evolved to occupy and create more habitats, more niches, each increase requiring new cooperative relationships between organisms—new roles, all of which were beneficial. In the earth's history can be seen the orderings which life has accomplished: the increase to life forms, habitats and roles, symbiotic relationships, and the dynamic equilibrium in the system—the total an increase in order. This is creation.

In the early earth, the sunlight which fell upon the planet equaled the degraded energy which was radiated from it. Since the beginning of plantlife, some of the sun's energy has been entrapped by photosynthesis and employed with matter to constitute the ordered beings of plants; thence, to the animals and decomposers, and all of the orderings which they have accomplished. This energy will surely be degraded, but the entrapped energy, with matter, is manifest in all life forms past and present, and in all of the orderings which they have accomplished. Thus, creation equals the energy which has been temporarily entrapped and used with matter to accomplish all of the ordering of physical, biological, and cultural evolution. This, physicists describe as negentropy, in contrast with the inevitable degradation of energy which is described as entropy.

By this we see the world as a creative process involving all matter and all life-forms in all time past and in the present. Thus, creation reveals two forms: first, the physical entrapment and ordering which is accomplished primarily by plants and by the simplest animals; and, second, apperception and the resulting ordering for which an increased capacity is observed as species rise in the phylogenetic scale. In this, man is seen to be especially endowed. This view of the world as a creative process involving all of its denizens, including man, in a cooperative enterprise, is foreign to the Western tradition that insists upon the exclusive divinity of man, his independent superiority, dominion, and license to subjugate the earth. It is this man in whose image was God made. This concept of nature as a creative, interacting process in which man is involved with all other life-forms is the ecological view. It is, I submit, the best approximation of the world that has been presented to us, and the indispensable approach to determining the role of man in the biosphere. It is indispensable also for investigation, not only of the adaptations which man accomplishes, but of their forms.

The place, the plants, the animals, and man, and the orderings which they have accomplished over time, are revealed in form. To understand this it is necessary to invoke all physical, biological, and cultural evolution. Form and process are indivisible aspects of a single phenomenon: being. Norbert Weiner described the world as consisting of "To Whom It May Concern" messages, but these are clothed in form. Process and fitness (which is the criterion of process) are revealed in form; form contains meaning. The artifact, tool, room, street, building, town or city, garden or region, can be examined in terms of process, manifest in form, which may be unfit, fit, or most fitting. The last of these, when made by man, is art.

The role of man is to understand nature, which is also to say man, and to intervene to enhance its creative processes. He is the prospective steward of the biosphere. The fruits of the anthropocentric view are in the improvement of the social environment, and great indeed are their values, but an encomium on social evolution is not my competence, and I leave the subject with the observation that, while Madison, Jefferson, Hamilton, and Washington might well take pride in many of our institutions, it is likely that they would recoil in horror from the face of the land of the free.

An indictment of the physical environment is too easy, for postindustrial cities are such squalid testimony to the bondage of toil and to the insensitivity of man, that the most casual examination of history reveals the modern city as a travesty of its antecedents and a denial of its role as the proudest testimony to peoples and their cultures. The city is no longer the preferred residence for the polite, the civilized, and the urbane, all of which say "city." They have fled to the illusion of the suburb, escaping the iridescent shills, neon vulgarity of the merchants, usurious slumlords, cynical polluters (household names for great corporations, not yet housebroken), crime, violence and corruption. Thus, the city is the home of the poor, who are chained to it, and the repository of dirty industry and the commuter's automobile. Give us your poor and oppressed, and we will give them Harlem and the Lower East Side, Bedford-Stuyvesant, the South Side of Chicago, and the North of Philadelphia—or, if they are very lucky, Levittown. Look at one of these habitats through the Cornell Medical School study of midtown Manhattan, where 20 percent of a sample population was found to be indistinguishable from the patients in mental institutions, and where a further 60 percent evidenced mental disease. Observe the environments of physical, mental, and social pathology. What of the countryside? Well, you may drive from the city and search for the rural landscape, but to do so you will follow the paths of those who preceded you, and many of them stayed to build. But those who did so *first* are now deeply embedded in the fabric of the city. So as you go you will transect the annular rings of the thwarted and disillusioned who are encapsulated in the city as nature endlessly eludes pursuit. You can tell when you have reached the edge of the rural scene for there are many emblems: the cadavers of old trees, piled in untidy heaps beside the magnificent machines for land despoliation, at the edge of the razed deserts; forests felled; marshes filled; farms obliterated; streams culverted; and the sweet rural scene transformed into the ticky-tacky vulgarity of the merchants' creed and expression. What of the continent? Well, Lake Erie is on the verge of becoming septic, New York suffers from water shortages as the Hudson flows foully past, and the Delaware is threatened by salt water intrusion. Smog, forest fires, and mud slides have become a way of life for Los Angeles. In San Francisco, the Bay is being filled and men build upon unconsolidated sediments, the most perilous foundations in this earthquake-prone area. DDT is in arctic ice and ocean deeps, radioactive wastes rest on the continental shelf, the Mississippi is engorged with five cubic miles of topsoil each year, the primeval forests are all but gone, flood and drought become increasingly common, the once-deep prairie soils are thinner now and we might as well recognize that itinerant investment farming is just another extractive industry.

This is the face of our Western inheritance—Judaism, Christianity, Humanism, and the Materialism which is better named Economic Determinism. The countryside, the last great cornucopia of the world's bounty, ravaged; and the city of man (God's Junkyard, or call it Bedlam) a vast demonstration of man's inhumanity to man, where existence, sustained by modern medicine and social legislation, is possible in spite of the physical environment. Yet we are the inheritors of enormous beauty, wealth, and variety. Our world is aching for the glorious cities of civilized and urbane men. Land and resources are abundant. We could build a thousand new cities in the most wonderful locations—on mountains and plains, on rocky ocean promontories, on desert and delta, by rivers and lakes, on islands and plateaus. It is within our compass to select the widest range of the most desirable lands and promulgate policies and regulations to ensure the realization of these cities, each in response to the nature of its site. We can manage the land for its health, productivity and beauty. All of these things are within the capacity of this people now. It is necessary to resolve to fulfill the American Revolution and to create the fair image that can be the land of the free and the home of the brave. But to resolve is not enough; it is also necessary that society at large understand nature as a process, having values, limiting factors, opportunities, and constraints; that creation and destruction are real; that there are criteria by which we can discern the direction and tests of evolution; and, finally, that there are formal implications revealed in the environment which affect the nature and form of human adaptations.

What inherited values have produced this plight, from which we must be released if the revolution is to be completed? Surely it is the very core of our tradition, the Judeo-Christian-Humanist view which is so unknowing of nature and of man, which has bred and sustained his simple-minded anthropocentrism and anthropomorphism. It is this obsolete view of man and nature which is the greatest impediment to our emancipation as managers of the countryside, city-builders, and artists. If it requires little effort to mobilize a sweeping indictment of the physical environment which is man's creation, it takes little more to identify the source of the value system which is the culprit. Whatever the origins, the text is quite clear in Judaism, was absorbed all but unchanged into Christianity, and was inflated in Humanism to become the implicit attitude of Western man to nature and the environment. Man is exclusively divine, all other creatures and things occupy lower and generally inconsequential status; man is given dominion over all creatures and things; he is enjoined to subdue the earth. Here is the best of all possible texts for him who would contemplate biocide, carelessly extirpate great realms of life, create Panama Canals, or dig Alaskan harbors with atomic demolition. Here is the appropriate injunction for the land rapist, the befouler of air and water, the uglifier, and the gratified bulldozer. Dominion and subjugation, or better call it conquest, are their creeds. It matters little that theologians point to the same source for a different text, and choose rather the image of man the steward who should dress the garden and keep it. It matters little that Buber and Heschel, Teilhard de Chardin, Weigel and Tillich retreat from the literality of the dominion and subjugation text, and insist that this is allegory. It remains the literal injunction which has been so warmly welcomed and enshrined at the core of the Western view. This environment was created by the man who believes that the cosmos is a pyramid erected to support man on its pinnacle, that reality exists only because man can perceive it, that God is made in the image of man, and that the world consists solely of a dialog between men. Surely this is an infantilism which is unendurable. It is a residue from a past of inconsequence when a few puny men cried of their supremacy to an unhearing and uncaring world. One longs for a psychiatrist who can assure man that his deep-seated cultural inferiority is no longer necessary or appropriate. He can now stand erect among the creatures and reveal his emancipation. His ancient vengeance and strident cries are a product of an earlier insignificance and are now obsolete. It is not really necessary to destroy nature in order to obtain God's favor or even his undivided attention. To this ancient view the past two centuries have added only materialism—an economic determinism which has merely sustained earlier views.

The face of the city and the land are the best testimony to the concept of conquest and exploitation—the merchants' creed. The Gross National Product is the proof of its success, money is its measure,

convenience is its cohort, the short term is its span, and the devil take
the hindmost is its morality. The economists, with some conspicuous
exceptions, have become the spokesmen for the merchants' creed and
in concert they ask with the most barefaced effrontery that we accommodate our values to theirs. Neither love nor compassion, health
nor beauty, dignity nor freedom, grace nor delight are true unless they
can be priced. If not, they are described as nonprice benefits and relegated to inconsequence, and the economic model proceeds towards
its self-fulfillment—which is to say more despoliation. The major criticism of this model is not that it is partial (which is conceded by its
strongest advocates), but more that the features which are excluded
are among the most important human values, and also the requirements for survival. If the ethics of society insist that it is man's bounden
duty to subdue the earth, then it is likely that he will obtain the tools
with which to accomplish this. If there is established a value system
based upon exploitation of the earth, then the essential components
for survival, health, and evolution are likely to be discounted, as they
are. It can then come as no surprise to us that the most scabrous slum
is more highly valued than the most beautiful landscape, that the most
loathsome roadside stand is more highly valued than the richest farmland, and that this society should more highly prize tomato stakes than
the primeval redwoods whence they come.

It is, in part, understandable why our economic value system is
completely blind to the realities of the biophysical world—why it ex-
cludes from consideration, not only the most important human aspirations, but even those processes which are indispensable for survival.
The origins of society and exchange began in an early world where man
was a trifling inconsequence in the face of an overwhelming nature. He
knew little of its operation. He bartered his surpluses of food and hides,
cattle, sheep and goats; and valued such scarcities as gold, silver, myrrh
and frankincense. In the intervening millennia the valuations attributed
to commodities have increased in range and precision and the understanding of the operation of this limited sphere has increased dra-
matically. Yet, we are still unable to identify and evaluate the processes
which are indispensable for survival. When you give money to a broker
to invest you do so on the understanding that this man understands a
process well enough to make the investment a productive one. Who
are the men to whom you entrust the responsibility for ensuring a
productive return on the world's investment? Surely, those who understand physical and biological processes realize that these are creative.
The man who views plants as the basis of negentropy in the world and
the base of the food chain, as the source of atmospheric oxygen, fossil
fuels and fibers, is a different man from one who values only economic
plants, or that man who considers them as decorative but irrelevant

aspects of life. The man who sees the sun as the source of life and the hydrologic cycle as its greatest work, is a different man from one who values sunlight in terms of a recreation industry, a portion of agricultural income, or from that man who can obscure sky and sunlight with air pollution, or who carelessly befouls water. The man who knows that the great recycling of matter, the return stroke in the world's cycles, is performed by the decomposer bacteria, views soils and water differently from the man who values a few bacteria in antibiotics, or he who is so unknowing of bacteria that he can blithely sterilize soils or make streams septic. That man who has no sense of the time which it has taken for the elaboration of life and symbiotic arrangements which have evolved, can carelessly extirpate creatures. That man who knows nothing of the value of the genetic pool, the greatest resource which we bring to the future, is not likely to fear radiation hazard or to value life. Clearly, it is illusory to expect the formulation of a precise value system which can include the relative value of sun, moon, stars, the changing seasons, physical processes, life-forms, their roles, their symbiotic relationships, or the genetic pool. Yet, without precise evaluation, it is apparent that there will be a profound difference in attitude—indeed, a profoundly different value system—between those who understand the history of evolution and the interacting processes of the biosphere, and those who do not.

The simpler people who were our ancestors (like primitive peoples today) did not subscribe to anthropocentric views, nor did the eighteenth-century English landscape tradition, which is the finest accomplishment of Western art in the environment, and which derives from a different hypothesis. The vernacular architecture in the Western tradition and the attitudes of the good farmer come from yet another source, one which has more consonance with the Orient than the West. But the views which ensured successes for the hunter and gatherer, for the vernacular farmer, and for the creation of a rich and beautiful pastoral landscape are inadequate to deal with twentieth-century problems of an inordinate population growth, accelerating technology, and transformation from a rural to an urban world. We need a general theory which encompasses physical, biological, and cultural evolution; which contains an intrinsic value system; which includes criteria of creativity and destruction and, not least, principles by which we can measure adaptations and their form. Surely, the minimum requirement for an attitude to nature and to man is that it approximate reality. Clearly, our traditional view does not. If one would know of these things, where else should one turn but to science. If one wishes to know of the phenomenal world, where better to ask than the natural sciences; if you would know of the interactions between organism and environment, then turn to the ecologist, for this is his competence. From the ecological view, one can conclude that by living one is united physically to the origins of life. If life originated from matter, then by living one is united with the primeval hydrogen. The earth has been the one home for all of its evolving processes and for all of its inhabitants; from hydrogen to man, it is only the bathing sunlight which changes. The planet contains our origins, our history, our milieu—it is our home. It is in this sense that ecology, derived from oikos, is the science of the home. Can we review physical and biological evolution to discern the character of these processes, their direction, the laws which obtain, the criteria for survival and success? If this can be done, there will also be revealed an intrinsic value system and the basis for form. This is the essential ingredient of an adequate view of the world: a value system which corresponds to the creative processes of the world and both a diagnostic and constructive view of human adaptations and their form.

The evolution of the world reveals movement from more to less random, from less to more structural, from simplicity to diversity, from few to many life-forms—in a word, toward greater negentropy. This can be seen in the evolution of the elements, the compounds, and of life. It is accomplished by physical processes, as in the early earth when matter liquefied and coalesced, forming the concentric cores of the planet. Vulcanism revealed the turbulence of early adaptations toward equilibrium. So, too, did the creation of the oceans. Evaporation and precipitation initiated the processes of erosion and sedimentation in which matter was physically sorted and ordered. When, from the aluminosilicate clays in the shallow bays, there emerged that novel organization, life, there developed a new agency for accomplishing ordering. The chloroplast of the plant was enabled to transmute sunlight into a higher ordering, sustaining all life. The atmosphere, originally hostile to life, was adapted by life to sustain and protect it, another form of ordering. The emergence of the decomposers, bacteria and fungi, permitted the wastes of life forms—and their substance after death—to be recycled and utilized by the living, the return stroke in the cycle of matter in the biosphere. The increasing number of organisms in the oceans and on land represent negentropy in their beings and in the ordering which they accomplish. We can now see the earth as a process by which the falling sunlight is destined for entropy, but is arrested and entrapped by physical processes and creatures, and reconstituted into higher and higher levels of order as evolution proceeds. Entropy is the law and demands its price, but while all energy is destined to become degraded, physical and biological systems move to higher order—from instability towards steady-state—in sum, to more negentropy. Evolution is thus a creative process in which all physical processes and life forms participate. Creation involves the raising of matter and energy from lower to higher levels of order. Retrogression and destruction consist of reduction from the higher levels of order to entropy.

As life can only be transmitted by life, then the spore, seed, egg, and sperm contain a record of the entire history of life. The journey was shared with the worms, the coelenterates, the sponges, and, later, with the cartilaginous and bony fishes. The reptilian line is ours, the common ancestor that we share with the birds. We left this path to assume mammalian form, live births, the placenta, and suckling of the young; the long period of infantile dependence marks us. From this branching line the monotremes, marsupials, edentates, and pangolins followed their paths, and we proceeded on the primate way. Tree shrew, lemur, tarsier and anthropoid, are our lineage. We are the line of man—the raised ape, the enlarged brain, the toolmaker—he of speech and symbols, conscious of the world and of himself. It is all written on the sperm and on the egg although the brain knows little of this journey. We have been through these stages in time past and the imprint of the journey is upon us. We can look at the world and see our kin; for we are united, by living, with all life, and are from the same origins. Life has proceeded from simple to complex, although the simplest forms have not been superseded, only augmented. It has proceeded from uniform to diverse, from few to many species. Life has revealed evolution as a progression from greater to lesser entropy. In the beginning was the atom of hydrogen with one electron. Matter evolved in the cosmic cauldrons, adding electron after electron, and terminating in the heaviest and most ephemeral of elements. Simple elements conjoined as compounds, thus reaching the most complex of these as amino acids, which is to say life. Life reached unicellular form and proceeded through tissue and organ to complex organisms. There were few species in the beginning and now they are myriad; there were few roles and now they are legion. There were once large populations of few species; now there is a biosphere consisting of multitudes of communities composed of innumerable interacting species. Evolution has revealed a progression from simple to complex, from uniform to diverse, from unicellular to multicelled, from few to many species, from few to many ecosystems, and the relations between these processes have also evolved toward increased complexity.

What holds the electrons to the nucleus? The molecules in rocks, air, and water may have ten atoms, but the organic molecule may have a thousand. Where is the catalytic enzyme which locks and unlocks the molecules? The single cell is very complex indeed; what orchestrates the cytoplasm and nucleus, nucleolus, mitochondria, chromosomes, centrosomes, Golgi elements, plastids, chromoplasts, leucoplasts and, not least, chloroplasts? The lichen shows an early symbiosis at the level of the organism as the alga and the fungus unite. The plant and the decomposer enter into symbiosis to utilize energy and matter, to employ the first and recycle the latter. The animal enters the cycle, consuming the plant, to be consumed by the decomposer and thence by the plant. Each creature must adapt to the others in that concession of autonomy toward the end of survival that is symbiosis. Thus parasite and host, predator and prey, and those creatures of mutual benefit develop symbioses to ensure survival. The world works through cooperative mechanisms in which the autonomy of the individual, be it cell, organ, organism, species, or community is qualified toward the survival and evolution of higher levels of order culminating in the biosphere. Now these symbiotic relationships are beneficial to the sum of organisms although clearly many of them are detrimental to individuals and species. While the prey is not pleased with the predator or the host far from enamored of the parasite or the pathogen, these are regulators of populations and the agents of death—that essential return phase in the cycle of matter, which fuels new life and evolution. Only in this sense can the predator, parasite, and pathogen be seen as important symbiotic agents, essential to the creative processes of life and evolution. If evolution has proceeded from simple to complex, this was accomplished through symbiosis. As the number of species increased, so then did the number of roles and the symbiotic arrangements between species. If stability increases as evolution proceeds, then this is the proof of increased symbiosis. If conservation of energy is essential to the diminution of entropy, then symbioses are essential to accomplish this. Perhaps it is symbiosis or, better, altruism that is the arrow of evolution.

This view of the world, creation, and evolution reveals as the principal actors, the sun, elements and compounds, the hydrologic cycle, the plant, decomposers, and the animals. Further, if the measure of creation is negentropy, then it is the smallest marine plants which perform the bulk of the world's work, which produce the oxygen of the atmosphere, the basis of the great food chains. On land it is the smallest herbs. Among the animals the same is true; it is the smallest of marine animals and the terrestrial herbivores which accomplish the greatest creative effort of raising the substance of plants to higher orders. Man has little creative role in this realm although his destructive potential is considerable. However, energy can as well be considered as information. The light which heats the body can inform the perceptive creature. When energy is so considered, then the apperception of information as meaning, and response to it, is also seen as ordering, as antientropic. Noise to the unperceptive organism, through perception becomes information from which is derived meaning. In an appraisal of the world's work of apperception, it is seen that the simpler organisms, which create the maximum negentropy, are low on the scale of apperception which increases as one rises on the evolutionary scale. Man, who had no perceptible role as a creator of negentropy, becomes prominent as a perceptive and conscious being. We have seen that the evolution from the unicellular to the multicellular organism involved symbiotic relationships. Hans Selye has described intercellular altruism as the cooperative mechanisms which make thirty billion, billion human cells into a single integrated organism. He also has described interpersonal altruism. Surely one must conclude that the entire biosphere exhibits altruism. In this sense, the life forms which now exist on earth, and the symbiotic roles which they have developed, constituted the highest ordering which life forms have yet been able to achieve. The human organism exists as a result of the symbiotic relationships in which cells assume different roles as blood, tissues, and organs, integrated as a single organism. So, too, can the biosphere be considered as a single superorganism in which the oceans and the atmosphere, all creatures, and communities play roles analogous to cells, tissues, and organs. That which integrates either the cell in the organism or the organism in the biosphere is a symbiotic relationship. In sum, these are beneficial. This then is the third measure, the third element, after order and complexity, of the value system: the concession of some part of the autonomy of the individual in a cooperative arrangement with other organisms which have equally qualified their individual freedom toward the end of survival and evolution. We can see this in the alga and fungus composing the lichen, in the complex relationships in the forest, and in the sea. Symbiosis is the indispensable value in the survival of life forms, ecosystems, and the entire biosphere. Man is superbly endowed to be that conscious creature who can perceive the phenomenal world, its operation, its direction, the roles of the creatures, and physical processes. Through his apperception, he is enabled to accomplish adaptations which are the symbioses of man-nature. This is the promise of his apperception and consciousness. This examination of evolution reveals direction in retrospect— that the earth and its denizens are involved in a creative process of which negentropy is the measure. It shows that creation does have attributes which include evolution toward complexity, diversity, stability (steady-state), increase in the number of species, and increase in symbiosis. Survival is the first test, creation is the next; and this may be accomplished by arresting energy, by apperception, or by symbiosis. This reveals an intrinsic value system with a currency: energy; an inventory which includes matter and its cycles, life forms and their roles, and cooperative mechanisms.

All of the processes which have been discussed reveal form; indeed, form and process are indivisible aspects of a single phenomenon. That which can be seen reveals process. Much of this need not be superficially visible; it may lie beneath the skin, below the level of vision, or only in invisible paths which bespeak the interactions of organisms. Yet, the place, the plants, animals, men, and their works, are revealed in form.

All of the criteria used to measure evolutionary success apply to form. Simplicity and uniformity reveal a primitive stage, while complexity and diversity are evidence of higher evolutionary forms: few elements or species as opposed to many, few interactions rather than the multitude of advanced systems. Yet, there is need for a synoptic term which can include the presence or absence of these attributes in form. For this, we can use "fitness" both in the sense that Henderson employs it, and also in Darwinian terms. Thus, the environment is fit, and can be made more fitting; the organism adapts to fit the environment. Lawrence Henderson speaks of the fitness of the environment for life in the preface to his book, *The Fitness of the Environment.*

> Darwinian fitness is compounded of a mutual relationship between the organism and the environment. Of this, fitness of environment is quite as essential a component of the fitness which arises in the process of organic evolution; and in fundamental characteristics the actual environment is the fittest possible abode for life.

Henderson supports his proposition by elaborating on the characteristics of carbon, hydrogen, oxygen, water, and carbolic acid, saying that "no other environment consisting of primary constituents, made up of other known elements, or lacking water and carbolic acid, could possess a like number of fit characteristics, or in any manner such great fitness to promote complexity, durability, and the active metabolism and the organic mechanism we call life." The environment is fit for life and all of the manifestations which it has taken, and does take. Conversely, the surviving and successful organism is fitted to the environment. Thus, we can use fitness as a criterion of the environment, organisms and their adaptations, as revealed in form. Form can reveal past processes and help to explain present realities. Mountains show their age and composition in their form; rivers demonstrate their age and reflect the physiography of their passage; the distribution and characteristics of soils are comprehensible in terms of historical geology, and climate and hydrology. The pattern and distribution of plants respond to environmental variables represented in the foregoing considerations, while animals respond to these and to the nature of the plant communities. Man is as responsive, but he is selective; the pattern and distribution of man is likely to be comprehensible in these same terms. The term "fitness" has a higher utility than art for the simple reason that it encompasses all things—inert and living, nonhuman, and those made by man—while art is limited to the last. Moreover, it offers a longer view and more evidence. Nature has been in the business of form since the beginning, and man is only one of its products. The fact that things and creatures exist is proof of their evolutionary fitness at the time, although among them there will be those more or less fit. There will be those which are unfit and will not persist, those are the misfits; then, those which are fit; and finally, the most fitting—all revealed in form. Form is also meaningful form. Through it, process and roles are revealed, but the revelation is limited by the capacity of the observer to perceive. Arctic differs from rain forest, tundra from ocean, forest from desert, plateau from delta; each is itself because. The platypus is different from seaweed, diatom from whale, monkey from man . . . because. Negro differs from Oriental, Eskimo from Caucasoid, Mongoloid from Australoid . . . because; and all of these are manifest in form. When process is understood, differentiation and form become comprehensible. Processes are dynamic, and so coastlines advance and recede as do ice sheets, lakes are in process of filling while others form, mountains succumb to erosion and others rise. The lake becomes marsh, the estuary a delta, the prairie becomes desert, the scrub turns into forest, a volcano creates an island, while continents sink. The observation of process, through form and the response, represents the evolution of information to meaning. If evolutionary success is revealed by the existence of creatures, then their fitness will be revealed in form; visible in organs, in organisms, and in communities of these. If this is so, then natural communities of plants and animals represent the most fitting adaptation to available environments. They are most fitting and will reveal this in form. Indeed, in the absence of man, these would be the inevitable expression. Thus, there is not only an appropriate ecosystem for any environment, and successional stages towards it, but such communities will reveal their fitness in their expression. This is a conclusion of enormous magnitude to those who are concerned with the land and its aspect: that there is a natural association of creatures for every environment. This could be called the intrinsic identity of the given form. If this is so, then there will be organs, organisms, and communities of special fitness, and these will, of course, be revealed in form. This might well be described as the ideal. The creation of adaptations which seek to be metaphysical symbols is, in essence, the concern with representing the ideal. Adaptation of the environment is accomplished by all physical processes and by all life. Yet, certain of these transformations are more visible than others, and some are analogous to those accomplished by man. The chambered nautilus, the bee, and the coral are all engaged in the business of using inert material to create adaptive environments. These reveal the individual, a society, or a population. Can the criteria of fitness be applied then to the artifact? We can accept that the stilt's legs, the flamingo's beak, and the mouth of the baleen whale are all splendid adaptations, and visibly so. It is no great leap to see the tennis serve, the left hook, and the jumping catch, as of the same realm as the impala's bound, the diving cormorant, or the leopard's lunge. Why then should we distinguish between the athletic gesture and the artifacts which are employed with them: the golf club, bat, glove, or tennis racquet? The instrument is only an extension of the limb. If this is so, then we can equally decide if the hammer and saw are fit, or the knife, fork and spoon. We can conclude that the tail-powered jet is more fit for the air than the clawing propellors. If we can examine tools, then we can as well examine the environments for activities: the dining room for dining, the bedroom for sleeping or for loving, the house, street, village, town, or city. Are they unfit, misfit, fit, or most fitting? It appears that any natural environment will have an appropriate expression of physical processes, revealed in physiography, hydrology, soils, plants, and animals. There should then be an appropriate morphology for man-site, and this should vary with environments. There will then be a fitting-for-man environment. One would expect that as the plants and animals vary profoundly from environment to environment, this should also apply to man. One would then expect to find distinct morphologies for man-nature in each of the major physiographic regions. The house, village, town, and city should vary from desert to delta, from mountain to plain. One would expect to find certain generic unity within these regions, but marked differentiation between them. If fitness is a synoptic measure of evolutionary success, what criteria can we use to measure it? We have seen that it must meet the simplicity-complexity, uniformity-diversity, instability-stability, independence-interdependence tests. Yet, in the view of Dr. Ruth Patrick, as demonstrated by her study of aquatic systems, these may all be subsumed under two terms: ill-health and health. A movement toward simplicity, uniformity, instability, and a low number of species characterizes disease. The opposites are evidence of health. This corresponds to common usage: ill-health is unfit; fitness and health are synonymous. Thus, if we would examine the works of man and his adaptations to the countryside, perhaps the most synoptic criteria are disease and health. We can conclude that that which sustains health represents a fitting between man and the environment. We would expect that this fitness be revealed in form. This criterion might well be the most useful to examine the city of man: wherein does pathology reside? What are its corollaries in the physical and social environment? What characterizes an environment of health? What are its institutions? What is its form? Know this, and we may be able to diagnose and prescribe with an assurance which is absent today.

What conclusions can one reach from this investigation? The first is that the greatest failure of Western society, and of the postindustrial period in particular, is the despoliation of the natural world and the inhibition of life which is represented by modern cities. It is apparent that this is the inevitable consequence of the values that have been our inheritance. It is clear, to me if to no one else, that these values have little correspondence to reality and perpetrate an enormous delusion as to the world, its work, the importance of the roles that are performed, and, not least, the potential role of man. In this delusion the economic model is conspicuously inadequate, excluding as it does the most important human aspirations and the realities of the biophysical world. The remedy requires that the understanding of this world which now reposes in the natural sciences be absorbed into the conscious value system of society, and that we learn of the evolutionary past and the roles played by physical processes and life-forms. We must learn of the criteria for creation and destruction, and of the attributes of both. We need to formulate an encompassing value system which corresponds to reality and which uses the absolute values of energy, matter, life-forms, cycles, roles, and symbioses.

We can observe that there seem to be three creative roles. The first is the arresting of energy in the form of negentropy, which offers little opportunity to man. Second, is apperception and the ordering which can be accomplished through consciousness and understanding. Third, is the creation of symbiotic arrangements for which man is superbly endowed. It can be seen that form is only a particular mode for examining process and the adaptations to the environment accomplished by process. Form can be the test used to determine processes as primitive or advanced, to ascertain if they are evolving or retrogressing. Fitness appears to have a great utility for measuring form: unfit, fit, or most fitting. When one considers the adaptations accomplished by man, they are seen to be amenable to this same criterion but, also, synoptically measurable in terms of health. Identify the environment of pathology; it is unfit, and will reveal this in form. Where is the environment of health— physical, mental, and social? This, too, should reveal its fitness in form. How can this knowledge be used to affect the quality of the environment? The first requirement is an ecological inventory in which physical processes and life-forms are identified and located within ecosystems, which consist of discrete but interacting natural processes. These data should then be interpreted as a value system with intrinsic values, offering both opportunities and constraints to human use, and implications for management and the forms of human adaptations.

The city should be subject to the same inventory and its physical, biological, and cultural processes should be measured in terms of fitness and unfitness, health and pathology. This should become the basis for the morphology of man-nature and man-city. We must abandon the self-mutilation which has been our way, reject the title of planetary disease which is so richly deserved, and abandon the value system of our inheritance which has so grossly misled us. We must see nature as process within which man exists, splendidly equipped to become the manager of the biosphere; and give form to that symbiosis which is his greatest role, man the world's steward.

Thomas Merton

the wild places

Man is a creature of ambiguity. His salvation and his sanity depend on his ability to harmonize the deep conflicts in his thought, his emotions, his personal mythology. Honesty and authenticity do not depend on complete freedom from contradictions—such freedom is impossible —but on recognizing our self-contradictions and not masking them with bad faith. The conflicts in individuals are not entirely of their own making. On the contrary, many of them are imposed, ready-made, by an ambivalent culture. This poses a very special problem, because he who accepts the ambiguities of his culture without protest and without criticism is rewarded with a sense of security and moral justification. A certain kind of unanimity satisfies our emotions and easily substitutes for truth. We are content to think like the others, and in order to protect our common psychic security we readily become blind to the contradictions—or even the lies—that we have all decided to accept as "plain truth."

One of the more familiar ambiguities in the American mind operates in our frontier mythology, which has grown in power in proportion as we have ceased to be a frontier or even a rural people. The pioneer, the frontier culture hero, is a product of the wilderness. But at the same time he is a destroyer of the wilderness. His success as pioneer depends on his ability to fight the wilderness and win. Victory consists in reducing the wilderness to something else, a farm, a village, a road, a canal, a railway, a mine, a factory, a city—and finally an urban nation. A recent study, *Wilderness and the American Mind*, by Roderick Nash[1] is an important addition to an already significant body of literature about this subject. It traces the evolution of the wilderness idea from the first Puritan settlers via Thoreau and Muir to the modern

Reprinted, by permission, from the July 1968 issue of The Center Magazine, *a publication of the Center for the Study of Democratic Institutions in Santa Barbara, California.*

[1] Yale University Press: 1967.

ecologists and preservationists—and to their opponents in big business and politics. The really crucial issues of the present moment in ecology are barely touched. The author is concerned with the wilderness idea and with the "irony of pioneering [which was] that success necessarily involved the destruction of the primitive setting that made the pioneer possible."

Mr. Nash does not develop the tragic implications of this inner contradiction, but he states them clearly enough for us to recognize their symptomatic importance. We all proclaim our love and respect for wild nature, and in the same breath we confess our firm attachment to values that inexorably demand the destruction of the last remnant of wilderness. But when people like Rachel Carson try to suggest that our capacity to poison the nature around us is some indication of a sickness in ourselves, we dismiss them as fanatics.

One of the interesting things about this ambivalence toward nature is that it is rooted in our Biblical, Judeo-Christian tradition. We might remark at once that it is neither genuinely Biblical nor Jewish nor Christian. Mr. Nash is perhaps a little one-sided in his analysis here. But a certain kind of Christian culture has clearly resulted in a Manichean hostility toward created nature. This, of course, we all know well enough. (The word "Manichean" has become a cliché of reproof like "Communist" or "racist.") But the very ones who use the cliché most may be the ones who are still unknowingly tainted, on a deep level, with what they condemn. I say on a deep level, an unconscious level. For there is a certain popular, superficial, and one-sided "Christian worldliness" that is, in its hidden implication, profoundly destructive of nature and of God's good creation" even while it claims to love and extol them.

The Puritans inherited a half-conscious bias against the realm of nature, and the Bible gave them plenty of texts that justified what Mr. Nash calls "a tradition of repugnance" for nature in the wild. In fact, they were able to regard the "hideous and desolate wilderness" of America as though it were filled with conscious malevolence against them. They hated it as a *person*, an extension of the Evil One, the Enemy opposed to the spread of the Kingdom of God. And the wild Indian who dwelt in the wilderness was also associated with evil. The wilderness itself was the domain of moral wickedness. It favored spontaneity—therefore sin. The groves (like those condemned in the Bible) suggested wanton and licentious rites to imaginations haunted by repressed drives. To fight the wilderness was not only necessary for physical survival, it was above all a moral and Christian imperative. Victory over the wilderness was an ascetic triumph over the forces of impulse and of lawless appetite. How could one be content to leave any part of nature just as it was, since nature was "fallen" and "corrupt"? The elementary Christian duty of the Puritan settler was to combat, reduce, destroy, and transform the wilderness. This was "God's work." The Puritan, and after him the pioneer, had an opportunity to prove his worth—or indeed his salvation and election—by the single-minded zeal with which he carried on this obsessive crusade against wildness. His reward was prosperity, real estate, money, and ultimately the peaceful "order" of civil and urban life. In a seventeenth-century Puritan book with an intriguing title, *Johnson's Wonder Working Providence*— ("The Great Society"?)—we read that it was Jesus Himself, working through the Puritans, who "turned one of the most hideous, boundless and unknown wildernesses in the world . . . to a well-ordered Commonwealth."

Max Weber and others have long since helped us recognize the influence of the Puritan ethos on the growth of capitalism. This is one more example. American capitalist culture is firmly rooted in a secularized Christian myth and mystique of struggle with nature. The basic article of faith in this mystique is that you prove your worth by overcoming and dominating the natural world. You justify your existence and you attain bliss (temporal, eternal, or both) by transforming nature into wealth. This is not only good but self-evident. Until transformed, nature is useless and absurd. Anyone who refuses to see this or acquiesce in it is some kind of half-wit—or, worse, a rebel, an anarchist, a prophet of apocalyptic disorders.

Let us immediately admit that superimposed on this is another mystique: a mystique of America the beautiful. America whose mountains are bigger and better than those of Switzerland, scenic America which is to be seen first, last, and always in preference to foreign parts, America which must be kept lovely for Lady Bird. (So don't throw that beer can in the river, even though the water is polluted with all kinds of industrial waste. Business can mess up nature, but not *you*, Jack!) This mystique—this cult of nature—took shape in the nineteenth century.

The romantic love of wild American nature began in the cities and was an import from Europe. It had a profound effect on American civilization. Not only did poets like William Cullen Bryant proclaim that the "groves were God's first temples," and not only did the nineteenth-century landscape painters make America realize that the woods and mountains were worth looking at; not only did Fenimore Cooper revive the ideal of the Noble Primitive who grew up in the "honesty of the woods" and was better than city people; but also it was now the villain in the story (perhaps a city slicker) who ravished the forest and callously misused the good things of nature.

The Transcendentalists, above all, reversed the Puritan prejudice against nature, and began to teach that in the forests and mountains

God was nearer than in the cities. The silence of the woods whispered, to the man who listened, a message of sanity and healing. While the Puritans had assumed that man, being evil, would only revert to the most corrupt condition in the wilderness, the Transcendentalists held that since he was naturally good, and the cities corrupted his goodness, he needed contact with nature in order to recover his true self.

All this quickly turned into cliché. Nevertheless, the prophetic work of Henry Thoreau went deeper than a mere surface enthusiasm for scenery and fresh air. It is true that Walden was not too far from Concord and was hardly a wilderness even in those days. But Thoreau did build himself a house in the woods and did live at peace with the wild things around the pond. He also proved what he set out to prove: that one could not only survive outside the perimeter of town or farm life but live better and happier there. On the other hand, having explored the Maine woods, he had enough experience of the real wilds to recognize that life there could be savage and dehumanizing. Hence he produced a philosophy of balance which, he thought, was right and necessary for America. He already saw that American capitalism was set on a course that would ultimately ravage all wild nature on the continent— perhaps even in the world—and he warned that some wildness must be preserved. If it were not, man would destroy himself in destroying nature.

Thoreau realized that civilization was necessary and right, but he believed that an element of wildness was a necessary component in civilized life itself. The American still had a priceless advantage over the European. He could "combine the hardiness of the Indian with the intellectualness of civilized man." For that reason, Thoreau added, "I would not have every part of a man cultivated." To try to subject everything in man to rational and conscious control would be to warp, diminish, and barbarize him. So, too, the reduction of all nature to use for profit would end in the dehumanization of man. The passion and savagery that the Puritan had projected onto nature turned out to be within man himself. And when man turned the green forests into asphalt jungles the price he paid was that they were precisely that: jungles. The savagery of urban man, untempered by wilderness discipline, was savagery for its own sake.

It has been consistently proved true that what early nature philosophers like Thoreau said, in terms that seemed merely poetic or sentimental, turned out to have realistic and practical implications. Soon a few people began to realize the bad effects of deforestation. As early as 1864 the crucial importance of the Adirondack woods for New York's water supply was recognized. About this time, too, the movement to set up national parks was begun, though not always for the right reasons.

The arguments for and against Yellowstone Park (1872) are instructive. First of all, the area was "no use for business anyway." And then the geysers, hot springs, and other "decorations" were helpful manifestations of scientific truth. Then, of course, the place would provide "a great breathing place for the national lungs." Against this, one representative advanced a typical argument: "I cannot understand the sentiment which favors the retention of a few buffaloes to the development of mining interests amounting to millions of dollars."

John Muir is the great name in the history of American wilderness preservation. Muir's Scotch Calvinist father was the kind of man who believed that only a sinner or a slacker would approach the wilderness without taking an axe to it. To leave wild nature unattacked or unexploited was, in his eyes, not only foolish but morally reprehensible. It is curious, incidentally, that this attitude has been associated rather consistently with the American myth of virility. To be in the wilderness without fighting it, or at least without killing the animals in it, is regarded as a feminine trait. When a dam was about to be built in a canyon in Yosemite Park in 1913 to provide additional water for San Francisco, those who opposed it were called "short haired women and long haired men." Theodore Roosevelt, though a friend of John Muir, associated camping and hunting in the wilds with his virility cult, and this has remained a constant in the American mystique.

Muir traveled on foot through a thousand miles of wild country from Indiana to the Gulf of Mexico. The reason he gave for the journey was that "there is a love of wild nature in everybody, an ancient mother love, showing itself whether recognized or no, and however covered by cares and duties." This was not mere regression, but a recognition of the profoundly ambiguous imbalance in the American mind. Muir saw intuitively that the aggressive, compulsive attitude of the American male toward nature reflected not strength but insecurity and fear. The American cult of success implied a morbid fear of failure and resulted in overkill mentality so costly not only to nature but to every real or imaginary competitor. A psychological study of John Muir would reveal some very salutary information for modern America.

An investigation of the wilderness mystique and of the contrary mystique of exploitation and power reveals the tragic depth of the conflict that now exists in the American mind. The ideal of freedom and creativity that has been celebrated with such optimism and self-assurance runs the risk of being turned completely inside out if the natural ecological balance, on which it depends for its vitality, is destroyed. Take away the space, the freshness, the rich spontaneity of a wildly flourishing nature, and what will become of the creative pioneer mystique? A pioneer in a suburb is a sick man tormenting himself with projects of virile conquest. In a ghetto he is a policeman shooting every black man who gives him a dirty look. Obviously, the frontier is a thing of the past, the bison has vanished, and only by some miracle have a few Indians managed to survive. There are still some forests and wilderness areas, but we are firmly established as an urban culture. Nevertheless, the problem of ecology exists in a most acute form. The danger of fallout and atomic waste is only one of the more spectacular ones.

Much of the stupendous ecological damage that has been done in the last fifty years is completely irreversible. Industry and the military, especially in America, are firmly set on policies that make further damage inevitable. There are plenty of people who are aware of the need for "something to be done": but consider the enormous struggle that has to be waged, for instance in eastern Kentucky, to keep mining interests from completing the ruin of an area that is already a ghastly monument to human greed. When flash floods pull down the side of a mountain and drown a dozen wretched little towns in mud, everyone will agree that it's too bad the strip-miners peeled off the tops of the mountains with bulldozers. But when a choice has to be made, it is almost invariably made in the way that brings a quick return on somebody's investment—and a permanent disaster for everybody else.

Aldo Leopold, a follower of Muir and one of the great preservationists, understood that the erosion of American land was only part of a more drastic erosion of American freedom—of which it was a symptom. If "freedom" means purely and simply an uncontrolled power to make money in every possible way, regardless of consequences, then freedom becomes synonymous with ruthless, mindless exploitation. Aldo Leopold saw the connection and expressed it in the quiet language of ecology: "Is it not a bit beside the point to be so solicitous about preserving American institutions without giving so much as a thought to preserving the environment which produced them and which may now be one of the effective means of keeping them alive?"

Leopold brought into clear focus one of the most important moral discoveries of our time. This can be called the ecological conscience, which is centered in an awareness of man's true place as a dependent member of the biotic community. The tragedy that has been revealed in the ecological shambles created by business and war is a tragedy of ambivalence, aggression, and fear cloaked in virtuous ideas and justified by pseudo-Christian clichés. Or rather a tragedy of pseudo-creativity deeply impregnated with hatred, megalomania, and the need for domination. Its psychological root doubtless lies in the profound dehumanization and alienation of modern Western man, who has gradually come to mistake the artificial value of inert objects and abstractions (goods, money, property) for the power of life itself. Against this ethic Aldo

Leopold laid down a basic principle of the ecological conscience: "A thing is right when it tends to preserve the integrity, stability, and beauty of the biotic community. It is wrong when it tends otherwise."

In the light of this principle, an examination of our social, economic, and political history in the last hundred years would be a moral nightmare, redeemed only by a few gestures of good will on the part of those who obscurely realize that there *is* a problem. Yet compared to the magnitude of the problem, their efforts are at best pitiful: and what is more, the same gestures are made with great earnestness by the very people who continue to ravage, destroy, and pollute the country. They honor the wilderness myth while they proceed to destroy nature.

Can Aldo Leopold's ecological conscience become effective in America today? The ecological conscience is also essentially a peacemaking conscience. A country that seems to be more and more oriented to permanent hot or cold war-making does not give much promise of developing either one. But perhaps the very character of the war in Vietnam—with crop poisoning, the defoliation of forest trees, the incineration of villages and their inhabitants with napalm—presents a stark enough example to remind us of this most urgent moral need.

Aldo Leopold

the conservation ethic

When godlike Odysseus returned from the wars in Troy, he hanged all on one rope some dozen slave-girls of his household whom he suspected of misbehavior during his absence.

This hanging involved no question of propriety, much less of justice. The girls were property. The disposal of property was then, as now, a matter of expediency, not of right and wrong.

Criteria of right and wrong were not lacking from Odysseus' Greece: witness the fidelity of his wife through the long years before at last his black-prowed galleys clove the wine-dark seas for home. The ethical structure of that day covered wives, but had not yet been extended to human chattels. During the three thousand years which have since elapsed, ethical criteria have been extended to many fields of conduct, with corresponding shrinkages in those judged by expediency only.

This extension of ethics, so far studied only by philosophers, is actually a process in ecological evolution. Its sequences may be described in biological as well as philosophical terms. An ethic, biologically, is a limitation on freedom of action in the struggle for existence. An ethic, philosophically, is a differentiation of social from antisocial conduct. These are two definitions of one thing. The thing has its origins in the tendency of interdependent individuals or societies to evolve modes of coöperation. The biologist calls these symbioses. Man elaborated certain advanced symbioses called politics and economics. Like their simpler biological antecedents, they enable individuals or groups to exploit each other in an orderly way. Their first yardstick was expediency.

The complexity of coöperative mechanisms increased with population density, and with the efficiency of tools. It was simpler, for example, to define the antisocial uses of sticks and stones in the days of the mastodons than of bullets and billboards in the age of motors.

At a certain stage of complexity, the human community found expe-

Reprinted, by permission, from the October 1933 issue of the Journal of Forestry, *the magazine of the Society of American Foresters.*

diency yardsticks no longer sufficient. One by one it has evolved and superimposed upon them a set of ethical yardsticks. The first ethics dealt with the relationship between individuals. The Mosaic Decalogue is an example. Later accretions dealt with the relationship between the individual and society. Christianity tries to integrate the individual to society, democracy to integrate social organization to the individual.

There is as yet no ethic dealing with man's relationship to land and to the nonhuman animals and plants which grow upon it. Land, like Odysseus' slave-girls, is still property. The land relation is still strictly economic, entailing privileges but not obligations.

The extension of ethics to this third element in human environment is, if we read evolution correctly, an ecological possibility. It is the third step in a sequence. The first two have already been taken. Civilized man exhibits in his own mind evidence that the third is needed. For example, his sense of right and wrong may be aroused quite as strongly by the desecration of a nearby woodlot as by a famine in China, a near-pogrom in Germany, or the murder of the slave-girls in ancient Greece. Individual thinkers since the days of Ezekial and Isaiah have asserted that the despoliation of land is not only inexpedient but wrong. Society, however, has not yet affirmed their belief. I regard the present conservation movement as the embryo of such an affirmation. I here discuss why this is, or should be, so.

Some scientists will dismiss this matter forthwith, on the ground that ecology has no relation to right and wrong. To such I reply that science, if not philosophy, should by now have made us cautious about dismissals. An ethic may be regarded as a mode of guidance for meeting ecological situations so new or intricate, or involving such deferred reactions, that the path of social expediency is not discernible to the average individual. Animal instincts are just this. Ethics are possibly a kind of advanced social instinct in the making.

Whatever the merits of this analogy, no ecologist can deny that our land relation involves penalties and rewards which the individual does not see, and needs modes of guidance which do not yet exist. Call these what you will, science cannot escape its part in forming them.

Ecology—Its Role in History

A harmonious relation to land is more intricate, and of more consequence to civilization, than the historians of its progress seem to realize. Civilization is not, as they often assume, the enslavement of a stable and constant earth. It is a state of *mutual and interdependent co-operation* between human animals, other animals, plants, and soils, which may be disrupted at any moment by the failure of any of them. Land despoliation has evicted nations, and can on occasion do it again. As long as six virgin continents awaited the plow, this was perhaps no tragic matter—eviction from one piece of soil could be recouped by despoiling another. But there are now wars and rumors of wars which foretell the impending saturation of the earth's best soils and climates. It thus becomes a matter of some importance, at least to ourselves, that our dominion, once gained, be self-perpetuating rather than self-destructive.

This instability of our land relation calls for example. I will sketch a single aspect of it: the plant succession as a factor in history.

In the years following the Revolution, three groups were contending for control of the Mississippi valley: the native Indians, the French and English traders, and American settlers. Historians wonder what would have happened if the English at Detroit had thrown a little more weight into the Indian side of those tipsy scales which decided the outcome of the colonial migration into the cane lands of Kentucky. Yet who ever wondered why the cane lands, when subjected to the particular mixture of forces represented by the cow, plow, fire, and axe of the pioneer, became bluegrass? What if the plant succession inherent in this "dark and bloody ground" had, under the impact of these forces, given us some worthless sedge, shrub, or weed? Would Boone and Kenton have held out? Would there have been any overflow into Ohio? Any Louisiana Purchase? Any transcontinental union of new states? Any Civil War? Any machine age? Any depression? The subsequent drama of American history, here and elsewhere, hung in large degree on the reaction of particular soils to the impact of particular forces exerted by a particular kind and degree of human occupation. No statesman-biologist selected those forces, nor foresaw their effects. That chain of events which in the Fourth of July we call our National Destiny hung on a "fortuitous concourse of elements," the interplay of which we now dimly decipher *by hindsight only*.

Contrast Kentucky with what hindsight tells us about the Southwest. The impact of occupancy here brought no bluegrass, nor other plant fitted to withstand the bumps and buffetings of misuse. Most of these soils, when grazed, reverted through a successive series of more and more worthless grasses, shrubs, and weeds to a condition of unstable equilibrium. Each recession of plant types bred erosion; each increment to erosion bred a further recession of plants. The result today is a progressive and mutual deterioration, not only of plants and soils, but of the animal community subsisting thereon. The early settlers did not expect this; on the cienegas of central New Mexico some even cut artificial gullies to hasten it. So subtle has been its progress that few people know anything about it. It is not discussed at polite tea tables or go-getting luncheon clubs, but only in the arid halls of science.

All civilizations seem to have been conditioned upon whether the plant succession, under the impact of occupancy, gave a stable and habitable assortment of vegetative types, or an unstable and uninhabitable assortment. The swampy forests of Caesar's Gaul were utterly changed by human use—for the better. Moses' land of milk and honey was utterly changed—for the worse. Both changes are the unpremeditated resultant of the impact between ecological and economic forces. We now decipher these reactions retrospectively. What could possibly be more important than to foresee and control them?

We of the machine age admire ourselves for our mechanical ingenuity; we harness cars to the solar energy impounded in carboniferous forests; we fly in mechanical birds; we make the ether carry our words or even our pictures. But are these not in one sense mere parlor tricks compared with our utter ineptitude in keeping land fit to live upon? Our engineering has attained the pearly gates of a near-millennium, but our applied biology still lives in nomad's tents of the stone age. If our system of land use happens to be self-perpetuating, we stay. If it happens to be self-destructive we move, like Abraham, to pastures new.

Do I overdraw this paradox? I think not. Consider the transcontinental air mail which plies the skyways of the Southwest—a symbol of its final conquest. What does it see? A score of mountain valleys which were green gems of fertility when first described by Coronado, Espejo, Pattie, Abert, Sitgreaves, and Couzens. What are they now? Sandbars, wastes of cobbles and burroweed, a path for torrents. Rivers which Pattie says were clear, now muddy sewers for the wasting fertility of an empire. A "Public Domain," once a velvet carpet of rich buffalo grass and grama, now an illimitable waste of rattlesnake bush and tumbleweed, too impoverished to be accepted as a gift by the states within which it lies. Why? Because the ecology of this Southwest happened to be set on a hair-trigger. Because cows eat brush when the grass is gone, and thus postpone the penalties of overutilization. Because certain grasses, when grazed too closely to bear seed stalks, are weakened and give way to inferior grasses, and these to inferior shrubs, and these to weeds, and these to naked earth. Because rain which spatters upon vegetated soil stays clear and sinks, while rain which spatters upon devegetated soil seals its interstices with colloidal mud and hence must run away as floods, cutting the heart out of country as it goes. Are these phenomena any more difficult to foresee than the paths of stars which science deciphers without the error of a single second? Which is the more important to the permanence and welfare of civilization?

I do not here berate the astronomer for his precocity, but rather the ecologist for his lack of it. The days of his cloistered sequestration are over.

> Whether you will or not,
> You are a king, Tristram, for you are one

Of the time-tested few that leave the world,
When they are gone, not the same place it was.
Mark what you leave.

Unforeseen ecological reactions not only make or break history in a
few exceptional enterprises—they condition, circumscribe, delimit, and
warp all enterprises, both economic and cultural, that pertain to land. In
the cornbelt, after grazing and plowing out all the cover in the interests
of "clean farming," we grew tearful about wildlife, and spent several
decades passing laws for its restoration. We were like Canute command-
ing the tide. Only recently has research made it clear that the imple-
ments for restoration lie not in the legislature, but in the farmer's tool-
shed. Barbed wire and brains are doing what laws alone failed to do.

In other instances we take credit for shaking down apples which
were, in all probability, ecological windfalls. In the Lake States and the
Northeast lumbering, pulping, and fire accidentally created some scores
of millions of acres of new second growth. At the proper stage we find
these thickets full of deer. For this we naively thank the wisdom of our
game laws.

In short, the reaction of land to occupancy determines the nature and
duration of civilization. In arid climates the land may be destroyed. In
all climates the plant succession determines what economic activities can
be supported. Their nature and intensity in turn determine not only
the domestic but also the wild plant and animal life, the scenery, and
the whole face of nature. We inherit the earth, but within the limits of
the soil and the plant succession we also *rebuild* the earth—without
plan, without knowledge of its properties, and without understanding of
the increasingly coarse and powerful tools which science has placed at
our disposal. We are remodeling the Alhambra with a steam shovel.

Ecology and Economics

The conservation movement is, at the very least, an assertion that
these interactions between man and land are too important to be left to
chance, even that sacred variety of chance known as economic law.

We have three possible controls: Legislation, self-interest, and ethics.
Before we can know where and how they will work, we must first understand the reactions. Such understanding arises only from research. At the
present moment research, inadequate as it is, has nevertheless piled up a
large store of facts which our land-using industries are unwilling, or
(they claim) unable, to apply. Why? A review of three sample fields
will be attempted.

Soil science has so far relied on self-interest as the motive for conservation. The landholder is told that it pays to conserve his soil and its

fertility. On good farms this economic formula has improved land practice, but on poorer soils vast abuses still proceed unchecked. Public acquisition of submarginal soils is being urged as a remedy for their misuse. It has been applied to some extent, but it often comes too late to check erosion, and can hardly hope more than to ameliorate a phenomenon involving in some degree *every square foot* on the continent. Legislative compulsion might work on the best soils where it is least needed, but it seems hopeless on poor soils where the existing economic setup hardly permits even uncontrolled private enterprise to make a profit. We must face the fact that, by and large, no defensible relationship between man and the soil of his nativity is as yet in sight.

Forestry exhibits another tragedy—or comedy—of *Homo sapiens,* astride the runaway Juggernaut of his own building, trying to be decent to his environment. A new profession was trained in the confident expectation that the shrinkage in virgin timber would, as a matter of self-interest, bring an expansion of timber-cropping. Foresters are cropping timber on certain parcels of poor land which happen to be public, but on the great bulk of private holdings they have accomplished little. Economics won't let them. Why? He would be bold indeed who claimed to know the whole answer, but these parts of it seem agreed upon: modern transport prevents profitable tree-cropping in cut-out regions until virgin stands in all others are first exhausted; substitutes for lumber have undermined confidence in the future need for it; carrying charges on stumpage reserves are so high as to force perennial liquidation, overproduction, depressed prices, and an appalling wastage of unmarketable grades which must be cut to get the higher grades; the mind of the forest owner lacks the point of view underlying sustained yield; the low wage standards on which European forestry rests do not obtain in America.

A few tentative gropings toward industrial forestry were visible before 1929, but these have been mostly swept away by the depression, with the net result that forty years of "campaigning" have left us only such actual tree-cropping as is underwritten by public treasuries. Only a blind man could see in this the beginnings of an orderly and harmonious use of the forest resource.

There are those who would remedy this failure by legislative compulsion of private owners. Can a landholder be successfully compelled to raise any crop, let alone a complex long-time crop like a forest, on land the private possession of which is, for the moment at least, a liability? Compulsion would merely hasten that avalanche of tax-delinquent land-titles now being dumped into the public lap.

Another and larger group seeks a remedy in more public ownership. Doubtless we need it—we are getting it whether we need it or not—but how far can it go? We cannot dodge the fact that the forest problem,

like the soil problem, *is coextensive with the map of the United States.*
How far can we tax other lands and industries to maintain forest lands
and industries artificially? How confidently can we set out to run a hun-
dred-yard dash with a twenty-foot rope tying our ankle to the starting
point? Well, we are bravely "getting set," anyhow.

The trend in wildlife conservation is possibly more encouraging than
in either soils or forests. It has suddenly become apparent that farmers,
out of self-interest, can be induced to crop game. Game crops are in
demand, staple crops are not. For farm species, therefore, the immediate
future is relatively bright. Forest game has profited to some extent by
the accidental establishment of new habitat following the decline of
forest industries. Migratory game, on the other hand, has lost heavily
through drainage and over-shooting; its future is black because motives
of self-interest do not apply to the private cropping of birds so mobile
that they "belong" to everybody, and hence to nobody. Only governments have interests coextensive with their annual movements, and the
divided counsels of conservationists give governments ample alibi for
doing little. Governments could crop migratory birds because their
marshy habitat is cheap and concentrated, but we get only an annual
crop of new hearings on how to divide the fast-dwindling remnant.

These three fields of conservation, while but fractions of the whole,
suffice to illustrate the welter of conflicting forces, facts, and opinions
which so far comprise the result of the effort to harmonize our machine
civilization with the land whence comes its sustenance. We have accomplished little, but we should have learned much. What?

I can see clearly only two things:

First, that the economic cards are stacked against some of the most
important reforms in land use.

Second, that the scheme to circumvent this obstacle by public ownership, while highly desirable and good as far as it goes, can never go far
enough. Many will take issue on this, but the issue is between two
conflicting conceptions of the end towards which we are working.

One regards conservation as a kind of sacrificial offering, made for
us vicariously by bureaus, on lands nobody wants for other purposes, in
propitiation for the atrocities which still prevail everywhere else. We
have made a real start on this kind of conservation, and we can carry it
as far as the tax-string on our leg will reach. Obviously, though, it con-
serves our self-respect better than our land. Many excellent people
accept it, either because they despair of anything better, or because they
fail to see the *universality of the reactions needing control.* That is to
say their ecological education is not yet sufficient.

The other concept supports the public program, but regards it as
merely extension, teaching, demonstration, an initial nucleus, a means to
an end, but not the end itself. The real end is a *universal symbiosis with*

land, economic and esthetic, public and private. To this school of thought public ownership is a patch but not a program.

Are we, then, limited to patchwork until such time as Mr. Babbitt has taken his Ph.D. in ecology and esthetics? Or do the new economic formulae offer a shortcut to harmony with our environment?

The Economic Isms

As nearly as I can see, all the new isms—Socialism, Communism, Fascism, and especially the late but not lamented Technocracy—outdo even Capitalism itself in their preoccupation with one thing: The distribution of more machine-made commodities to more people. They all proceed on the theory that if we can all keep warm and full, and all own a Ford and a radio, the good life will follow. Their programs differ only in ways to mobilize machines to this end. Though they despise each other, they are all, in respect of this objective, as identically alike as peas in a pod. They are competitive apostles of a single creed: *salvation by machinery.*

We are here concerned, not with their proposals for adjusting men and machinery to goods, but rather with their lack of any vital proposal for adjusting men and machines to land. To conservationists they offer only the old familiar palliatives: Public ownership and private compulsion. If these are insufficient now, by what magic are they to become sufficient after we change our collective label?

Let us apply economic reasoning to a sample problem and see where it takes us. As already pointed out, there is a huge area which the economist calls submarginal, because it has a minus value for exploitation. In its once-virgin condition, however, it could be "skinned" at a profit. It has been, and as a result erosion is washing it away. What shall we do about it?

By all the accepted tenets of current economics and science we ought to say "let her wash." Why? Because staple land crops are overproduced, our population curve is flattening out, science is still raising the yields from better lands, we are spending millions from the public treasury to retire unneeded acreage, and here is nature offering to do the same thing free of charge; why not let her do it? This, I say, is economic reasoning. *Yet no man has so spoken.* I cannot help reading a meaning into this fact. To me it means that the average citizen shares in some degree the intuitive and instantaneous contempt with which the conservationist would regard such an attitude. We can, it seems, stomach the burning or plowing-under of overproduced cotton, coffee, or corn, but the destruction of mother earth, however "submarginal," touches something deeper, some subeconomic stratum of the human intelligence wherein lies that something—perhaps the essence of civilization—which Wilson called "the decent opinion of mankind."

The Conservation Movement

We are confronted, then, by a contradiction. To build a better motor we tap the uttermost powers of the human brain; to build a better countryside we throw dice. Political systems take no cognizance of this disparity, offer no sufficient remedy. There is, however, a dormant but widespread consciousness that the destruction of land, and of the living things upon it, is wrong. A new minority have espoused an idea called conservation which tends to assert this as a positive principle. Does it contain seeds which are likely to grow?

Its own devotees, I confess, often give apparent grounds for skepticism. We have, as an extreme example, the cult of the barbless hook, which acquires self-esteem by a self-imposed limitation of armaments in catching fish. The limitation is commendable, but the illusion that it has something to do with salvation is as naive as some of the primitive taboos and mortifications which still adhere to religious sects. Such excrescences seem to indicate the whereabouts of a moral problem, however irrelevant they be in either defining or solving it.

Then there is the conservation-booster, who of late has been rewriting the conservation ticket in terms of "tourist bait." He exhorts us to "conserve outdoor Wisconsin" because if we don't the motorist on vacation will streak through to Michigan, leaving us only a cloud of dust. Is Mr. Babbitt trumping up hard-boiled reasons to serve as a screen for doing what he thinks is right? His tenacity suggests that he is after something more than tourists. Have he and other thousands of "conservation workers" labored through all these barren decades fired by a dream of augmenting the sales of sandwiches and gasoline? I think not. Some of these people have hitched their wagon to a star—and that is something.

Any wagon so hitched offers the discerning politician a quick ride to glory. His agility in hopping up and seizing the reins adds little dignity to the cause, but it does add the testimony of his political nose to an important question: is this conservation something people really want? The political objective, to be sure, is often some trivial tinkering with the laws, some useless appropriation, or some pasting of pretty labels on ugly realities. How often, though, does any political action portray the real depth of the idea behind it? For political consumption a new thought must always be reduced to a posture or a phrase. It has happened before that great ideas were heralded by growing pains in the body politic, semicomic to those onlookers not yet infected by them. The insignificance of what we conservationists, in our political capacity, say and do, does not detract from the significance of our persistent desire to do something. To turn this desire into productive channels is the task of time, and ecology.

The recent trend in wildlife conservation shows the direction in which ideas are evolving. At the inception of the movement fifty years ago, its underlying thesis was to save species from extermination. The means to this end were a series of restrictive enactments. The duty of the individual was to cherish and extend these enactments, and to see that his neighbor obeyed them. The whole structure was negative and prohibitory. It assumed land to be a constant in the ecological equation. Gunpowder and blood lust were the variables needing control.

There is now being superimposed on this a positive and affirmatory ideology, the thesis of which is to prevent the deterioration of environment. The means to this end is research. The duty of the individual is to apply its findings to land, and to encourage his neighbor to do likewise. The soil and the plant succession are recognized as the basic variables which determine plant and animal life, both wild and domesticated, and likewise the quality and quantity of human satisfactions to be derived. Gunpowder is relegated to the status of a tool for harvesting one of these satisfactions. Blood-lust is a source of motive-power, like sex in social organization. Only one constant is assumed, and that is common to both equations: the love of nature.

This new idea is so far regarded as merely a new and promising means to better hunting and fishing, but its potential uses are much larger. To explain this, let us go back to the basic thesis—the preservation of fauna and flora.

Why do species become extinct? Because they first become rare. Why do they become rare? Because of shrinkage in the particular environments which their particular adaptations enable them to inhabit. Can such shrinkage be controlled? Yes, once the specifications are known. How known? Through ecological research. How controlled? By modifying the environment with those same tools and skills already used in agriculture and forestry.

Given, then, the knowledge and the desire, this idea of controlled wild culture or "management" can be applied not only to quail and trout, but to *any living thing* from bloodroots to Bell's vireos. Within the limits imposed by the plant succession, the soil, the size of property, and the gamut of the seasons, the landholder can "raise" any wild plant, fish, bird, or mammal he wants to. A rare bird or flower need remain no rarer than the people willing to venture their skill in *building it a habitat*. Nor need we visualize this as a new diversion for the idle rich. The average dolled-up estate merely proves what we will some day learn to acknowledge: that bread and beauty grow best together. Their harmonious integration can make farming not only a business but an art; the land not only a food factory but an instrument for self-expression, on which each can play music of his own choosing.

It is well to ponder the sweep of this thing. It offers us nothing less than a renaissance—a new creative stage—in the oldest, and potentially the most universal, of all the fine arts. "Landscaping," for ages dissociated from economic land use, has suffered that dwarfing and distortion which always attends the relegation of esthetic or spiritual functions to parks and parlors. Hence it is hard for us to visualize a creative art of land beauty which is the prerogative, not of esthetic priests but of dirt farmers, which deals not with plants but with biota, and which wields not only spade and pruning shears, but also draws rein on those invisible forces which determine the presence or absence of plants and animals. Yet such is this thing which lies to hand, if we want it. In it are the seeds of change, including, perhaps, a rebirth of that social dignity which ought to inhere in land ownership, but which, for the moment, land skinning hardly deserve. In it, too, are perhaps the seeds of a new has passed to inferior professions, and which the current processes of fellowship in land, a new solidarity in all men privileged to plow, a realization of Whitman's dream to *"plant companionship as thick as trees along all the rivers of America."* What bitter parody of such companionship, and trees, and rivers, is offered to this our generation!

I will not belabor the pipedream. It is no prediction, but merely an assertion that the idea of controlled environment contains colors and brushes wherewith society may some day paint a new and possibly a better picture of itself. Granted a community in which the combined beauty and utility of land determines the social status of its owner, and we will see a speedy dissolution of the economic obstacles which now beset conservation. Economic laws may be permanent, but their impact reflects what people want, which in turn reflects what they know and what they are. The economic setup at any moment is in some measure the result, as well as the cause, of the then prevailing standard of living. Such standards change. For example: some people discriminate against manufactured goods produced by child labor or other antisocial processes. They have learned some of the abuses of machinery, and are willing to use their custom as a leverage for betterment. Social pressures have also been exerted to modify ecological processes which happened to be simple enough for people to understand—witness the very effective boycott of birdskins for millinery ornament. We need postulate only a little further advance in ecological education to visualize the application of like pressures to other conservation problems.

For example: the lumberman who is now unable to practice forestry because the public is turning to synthetic boards may be able to sell man-grown lumber "to keep the mountains green." Again: certain wools are produced by gutting the public domain; couldn't their competitors, who lead their sheep in greener pastures, so label their product? Must we view forever the irony of educating our sons with paper, the offal of which pollutes the rivers which they need quite as badly as books?

Would not many people pay an extra penny for a "clean" newspaper? Government may some day busy itself with the legitimacy of labels used by land industries to distinguish conservation products, rather than with the attempt to operate their lands for them.

I neither predict nor advocate these particular pressures—their wisdom or unwisdom is beyond my knowledge. I do assert that these abuses are just as real, and their correction every whit as urgent, as was the killing of egrets for hats. *They differ only in the number of links composing the ecological chain of cause and effect.* In egrets there were one or two links, which the mass-mind saw, believed, and acted upon. In these others there are many links; people do not see them, nor believe us who do. The ultimate issue, in conservation as in other social problems, is whether the mass-mind *wants* to extend its powers of comprehending the world in which it lives, or, granted the desire, *has the capacity to do so.* Ortega, in his "Revolt of the Masses," has pointed the first question with devastating lucidity. The geneticists are gradually, with trepidations, coming to grips with the second. I do not know the answer to either. I simply affirm that a sufficiently enlightened society, by changing its wants and tolerances, can change the economic factors bearing on land. It can be said of nations, as of individuals: "as a man thinketh, so is he."

It may seem idle to project such imaginary elaborations of culture at a time when millions lack even the means of physical existence. Some may feel for it the same honest horror as the Senator from Michigan who lately arraigned Congress for protecting migratory birds at a time when fellow humans lacked bread. The trouble with such deadly parallels is we can never be sure which is cause and which is effect. It is not inconceivable that the wave phenomena which have lately upset everything from banks to crime rates might be less troublesome if the human medium in which they run *readjusted its tensions.* The stampede is an attribute of animals interested solely in grass.

Paul Shepard

ecology and man—a viewpoint

Ecology is sometimes characterized as the study of a natural "web of life." It would follow that man is somewhere in the web or that he in fact manipulates its strands, exemplifying what Thomas Huxley called "man's place in nature." But the image of a web is too meager and simple for the reality. A web is flat and finished and has the mortal frailty of the individual spider. Although elastic, it has insufficient depth. However solid to the touch of the spider, for us it fails to denote the *eikos*—the habitation—and to suggest the enduring integration of the primitive Greek domicile with its sacred hearth, bonding the earth to all aspects of society.

Ecology deals with organisms in an environment and with the processes that link organism and place. But ecology as such cannot be studied, only organisms, earth, air, and sea can be studied. It is not a discipline: there is no body of thought and technique which frames an ecology of man.[1] It must be therefore a scope or a way of seeing. Such a *perspective* on the human situation is very old and has been part of philosophy and art for thousands of years. It badly needs attention and revival.

Man is in the world and his ecology is the nature of that *inness*. He is in the world as in a room, and in transience, as in the belly of a tiger or in love. What does he do there in nature? What does nature do there *in him*? What is the nature of the transaction? Biology tells us that the transaction is always circular, always a mutual feedback. Human ecology cannot be limited strictly to biological concepts, but it cannot ignore them. It cannot even transcend them. It emerges from biological reality and grows from the fact of interconnection as a general

[1] There is a branch of sociology called human ecology, but it is mostly about urban geography.

principle of life. It must take a long view of human life and nature as they form a mesh or pattern going beyond historical time and beyond the conceptual bounds of other humane studies. As a natural history of what it means to be human, ecology might proceed the same way one would define a stomach, for example, by attention to its nervous and circulatory connections as well as its entrance, exit, and muscular walls.

Many educated people today believe that only what is unique to the individual is important or creative, and turn away from talk of populations and species as they would from talk of the masses. I once knew a director of a wealthy conservation foundation who had misgivings about the approach of ecology to urgent environmental problems in America because its concepts of communities and systems seemed to discount the individual. Communities to him suggested only followers, gray masses without the tradition of the individual. He looked instead—or in reaction—to the profit motive and capitalistic formulas, in terms of efficiency, investment, and production. It seemed to me that he had missed a singular opportunity. He had shied from the very aspect of the world now beginning to interest industry, business, and technology as the biological basis of their—and our—affluence, and which his foundation could have shown to be the ultimate basis of all economics.

Individual man *has* his particular integrity, to be sure. Oak trees, even mountains, have selves or integrities too (a poor word for my meaning, but it will have to do). To our knowledge, those other forms are not troubled by seeing themselves in more than one way, as man is. In one aspect the self is an arrangement of organs, feelings, and thoughts—a "me"—surrounded by a hard body boundary: skin, clothes, and insular habits. This idea needs no defense. It is conferred on us by the whole history of our civilization. Its virtue is verified by our affluence. The alternative is a self as a center of organization, constantly drawing on and influencing the surroundings, whose skin and behavior are soft zones contacting the world instead of excluding it. Both views are real and their reciprocity significant. We need them both to have a healthy social and human maturity.

The second view—that of relatedness of the self—has been given short shrift. Attitudes toward ourselves do not change easily. The conventional image of a man, like that of the heraldic lion, is iconographic; its outlines are stylized to fit the fixed curves of our vision. We are hidden from ourselves by habits of perception. Because we learn to talk at the same time we learn to think, our language, for example, encourages us to see ourselves—or a plant or animal—as an isolated sack, a thing, a contained self. Ecological thinking, on the other hand, requires a kind of vision across boundaries. The epidermis of the skin is ecologically like a pond surface or a forest soil, not a shell so much as a delicate interpenetration. It reveals the self enobled and extended rather than threatened as part of the landscape and the ecosystem, because the beauty and complexity of nature are continuous with ourselves.

And so ecology as applied to man faces the task of renewing a balanced view where now there is man-centeredness, even pathology of isolation and fear. It implies that we must find room in "our" world for all plants and animals, even for their otherness and their opposition. It further implies exploration and openness across an inner boundary—an ego boundary—and appreciative understanding of the animal in ourselves which our heritage of Platonism, Christian morbidity, duality, and mechanism have long held repellent and degrading. The older counter-currents—relics of pagan myth, the universal application of Christian compassion, philosophical naturalism, nature romanticism and pantheism—have been swept away, leaving only odd bits of wreckage. Now we find ourselves in a deteriorating environment which breeds aggressiveness and hostility toward ourselves and our world.

How simple our relationship to nature would be if we only had to choose between protecting our natural home and destroying it. Most of our efforts to provide for the natural in our philosophy have failed—run aground on their own determination to work out a peace at arm's length. Our harsh reaction against the peaceable kingdom of sentimental romanticism was evoked partly by the tone of its dulcet facade but also by the disillusion to which it led. Natural dependence and contingency suggest togetherness and emotional surrender to mass behavior and other lowest common denominators. The environmentalists matching culture and geography provoke outrage for their over-simple theories of cause and effect, against the sciences which sponsor them and even against a natural world in which the theories may or may not be true. Our historical disappointment in the nature of nature has created a cold climate for ecologists who assert once again that we are limited and obligated. Somehow they must manage in spite of the chill to reach the centers of humanism and technology, to convey there a sense of our place in a universal vascular system without depriving us of our self-esteem and confidence.

Their message is not, after all, all bad news. Our natural affiliations define and illumine freedom instead of denying it. They demonstrate it better than any dialectic. Being more enduring than we individuals, ecological patterns—spatial distributions, symbioses, the streams of energy and matter and communication—create among individuals the tensions and polarities so different from dichotomy and separateness. The responses, or what theologians call "the sensibilities" of creatures (including ourselves) to such arrangements grow in part from a healthy union of the two kinds of self already mentioned, one emphasizing integrity, the other relatedness. But it goes beyond that to something better known to twelfth century Europeans or Paleolithic hunters than to ourselves. If nature is not a prison and earth a shoddy way-station, we must find the faith and force to affirm its metabolism as our own— or rather, our own as part of it. To do so means nothing less than a shift in our whole frame of reference and our attitude towards life itself, a wider perception of the landscape as a creative, harmonious being where relationships of things are as real as the things. Without losing our sense of a great human destiny and without intellectual surrender, we must affirm that the world is a being, a part of our own body.[2]

Such a being may be called an ecosystem or simply a forest or landscape. Its members are engaged in a kind of choreography of materials and energy and information, the creation of order and organization. (Analogy to corporate organization here is misleading, for the distinction between social (one species) and ecological (many species) is fundamental.) The pond is an example. Its ecology includes all events: the conversion of sunlight to food and the food-chains within and around it, man drinking, bathing, fishing, plowing the slopes of the watershed, drawing a picture of it, and formulating theories about the world based on what he sees in the pond. He and all the other organisms at and in the pond act upon one another, engage the earth and atmosphere, and are linked to other ponds by a network of connections like the threads of protoplasm connecting cells in living tissues.

The elegance of such systems and delicacy of equilibrium are the outcome of a long evolution of interdependence. Even society, mind and culture are parts of that evolution. There is an essential relationship between them and the natural habitat: that is, between the emergence of higher primates and flowering plants, pollinating insects, seeds, humus, and arboreal life. It is unlikely that a manlike creature could arise by any other means than a long arboreal sojourn following and followed by a time of terrestriality. The fruit's complex construction and the mammalian brain are twin offspring of the maturing earth, impossible, even meaningless, without the deepening soil and the mutual development of savannas and their faunas in the last geological epoch. Internal complexity, as the mind of a primate, is an extension of natural complexity, measured by the variety of plants and animals and the variety of nerve cells—organic extensions of each other.

The exuberance of kinds as the setting in which a good mind could evolve (to deal with a complex world) was not only a past condition. Man did not arrive in the world as though disembarking from a train in the city. He continues to arrive, somewhat like the birth of art, a train

[2] See Alan Watts, "The World is Your Body," in *The Book on the Taboo Against Knowing Who You Are*. New York: Pantheon Books, 1966 [reprinted in this volume, pp. 181–93].

in Roger Fry's definition, passing through many stations, none of which is wholly left behind. This idea of natural complexity as a counterpart to human intricacy is central to an ecology of man. The creation of order, of which man is an example, is realized also in the number of species and habitats, an abundance of landscapes lush and poor. Even deserts and tundras increase the planetary opulence. Curiously, only man and possibly a few birds can appreciate this opulence, being the world's travelers. Reduction of this variegation would, by extension then, be an amputation of man. To convert all "wastes"—all deserts, estuaries, tundras, ice fields, marshes, steppes and moors—into cultivated fields and cities would impoverish rather than enrich life esthetically as well as ecologically. By esthetically, I do not mean that weasel term connoting the pleasure of baubles. We have diverted ourselves with litterbug campaigns and greenbelts in the name of esthetics while the fabric of our very environment is unravelling. In the name of conservation, too, such things are done, so that conservation becomes ambiguous. Nature is a fundamental "resource" to be sustained for our own well-being. But it loses in the translation into usable energy and commodities. Ecology may testify as often against our uses of the world, even against conservation techniques of control and management for sustained yield, as it does for them. Although ecology may be treated as a science, its greater and overriding wisdom is universal.

That wisdom can be approached mathematically, chemically, or it can be danced or told as a myth. It has been embodied in widely scattered economically different cultures. It is manifest, for example, among pre-Classical Greeks, in Navajo religion and social orientation, in Romantic poetry of the eighteenth and nineteenth centuries, in Chinese landscape painting of the eleventh century, in current Whiteheadian philosophy, in Zen Buddhism, in the world view of the cult of the Cretan Great Mother, in the ceremonials of Bushman hunters, and in the medieval Christian metaphysics of light. What is common among all of them is a deep sense of engagement with the landscape, with profound connections to surroundings and to natural processes central to all life.

It is difficult in our language even to describe that sense. English becomes imprecise or mystical—and therefore suspicious—as it struggles with "process" thought. Its noun and verb organization shapes a divided world of static doers separate from the doing. It belongs to an idiom of social hierarchy in which all nature is made to mimic man. The living world is perceived in that idiom as an upright ladder, a "great chain of being," an image which seems at first ecological but is basically rigid, linear, condescending, lacking humility and love of otherness.

We are all familiar from childhood with its classifications of everything on a scale from the lowest to the highest: inanimate matter/vegetative life/lower animals/higher animals/men/angels/gods. It ranks animals themselves in categories of increasing good: the vicious and lowly parasites, pathogens and predators/the filthy decay and scavenging organisms/indifferent wild or merely useless forms/good tame creatures/and virtuous beasts domesticated for human service. It shadows the great man-centered political scheme upon the world, derived from the ordered ascendency from parishioners to clerics to bishops to cardinals to popes, or in a secular form from criminals to proletarians to aldermen to mayors to senators to presidents.

And so is nature pigeonholed. The sardonic phrase, "the place of nature in man's world," offers, tongue-in-cheek, a clever footing for confronting a world made in man's image and conforming to words. It satirizes the prevailing philosophy of antinature and human omniscience. It is possible because of an attitude which—like ecology—has ancient roots, but whose modern form was shaped when Aquinas reconciled Aristotelian homocentrism with Judeo-Christian dogma. In a later setting of machine technology, puritanical capitalism, and an urban ethos it carves its own version of reality into the landscape like a schoolboy initialing a tree. For such a philosophy nothing in nature has inherent merit. As one professor recently put it, "The only reason anything is done on this earth is for people. Did the rivers, winds, animals, rocks, or dust ever consider my wishes or needs? Surely, we do all our acts in an earthly environment, but I have never had a tree, valley, mountain, or flower thank me for preserving it." [3] This view carries great force, epitomized in history by Bacon, Descartes, Hegel, Hobbes, and Marx.

Some other post-Renaissance thinkers are wrongly accused of undermining our assurance of natural order. The theories of the heliocentric solar system, of biological evolution, and of the unconscious mind are held to have deprived the universe of the beneficence and purpose to which man was a special heir and to have evoked feelings of separation, of antipathy towards a meaningless existence in a neutral cosmos. Modern despair, the arts of anxiety, the politics of pathological individualism and predatory socialism were not, however, the results of Copernicus, Darwin and Freud. If man was not the center of the universe, was not created by a single stroke of Providence, and is not ruled solely by rational intelligence, it does not follow therefore that nature is defective where we thought it perfect. The astronomer, biologist and psychiatrist each achieved for mankind corrections in sensibility. Each showed the interpenetration of human life and the universe to be richer and more mysterious than had been thought.

Darwin's theory of evolution has been crucial to ecology. Indeed, it

---

[3] Clare A. Gunn in *Landscape Architecture*, July 1966, p. 260.

might have helped rather than aggravated the growing sense of human alienation had its interpreters emphasized predation and competition less (and, for this reason, one is tempted to add, had Thomas Huxley, Herbert Spencer, Samuel Butler and G. B. Shaw had less to say about it). Its bases of universal kinship and common bonds of function, experience and value among organisms were obscured by pre-existing ideas of animal depravity. Evolutionary theory was exploited to justify the worst in men and was misused in defense of social and economic injustice. Nor was it better used by humanitarians. They opposed the degradation of men in the service of industrial progress, the slaughter of American Indians, and child labor, because each treated men 'like animals." That is to say, men were not animals, and the temper of social reform was to find good only in attributes separating men from animals. Kindness both towards and among animals was still a rare idea in the nineteenth century, so that using men as animals could mean only cruelty.

Since Thomas Huxley's day the nonanimal forces have developed a more subtle dictum to the effect that, "Man may be an animal, but he is more than an animal, too!" The *more* is really what is important. This appealing aphorism is a kind of anesthetic. The truth is that we are ignorant of what it is like or what it means to be any other kind of creature than we are. If we are unable to truly define the animal's experience of life or "being an animal" how can we isolate our animal part?

The rejection of animality is a rejection of nature as a whole. As a teacher, I see students develop in their humanities studies a proper distrust of science and technology. What concerns me is that the stigma spreads to the natural world itself. C. P. Snow's "Two Cultures," setting the sciences against the humanities, can be misunderstood as placing nature against art. The idea that the current destruction of people and environment is scientific and would be corrected by more communication with the arts neglects the hatred for this world carried by our whole culture. Yet science as it is now taught does not promote a respect for nature. Western civilization breeds no more ecology in Western science than in Western philosophy. Snow's two cultures cannot explain the antithesis that splits the world, nor is the division ideological, economic or political in the strict sense. The antidote he proposes is roughly equivalent to a liberal education, the traditional prescription for making broad and well-rounded men. Unfortunately, there is little even in the liberal education of ecology-and-man. Nature is usually synonymous with either natural resources or scenery, the great stereotypes in the minds of middle-class, college-educated Americans.

One might suppose that the study of biology would mitigate the humanistic—largely literary—confusion between materialism and a concern for nature. But biology made the mistake at the end of the seventeenth century of adopting a *modus operandi* or life style from physics, in which the question why was not to be asked, only the question how. Biology succumbed to its own image as an esoteric prologue to technics and encouraged the whole society to mistrust naturalists. When scholars realized what the sciences were about it is not surprising that they threw out the babies with the bathwater: the information content and naturalistic lore with the rest of it. This is the setting in which academia and intellectual America undertook the single-minded pursuit of human uniqueness, and uncovered a great mass of pseudo distinctions such as language, tradition, culture, love, consciousness, history and awe of the supernatural. Only men were found to be capable of escape from predictability, determinism, environmental control, instincts and other mechanisms which "imprison" other life. Even biologists, such as Julian Huxley, announced that the purpose of the world was to produce man, whose social evolution excused him forever from biological evolution. Such a view incorporated three important presumptions: that nature is a power structure shaped after human political hierarchies; that man has a monopoly of immortal souls; and omnipotence will come through technology. It seems to me that all of these foster a failure of responsible behavior in what Paul Sears calls "the living landscape" except within the limits of immediate self-interest.

What ecology must communicate to the humanities—indeed, as a humanity—is that such an image of the world and the society so conceived are incomplete. There is overwhelming evidence of likeness, from molecular to mental, between men and animals. But the dispersal of this information is not necessarily a solution. The Two Culture idea that the problem is an information bottleneck is only partly true; advances in biochemistry, genetics, ethnology, paleoanthropology, comparative physiology and psychobiology are not self-evidently unifying. They need a unifying principle not found in any of them, a wisdom in the sense that Walter B. Cannon used the word in his book *Wisdom of the Body*,[4] about the community of self-regulating systems within the organism. If the ecological extension of that perspective is correct, societies and ecosystems as well as cells have a physiology, and insight into it is built into organisms, including man. What was intuitively apparent last year—whether esthetically or romantically—is a find of this year's inductive analysis. It seems apparent to me that there is an ecological instinct which probes deeper and more comprehensively than science, and which anticipates every scientific confirmation of the natural history of man.

It is not surprising, therefore, to find substantial ecological insight

[4] New York: W. W. Norton, 1932.

in art. Of course there is nothing wrong with a poem or dance which is ecologically neutral; its merit may have nothing to do with the transaction of man and nature. It is my impression, however, that students of the arts no longer feel that the subject of a work of art—what it "represents"—is without importance, as was said about forty years ago. But there are poems and dances as there are prayers and laws attending to ecology. Some are more than mere comments on it. Such creations become part of all life. Essays on nature are an element of a functional or feedback system influencing men's reactions to their environment, messages projected by men to themselves through some act of design, the manipulation of paints or written words. They are natural objects, like bird nests. The essay is as real a part of the community— in both the one-species sociological and many-species ecological senses— as are the songs of choirs and crickets. An essay in an Orphic sound, words that make knowing possible, for it was Orpheus as Adam who named and thus made intelligible all creatures.

What is the conflict of Two Cultures if it is not between science and art or between national ideologies? The distinction rather divides science and art within themselves. An example within science was the controversy over the atmospheric testing of nuclear bombs and the effect of radioactive fallout from the explosions. Opposing views were widely published and personified when Linus Pauling, a biochemist, and Edward Teller, a physicist, disagreed. Teller, one of the "fathers" of the bomb, pictured the fallout as a small factor in a world-wide struggle, the possible damage to life in tiny fractions of a percent, and even noted that evolutionary progress comes from mutations. Pauling, an expert on the hereditary material, knowing that most mutations are detrimental, argued that a large absolute number of people might be injured, as well as other life in the world's biosphere.

The humanness of ecology is that the dilemma of our emerging world ecological crises (overpopulation, environmental pollution, etc.) is at least in part a matter of values and ideas. It does not divide men as much by their trades as by the complex of personality and experience shaping their feelings towards other people and the world at large. I have mentioned the disillusion generated by the collapse of unsound nature philosophies. The antinature position today is often associated with the focusing of general fears and hostilities on the natural world. It can be seen in the behavior of control-obsessed engineers, corporation people selling consumption itself, academic superhumanists and media professionals fixated on political and economic crisis; neurotics working out psychic problems in the realm of power over men or nature, artistic symbol-manipulators disgusted by anything organic. It includes many normal, earnest people who are unconsciously defending themselves or their families against a vaguely threatening universe. The dangerous eruption of humanity in a deteriorating environment does not show itself as such in the daily experience of most people, but is felt as general tension and anxiety. We feel the pressure of events not as direct causes but more like omens. A kind of madness arises from the prevailing nature-conquering, nature-hating and self- and world-denial. Although in many ways most Americans live comfortable, satiated lives, there is a nameless frustration born of an increasing nullity. The aseptic home and society are progressively cut off from direct organic sources of health and increasingly isolated from the means of altering the course of events. Success, where its price is the misuse of landscapes, the deterioration of air and water and the loss of wild things, becomes a pointless glut, experience one-sided, time on our hands an unlocalized ache.

The unrest can be exploited to perpetuate itself. One familiar prescription for our sick society and its loss of environmental equilibrium is an increase in the intangible Good Things: more Culture, more Security and more Escape from pressures and tempo. The "search for identity" is not only a social but an ecological problem having to do with a sense of place and time in the context of all life. The pain of that search can be cleverly manipulated to keep the *status quo* by urging that what we need is only improved forms and more energetic expressions of what now occupy us: engrossment with ideological struggle and military power, with productivity and consumption as public and private goals, with commerce and urban growth, with amusements, with fixation on one's navel, with those tokens of escape or success already belabored by so many idealists and social critics so ineffectually.

To come back to those Good Things: the need for culture, security and escape are just near enough to the truth to take us in. But the real cultural deficiency is the absence of a true *cultus* with its significant ceremony, relevant mythical cosmos, and artifacts. The real failure in security is the disappearance from our personal lives of the small human group as the functional unit of society and the web of other creatures, domestic and wild, which are part of our humanity. As for escape, the idea of simple remission and avoidance fails to provide for the value of solitude, to integrate leisure and natural encounter. Instead of these, what are foisted on the puzzled and troubled soul as Culture, Security and Escape are more art museums, more psychiatry, and more automobiles.

The ideological status of ecology is that of a resistance movement. Its Rachel Carsons and Aldo Leopolds are subversive (as Sears recently called ecology itself[5]). They challenge the public or private right to pollute the environment, to systematically destroy predatory animals, to spread chemical pesticides indiscriminately, to meddle chemically with

[5] Paul B. Sears, "Ecology—a subversive subject," *BioScience*, 14(7):11 July 1964.

food and water, to appropriate without hindrance space and surface for technological and military ends; they oppose the uninhibited growth of human populations, some forms of "aid" to "underdeveloped" peoples, the needless addition of radioactivity to the landscape, the extinction of species of plants and animals, the domestication of all wild places, large-scale manipulation of the atmosphere or the sea, and most other purely engineering solutions to problems of and intrusions into the organic world.

If naturalists seem always to be *against* something it is because they feel a responsibility to share their understanding, and their opposition constitutes a defense of the natural systems to which man is committed as an organic being. Sometimes naturalists propose projects too, but the project approach is itself partly the fault, the need for projects a consequence of linear, compartmental thinking, of machine-like units to be controlled and manipulated. If the ecological crisis were merely a matter of alternative techniques, the issue would belong among the technicians and developers (where most schools and departments of conservation have put it).

Truly ecological thinking need not be incompatible with our place and time. It does have an element of humility which is foreign to our thought, which moves us to silent wonder and glad affirmation. But it offers an essential factor, like a necessary vitamin, to all our engineering and social planning, to our poetry and our understanding. There is only one ecology, not a human ecology on one hand and another for the sub-human. No one school or theory or project or agency controls it. For us it means seeing the world mosaic from the human vantage without being man-fanatic. We must use it to confront the great philosophical problems of man—transience, meaning, and limitation—without fear. Affirmation of its own organic essence will be the ultimate test of the human mind.

III

THE IMPACT OF
ECOLOGICAL VALUES

ECOLOGY, SCIENCE, AND TECHNOLOGY

The next few decades will almost certainly witness mounting dangers to the integrity of the biosphere as a life-support system for man. The reasons for this are located in population growth, spreading industrialization, increased use of both fossil and atomic fuels, continuing efforts in all parts of the world to raise per capita consumption, greater reliance on chemical methods to boost agricultural output, the development and implementation of superfluous technological gimmicks, and the proliferation of ever deadlier weapons systems.

The snowballing characteristic of these threats, in turn, demands that ecological values be integrated with government policies, urban and educational planning, consumption habits, individual life styles, philosophic and religious attitudes, and, finally, into societal myths and visions of the future. In the long run, if the nations of the world fail to act upon these values, by so much more will the odds favor the doomsday prophets, whose computers are beginning to establish the parameters beyond which human existence will no longer be possible.

While sweeping institutional and individual changes are prerequisites for survival in the long run, the hard facts indicate that there are no known ways (within the realms of sanity or probability) to arrest or reverse the growth of serious environmental problems in the short run.[1] At best we can hope to minimize the impact of the worst practices and

---

[1] The rate at which environmental deterioration takes place is not easily measured. As the formidable Frank Egler has observed, not only is the ecosystem "more complex than we think. It is more complex than we *can* think." See his article, "Pesticides—In Our Ecosystem," *American Scientist*, LII, no. 1 (March, 1964), 110–36.

poisons, and thus buy time until an international ecological conscience can guide environmental policies.

The most pressing need in the short run is to contain the negative effects of rampant technology as quickly as possible, humanize the applications of technology, minimize the overt abuses, and redirect technological research onto problems of survival. Closely affiliated objectives include the need to bring scientific research into a more humane perspective and to establish within the scientific community a freedom of expression that will subject military technology to stringent public evaluation of ecological consequences.

Another important problem concerns the implications of technology for the countries of the Third World. In these areas planners will require sophisticated ecological know-how in order to choose the types of programs that will be helpful, and to reject proposals that will annihilate cultural and environmental values. Already we have on record the tragic consequences for underdeveloped countries when misguided hopes for technological progress result in ecological catastrophe.[2] These decisions, unavoidably, will be extremely difficult to make and will involve many invidious choices. Nevertheless, the choices must finally be made on the basis of ecologically sound principles and in the interests of human and cultural values if irrevocable harm is to be avoided and the disasters of the past not repeated.

In the heavily industrialized nations, where commitments to technological methods of production and consumption are already irrevocable, survival will depend upon the speed with which the destructive side effects of technology can be brought under control. To achieve this objective will require both ecophilosophers and technologists to recognize the truth of Paul Shepard's observation that "Human ecology cannot be limited to strictly biological concepts, but it cannot ignore them. It cannot even transcend them." In short, success in breaking down technological arrogance, one of the true banes of the modern epoch, necessitates the closing of the gap between the humanities and technology, between technology and science.[3]

The scope of these challenges is brilliantly displayed in the essays of

---

[2] Good examples can be found in *The Unforeseen International Ecologic Boomerang*, eds. M. Taghi Farvar and John Milton and published in February, 1969, by *Natural History Magazine* as "A Natural History Special Supplement."

[3] I have purposely ignored the frequently proposed "Luddite" solution because there is no practical way of abolishing technology in the West until we have learned the sophisticated skills necessary to live without it. But I do not wish to suggest that the brilliant critiques of science and technology from Swift through Ellul may not lead to the conclusion that the fullest realization of human capacities is incompatible with a tradition of science and technology. The question in my opinion remains open.

zoologist *Lawrence Slobodkin and historian Lewis Mumford, who take different approaches toward understanding the relationship of science and technology to the environmental crisis. For Slobodkin, the value-oriented thinkers are grossly unrealistic and dangerously misleading when they look to "changes of heart" and religious conversions to solve the complicated problems indicated by scientific ecology. The key issue, Slobodkin argues, is to understand that the best approach to problems of human survival is neither "moral rearmament" nor fine intentions, but solid research, engineering, and technology. No degree of ecological good will can discover how to recycle materials, determine side effects, or comprehend nonlinear variables.*

Slobodkin's insistence on the need to improve the expertise of scientific and applied ecology in order to cope with the unbelievable difficulties of the technical issues involved is an objective that would be discredited only by neo-Luddites or earth mystics. Yet, Slobodkin's opinion that moral rearmament as an "ecological nostrum" is dangerous because of the "real problems of engineering and technology" fails to account realistically for the ways ecological knowledge would actually be used. As Lewis Mumford points out, science and technology are both spiritually impoverished and therefore dangerous when divorced from an overriding awareness of human origins, purposes, and values—an assertion that is easily confirmed by a brief review of twentieth-century history.

Further support for this assumption is provided by Mumford's observation that the scientist "is generally unprepared to recognize or deal with the institutionalized purposes that are actually controlling our society: forces such as finance capitalism, bureaucratic organization, mechanization, and automation." While Mumford is no Luddite, he is skeptical that the institutions of society are capable of making humane uses of science and technology. He strongly emphasizes that the salvation of man and earth will depend less on producing scientists and technicians, and more on "producing more whole men and women, at home in every part of the environment." Whatever gains are made toward finding technical solutions to ecological problems, we will still fail if we cannot locate these techniques within a context of human values.

Professor Mumford's passionate critique of the valueless technocracy running wild, contributing to the rape of the biosphere, cutting man off from nature and from his own natural history, relentlessly diminishing the value of life, is complemented by Paul Goodman's proposal that technology be placed where it belongs, as a branch of moral philosophy subject to the guidance of rational criteria derived from the humanities.

By combining the viewpoints of Slobodkin and Mumford, Good-

man's proposals illuminate both the problem of scientific parochialism and that of the individual scientist's responsibility for the uses made of his work. Traditionally, as Paul Shepard pointed out, Western science has tended to be obsessed with reductionist studies of nonliving matter, ignoring the broader problems posed by human existence. But unless scientific endeavor can break with orthodoxy and expand its scope to include man within "the interplay between the component parts of a system," we condemn ourselves to the "destructive mismanagement of human lives and of natural resources." [4]

Beyond expanding its horizons to include the whole living organism functioning in its total environment, the conscience of science must assume responsibility for informing the peoples of all the world about the ecological significance of ongoing military, political, technological, and commercial enterprises, regardless of the consequences for those institutions. As Barry Commoner makes clear, science can no longer tolerate secrecy, nor can individual scientists quietly abide military or commercial policies which, though politically or economically expedient, are tantamount to ecological murder.

[4] René Dubos, *So Human An Animal* (New York: Charles Scribner's Sons, 1968), pp. 208–22, provides an excellent discussion of scientific responsibilities, met and unmet.

Lawrence B. Slobodkin

aspects of the future of ecology

The General Problem

The future of ecology is tied to the future of mankind in an intimate and uncomfortable way. That is, physical and biochemical systems can be reasonably well insulated from environmental changes while, to the degree that ecology is concerned with naturally occurring interactions between organisms, it is highly vulnerable to all sorts of changes, most of which can be traced directly or indirectly to the activities of men. To study climax forests in America would have been reasonably simple one or two centuries ago, had it been of interest at that time, but a study of that sort is now almost impossible. To permit such study one or two centuries hence will require that we now establish reserve areas and maintain them in a natural state for the next one or two centuries. This will immediately bring up the administrative and political problems associated with the establishment of such areas: the conflicts of land use requirements that now exist and the very difficult questions relating to changes in land use pressures that are likely to arise in the next two centuries. Thus, even if one begins with the purest and most intellectual of ecological problems, one is very quickly forced to consider practical and political problems. Conversely, it is abundantly apparent that a most difficult and most important practical problem facing humanity at present is an ecological one, at least in the sense that its satisfactory solution will necessarily require consideration of intellectual problems which are identical, at least in form, with those that concern ecologists. I am referring to the cluster of problems associated with the high density of human population on earth.

There is an extremely dangerous possibility that the full complexity of the interaction between ecological thought and the practical business of mankind's survival will not be realized soon enough and with sufficient clarity by any of the decision-makers involved. It is my present

Reprinted, by permission, from BioScience, 13(1), 16–23.

71

concern to explain what I believe to be rather obvious and important aspects of these interactions. I am convinced that while ecology may, in fact must, continue to develop as an intellectual discipline, there must also be an increasing interaction between ecology and public affairs in the broadest sense. This interaction not only has intellectual appeal in its own right but is of overwhelming practical significance.

Practical Problems on the Social Level

We must distinguish between the practicality of a concept and its operationality. This distinction is of paramount importance for our present purpose.

Consider the following suggestions, each one of which was presented at the American Association for the Advancement of Science meetings in Washington in 1966 at plenary sessions of the AAAS as a whole.

1. *Since the expansive, exploitative, and basically antagonistic attitude of modern man to his environment is an outgrowth of the Judeo-Christian tradition, it cannot be halted until this attitude is changed on a profoundly personal level. The fundamental solution to the increasingly difficult problems created by man's expansion must be in a revision of our basic attitude toward nature. The attitude that must replace our present one is essentially that of St. Francis of Assisi.*

Note that this concept is practical in the sense that many of our problems would disappear if there were a mass conversion to the principles of St. Francis but is nonoperational in the sense that it is not clear what action should be immediately taken to encourage conversion to the ideas of St. Francis, even if one could avoid undesirable side effects.

2. *Since it is known that under suitable crowding, the reproductive activity of rodents comes to a halt, presumably, under suitable conditions of crowding, human reproduction activity will also come to a halt, therefore no particular measures need be taken.*

This is completely operational but there is some question of its practicality.

3. *What is required is to introduce and achieve the adoption of suitable birth control devices that are cheap, effective, inoffensive, and do not require indoor plumbing.*

This is, in fact, an often rediscovered nostrum. Its operationality is open to question at least for the majority of situations and people. Obviously, if birth control was very widely used, the problem would be ameliorated. It is not clear, however, how one effectively increases the use of birth control. There is also real danger in not taking cognizance of the secondary effects, politically and socially, of promulgating increased use of birth control.

The three statements listed were actually received with applause by an audience consisting of approximately 50 percent Ph.D.'s in science. All three statements were in one sense correct and valid. They are also mutually contradictory and simplistic. For the same audience to seem equally enthusiastic about all of them may imply that applause of a scientific audience is like that of the audience at a play—without reference to the empirical content of the script. It is also possible that scientific fascination with the intellectual may preclude the realization that the problems at issue are immedate and are firmly embedded in the problems of politics and engineering so that the proposed solutions must have similar immediacy. That is, any proposed solution which is not amenable to immediate activation or at least testing is illegitimate, both morally and intellectually.

Nevertheless, the three statements are all obviously concerned with a real problem and this problem becomes identical with that of ecology. The future of ecology becomes identical with the attempt at solving this problem. I hope this will become obvious.

I will begin the analysis at the furthest remove from the obviously ecological and will briefly indicate how attempts to find practical and operational solutions on one level generate questions on another, and also how motivations of pure intellectuality become entangled with political, ethical, and engineering considerations and the converse.

Without being an alarmist and without exaggeration of self-evident facts, I can state that starvation is a major problem in much of the world and shows no indication of becoming less so in many areas. It is not empirically obvious what fraction of the world's starvation is caused by economic factors such as poor food distribution,[1] excessive prices for food, or the obverse, excessively low incomes for hungry people or poor distribution of food-consuming populations with reference to the food and income-producing resources.

It is apparent, however, that improved transportation would solve part of the problem and that increased use of fertilizers, increased industrialization, and education would all to some degree alleviate the immediate problem of starvation.

Possibly there are ecological limits that come into immediate play at this point. For example, certain lands may not be improvable by fertilization. Also, it can be asserted, with a high probability, that if a large-scale assault is made on problems of transportation, fertilization,

---

[1] For example, I have been told by a traveler that fresh fruits and vegetables in some Indian markets are priced very high, the price declining as they become stale. When they are so stale as to have lost much of their food value, they are priced at a level which can be rapidly sold. In the process many fruits and vegetables are discarded as rotten.

and industrialization, it will further disturb or upset the existing ecological balance. Clearly, the consequence of disturbed ecological balance
is not as important as present starvation unless it can be shown that the
disturbance will result in greater starvation in the future. Even then it
becomes a moral or ethical problem as to how one weighs tomorrow's
disaster against today's malnutrition!

We will find throughout the analysis that *"correct" solutions, even
if they are feasible, may generate problems whose solutions may or may
not be feasible*. I will not call attention to this again.

Staying on the general level of public works, as problems of starvation
are solved or avoided, problems of pollution increase. I am sure it can
be documented that a dweller in an opulent city has blacker lungs than
a dweller in a poor one, that the concentration of carcinogens in an
American are higher than in a Kenyan, and that a bathing beach off
New York has a higher lead concentration than a bathing beach off
Calcutta (I will ignore garbage for the moment).

The public health problems associated with efficiency and urbanization are fantastic and fascinating: anome in Ypsilanti, Michigan; false
epilepsy seizures of Navajo boys at boarding school; ulcers and associated cancer in Chinese, etc. Thus, madness and psychosomatic death
may accompany efficiency and full bellies in surprising ways.

Perhaps lives are saved and the quality of life is improved by "non-
productive" areas such as parks, wastelands, and wilderness. It also
seems reasonably clear that a wilderness used as an adjunct to a mental
health program is to some degree not the kind of wilderness that one
wants for a research area, nor even the kind one would prefer for a
family vacation. Again, compromise must be made.

All of the considerations in this section assume that one can predict
the effect of particular regulations or activities on human and ecological
parameters. We will examine this assumption in part in the next section.
Even if this assumption is met, however, so that one knows what ought
to be done to gain a particular end and can present a complete statement of the consequences of these actions and can show that these consequences are beneficial and even palatable and pleasant, the actual
doing involves the political assent of the persons involved or some decision as to the moral and eventually practical consequences of a teleo-
logical suspension of the ethical in order to circumvent political barriers.

There are social, political, and moral problems generated by any
serious attempts to manipulate man's environment, even if the technological procedures for this manipulation are known and even if the
consequences of the manipulations can be predicted with high accuracy.
These problems are not solvable technologically or scientifically even in
principle. All that can be done technologically is to describe how to do
things and what the consequences of doing things might be. The actual

doing of them involves other kinds of commitments than the purely technological or intellectual ones.

The Technological or Ecological Engineering Level

Just as in the preceding section, the false assumption is made that technologists can answer all questions put to them. In this and subsequent sections the assumption is made that only the immediate problem of the section remains unsolved.

I will now list examples of some of the technological problems associated with high levels of human population.

Given any type of biological resource-producing area, an initial decision must be made as to whether this is to be used as a farm or as a hunting ground. In certain situations the decision is obvious for either biological or politico-historical reasons. For example, international waters cannot be treated as farms and privately owned agricultural land cannot be treated as hunting grounds. There are, however, situations which are borderline. For example, there is open discussion as to how some of the East African grasslands might be best used, and there is at least some possibility that there would be greater economic return and food production by abandoning use as farms in favor of wild animal range.

Conversely, there is serious consideration of using the sea lochs of Western Scotland as fish ponds, blocking off the seaward ends. The feasibility of this plan is contingent on several things—specifically on the ability to raise young plaice in the laboratory, on the feasibility of fertilizing the lochs so that the planted immature plaice may grow to maturity, and on the settlement of ownership questions.

It has recently been established that young plaice can be raised in quantity if they are provided with the nauplii of brine shrimp as food. The brine shrimp nauplii are hatched from eggs that are purchased from American suppliers. The suppliers collect the eggs at salt pans in California and in Utah. Due to increasing demands for brine shrimp nauplii by tropical fish hobbyists and, possibly, to real estate developments in and near what were salt pans, the supply of California eggs is no longer adequate to meet demand. The eggs from Utah produce nauplii which are toxic to the plaice larvae. The toxicity of the Utah shrimps has been traced to residual insecticides from the surrounding agricultural regions of the Great Salt Lake basin.

That is, the prospect of cheaper and more abundant fish in England is confronted with a bottleneck due to the use of insecticides in Utah!

Consider another technological problem—the relative advantage of different pest control procedures. Biological control methods (i.e., the introduction, establishment, and management of populations of predators, parasites, and competitors) has been reasonably successful in a variety of situations. It is often unsuccessful or at least requires a relatively long period of field experimentation before a suitable control pattern can be developed. It has the advantage of avoiding the peculiar side effects that may come from insecticides. Insecticides are immediately effective, may be cheaper in the short run, but require constant renewal, and, as pest organisms evolve in response to the insecticides, require constant revision of procedures. If more information were available on predator-prey interactions, the choice would be simpler.

I think it is clear that the motivation of the crop growers and insecticide manufacturers is the honest search for profit. If biological control mechanisms were clearly and demonstrably practically superior at producing cash profits to the growers, they would drive insecticides off the market and presumably provide cash profit to their producers.

The fact that biological control methods are generally not commercially competitive poses a problem not only of biological technology, but also of governmental and economic concern. For example, consider this quotation.

> People aren't supposed to like small bits of insect in their catsup even if they can't find them. Thus [The] Public Health [Service], which is trying to keep poisonous residues out of food stuffs, may be forcing the tomato grower to treat [with insecticides], with the result that the consumer has bug-free but not toxicant-free catsup.[2]

Also, research on chemical insecticides is a natural outgrowth of the research and development programs of the chemical and petroleum industries, while biological control research is not in such a comfortable relation with a profitable industry.

While there is general agreement that large amounts of non-nutritious chemicals designed to kill animals ought not be part of an ideal diet, there are real technological, economic, and legal reasons why the insecticides continue to be used. There is no obvious reason to conclude that morality and intelligence exist only on one side or the other of the insecticide versus biological control polemic.

In the case of a hunting or fishing area there is another, more or less related, family of problems. How does one determine whether or not the present fishing or hunting practice is optimal? Obviously, this depends on the definition of optimum; e.g., maximum income to fisherman or hunter, maximum protein, maximum sustainable yield. In fact, rather sophisticated theories are available for fisheries' studies, but these tend to remain problems of data quality on the one hand and enforceability on the other.

[2] Paul DeBach, *Biological Control of Insect Pests and Weeds* (New York: Reinhold, 1964), p. 712.

A related but distinct technological area is that of pollution control. The potential subtlety of the relation may perhaps be most readily visualized by one example. It has been found recently that extremely dilute solutions of detergents, while not interfering with the apparent health and survival of fish, do interfere with the cytological fine structure of the lateral line system. It has also been shown that the odor of water, sensed by the lateral line system, is used by some fishes to return to their birth streams for breeding. We then have the curious possibility of an extremely low level of a specific pollutant having a specific, potentially highly deleterious effect on a fishery. How many such highly specific effects exist is simply not known at present. The more obvious problems are those involving massive quantities of biological wastes, industrial wastes, and heat. The technology of disposal is not yet completely developed, and it may be safe to say that there is no waste removal process that is completely without drawbacks. At best, biological wastes are reducible to mineral form, but these mineral residues are precisely the things that will accelerate the growth of algae and other water plants which may themselves become a nuisance.

As the scale of the problem increases, the likelihood of fairly subtle side effects may also increase. Perhaps the prime example may prove to be the greenhouse effect[3] on earth surface temperature associated with the increase of atmospheric CO_2 content, as a combined result of industrial fuels and deforestation.

The scale of system that must be considered in developing a technology of waste management may be very large indeed. While the isolated settler can rely on a cesspool, manure pile, stream and rubbish dump, a series of small towns must begin apportioning the water and waste disposal facilities of an entire stream or stream system or watershed, and as industrialization proceeds, the scale of the problem is enhanced. One or two large paper mills in Czechoslovakia turn the waters of the Elbe brown as far downstream as Dresden.

The precise form that management should take remains obscure, and under most realistic assumptions must be aimed at minimizing the possible dangers of absence of management or mismanagement. These can sometimes be assessed in rather obvious ways from appearances, tastes, or smells. Occasionally, more subtle assessments of danger are necessary. Even in the absence of very definite theories it is usually a sound conjecture that unless a system is actively deteriorating there is no need for immediate revision of existing procedures—unless there exists strong argument to the contrary. For example, if there exists a

---

[3] This effect results from the relative opacity of CO_2 to infra-red radiation, thereby tending to lower the temperature specific rate of heat radiation from the earth to space.

certain level of water and air pollution, which is apparently neither toxic nor too displeasing on other grounds, there is no immediate necessity to alter sewage treatment procedures or air cleaning procedures. Conversely, if there is evidence of actual deterioration of air or water quality, on the grossest level of consideration, or of biological diversity on a somewhat more sophisticated level, then there exists immediate need for change in existing programs.

There now exists a technology which, at least in part, may be utilized by public agencies in carrying out action programs to deal with population increase-associated problems.

Appropriate action is contingent on certain kinds and qualites of data available on a continuing basis and on the development of predictive conclusions from these data.

Thus, just as the practical legislative programs depend on the development of certain kinds of engineering, so the engineering depends on the data and theory available from a somewhat more abstract level.

Monitoring Systems and Sensivity Studies

One of the goals of ecology is prediction of the effect of perturbations of all sorts on the environment, in particular, of man-caused perturbations. While a profound understanding of ecological problems would almost certainly help in this type of prediction, as we will see below, at a certain level profound understanding is simply not necessary. It is possible to develop a predictive system, adequate for most purposes in the following fashion:

1. Collect, on a routine basis, as much data of as many different kinds as possible about a particular system (stream or watershed or region of the earth.)

2. Choose some measurement which is of particular interest and measure it at the same times and places as you have measured the other data.

3. For each time and place set up a general regression equation which expresses your interesting measurement, Y, as the sum of each of the routine data multiplied by some unknown constant coefficient.

4. Feed the data from a number of times and places considerably greater than the number of unknown constants into a computer and have the computer discard those measurements which do not significantly contribute to determining the variance in the interesting measurement and provide best least squares estimates of the remaining coefficients.

5. A reasonable prediction of the effect of changes in Y on each of the routine measurements and the converse is now available, or, if Y and some sets of measurements are set arbitrarily, a reasonable estimate can be made of the probable values that will be taken by the remaining measurements.

If, for example, Y is human population size and there exists a set of convenient environmental measurements, a prediction of the effects of population increase on these measurements can be made. This does not require that there be any *known* logical or empirical relation whatsoever between the various measurements, but it does require that the precision of these measurements be fairly high.

This may be best explained by an example. Incoming freshmen at the University of Michigan are given a questionnaire known popularly as the "cooked-carrots test." This consists of a series of multiple choice questions which were made up in a completely arbitrary fashion, that is, with no attempt whatsoever at theoretical justification. The test is used to predict the future history of the students at the University and makes very good predictions. This is because the questions were given to a large number of students in a pretest and the career of these pretest students was then followed for four years. It was then possible to correlate the answer profiles of students with their academic performance. Particular types of profiles were correlated with, for example, "A—" students of English Literature. These profiles were sufficiently highly correlated so that, when an entering student was shown to have this profile, one could state with fair certainty that if he became an English Literature major he would achieve an A— academic average. Notice that no theory of pedagogy or competence is involved, only brute prediction.

Taking another example, it is possible to show that the number of species of birds on an island is reasonably well predicted by a multidimensional regression equation in which the area of the island, its height, and its distance from other land masses enter as data with suitable coefficients. This fact poses theoretical problems; for example, "Why is the relation between area and population size what it is rather than something else?" But it does not constitute an insightful theory in its own right. If the immediate concern is prediction, however, it does nicely.

It is clear when the above examples are considered that predictions based on them will generally work reasonably well, but that they do not take the place of actual models or theories for dealing with the unusual or unexpected. Consider, for example, a student who is going to create a new branch of zoology. We would not expect him to have the same "cooked-carrots" profile as our past students.

We will consider the problems raised by this weakness extensively in the next section.

A hypothetical example will make the important distinction between brute prediction and insightful theory apparent. A successful regression analysis of the abundance of some particular organisms on a series of environmental variables chosen at random would give the result that some would show a significant relation while others would not. Now, consider some environmental variable which had to be present in precisely correct levels for this species to survive at all. While this might be the primary thing to be careful of, with reference to the species in question, in the analysis it would not show up as a significant factor at all!

Taking an actual case, the noxious pest Klamath weed (*Hypericum perforatum*) was brought under control in the American West by introduction of a beetle (*Chrysolina quadrigemina*). When the situation had come to a steady state, both the beetle and the Klamath weed were relatively rare constituents of the biota and would have shown no particular significant relation (in the statistical sense) on a regression analysis, but obviously elimination of the beetle would have permitted the weed to return to its role as a pest.

Even within the confines of blind regression there exists the very real problem of deciding what properties are to be measured and how. Therefore, the primary usefulness of a regression system is to monitor the state of ecological systems so as to provide warning of deleterious changes before they become irreversible. In the absence of understanding or insight the only safe course is to keep constant tab on a large series of variables—preferably by means of automated measuring devices as yet to be designed—and to set some statistical standard for what would be considered a sufficiently great deviation from previously observed mean values or a sufficiently significant trend to require practical action of the sort indicated in previous sections. *Constancy of environmental variables generally represents, if not a good position, at least a non-deteriorating one. Any failure of constancy in the absence of strong evidence to the contrary must be considered as a danger sign.*

Obviously, the objection might be made that changes in certain measurable properties are of trivial importance. This is true but, unfortunately, distinguishing between the trivial and nontrivial is not itself obvious and the penalties associated with error in this distinction are too enormous to permit a wait-and-see approach.

Monitoring of environmental variables will, at least in principle, permit an assessment of environmental quality deterioration. It is expensive and technically difficult. It has the additional drawbacks that (a) variables which are not statistically significant at first glance may be of overwhelming empirical importance under certain circumstances, and

(b) while the need for corrective procedures can be seen from monitoring, the actual procedures to be taken must be indicated by other types of theory.

Pure Ecology

The problems of pure ecology must be partially solved before the engineering aspects of ecology can be fully effective, partially because ecological understanding is a prerequisite to effective engineering and partially because clear explanations of ecology are required before the legislatures and voters can be expected to support ecologically significant legislation and regulation.

Pure ecology, as the term is being used here, is concerned with the development of empirically significant theories and models which will permit understanding and prediction of such things as the control of abundance and of organisms, the pattern of interaction between species, and the effects of physical and biological perturbations on these things. The notion of "purity" is used here in the sense of a greater concern with the intellectual problems of theory construction as opposed to the practical problems of sewage disposal, fisheries theory, etc. This is not equivalent to saying that the interesting intellectual developments are not necessary for the solution of these practical problems; in fact, the reverse is true.

Inanimate systems, with the passage of time, typically come to either an equilibrium condition or to a steady state which is linearly dependent on external variables. Living systems, on the other hand, are characteristically not linear. Whole organisms or groups of whole organisms may respond to small changes in environmental conditions by large-scale alterations in their properties. These responses may be behavioral or may be mediated through physiological mechanisms.

Many organisms can be maintained in artificial or laboratory environments. It is generally the case that organisms introduced to such environments alter in abundance with the passage of time and come to some steady state abundance. The history of such artificial populations can be presented mathematically with greater or lesser facility. The mathematical formulations may be rather complex, involving feedbacks and functional dependencies of fairly subtle kinds. In addition, all populations that have been carefully studied have either a dispersive phase during the life of the animals, or they have some pattern of escape behavior which causes them to leave a crowded region. The escape behavior patterns may be triggered by subtle changes in either the environment or the other animals in the population. To build such patterns into the mathematical models makes very severe demands on mathematical notation, requiring nonlinearities and stipulation of elaborate boundary conditions for any given model, even if the relevant facts are known. The facts themselves are sometimes quite curious—the Koala bear's requirement for old eucalyptus leaves, the "putzer" fishes (*Ladroides dimidratus*) grooming stations to which other fish come to have their dead skin and parasites removed, the hydra that float away when they are hungry in a crowded environment, etc.

In short, even the relatively simple problem of growth pattern and control mechanism of organisms in simplified environments is not yet solved either on the biological level or on the level of a general mathematical theory of nonlinear feedback systems.

There are also problems of a very real kind that can be generated from either constructing more complex experimental situations or considering the effects of perturbations on simple systems by changes analogous to those occurring in nature as a result of human expansion.

The problem of pure ecology can also be approached from the other direction—that is, questions may be asked about natural systems with all their complexity intact; if properly formulated, these questions can then be answered in terms permitting predictions about natural systems. The measure of quality of this type of questioning is in the clarity and generality of the answers and in the soundness of the biological assumptions made. For example, on the basis of certain elementary observations it has been suggested that populations of terrestrial herbivore species in undisturbed natural situations will have a lower food consumption per year, relatively to the total food available, than will carnivores in the same or similar communities. This is a very specific, readily testable nontrivial conclusion derived from a uniquely specified sequence of theoretical steps. It also seems to be confirmed in nature. As another example, on the basis of stability considerations suggested by laboratory experiments it has been predicted that predators in nature will behave in a fashion very much like that prescribed by a rational theory of predation or fishing and will tend to take prey animals which would have died of other causes in any case. This prediction has been made without imputing either rationality or prescience to animals. While this theory has not, in fact, been adequately tested in the field, it has not been denied by the available data. In this case a regression equation relating the food consumption of the prey to the size of the prey populations, and the possible kinds of prey animals that might be taken defines the optimal category of prey removed as that associated with the lowest regression coefficient in a purely engineering sense. It has the further interesting property, for our present illustrative purpose, that it is possible to show that each of the regression coefficients can be replaced by a more complex expression which relates the relative value of taking a particular kind of prey to the growth and survivorship pattern of the prey population.

Thus, regression coefficients of the sort discussed in the previous section can, at least in principle, be replaced by insightful statements in such a way as to make clear the degree to which they may serve as valid guides to action.

This suggests the possible paradigm of the interaction between pure and applied ecology—namely, out of the pure research may arise theories which explain the significance of relatively simple and cheaply made measurements which, by themselves, do not provide obvious insights.

Many of the observations of pure ecology seem to suggest rather major practical conclusions, but as yet the precise operationality of these conclusions is open to question. For example, the diversity of life in the tropics seems considerably greater than that in the arctic, and there is also an impression that populations of tropical animals are less subject to violent fluctuations than those of the arctic. In all likelihood these impressions are valid, but there are questions as to the most useful operational meaning for the concepts "diverse" and "stable." From these impressions and the observations that pests and weeds seem able to invade cropland or other disturbed land, it is deduced that the stability of natural communities is related to the number of species in the system. If it could be determined that the stability is a consequence of the large number of species and not the reverse, this would be a very important guide to conservation practice. It is, however, possible to consider that stability in some sense permits a large number of species to be present, given some appropriate measure of stability. This is as yet an unclear area.

As a final example, one of the concerns of pure ecology, in conjunction with systematics and genetics, is the development of an evolutionary theory which will permit prediction, at least to some degree. This must take account of the interactions between organisms and their environment in the broadest sense. The consequences of success in developing such a theory are, in general, the ability to predict the effects of perturbations from unnatural sources, which is precisely what is required on a practical level.

In general, pure ecology suffers from a lack of financial support, from the difficulties associated with using mathematical systems designed for linear systems to describe nonlinear biological systems, and from a scarcity of sophisticated personnel. I hope it is clear from the examples given that the practical problems of ecology cannot be solved completely until the pure problems are at least partially solved.

There exists a series of "pure" ecology problems generated by primarily intellectual concerns. These are generally only partially solved at present, but even the partial solutions seem to produce generalities that are of appreciable practical significance in permitting insightful programs of prediction and management.

Conclusions

Background. Despite the brevity of presentation I hope enough examples have been provided to establish, or at least make plausible, the following conclusions:

1. The solutions of major practical problems of human survival are intimately associated with the solutions of the technological, biological, and mathematical problems which, taken together, constitute environmental biology or ecology, broadly defined.

2. The best intentions in the world can not provide simple, cheap, or automatic solutions to these problems; that is, the recommendation of the use of political persuasion or moral rearmament as an ecological nostrum is worse than futile. It is dangerous since there exist real problems of engineering and technology that require more than a "good heart" for their activation.

3. Current technology can do more than it has done, but it is limited as much by a shortage of basic scientific information as it is by a lack of financial and political support.

The scientific problems of ecology constitute major intellectual challenges, involving the development of theories and analyses that are not trivial consequences of physiology, genetics, or other branches of biology, but must be developed on their own. Extant ecological problems will not be automatically solved by "applying" extant mathematical, physiological, or philosophical insights but will require the painstaking collection of appropriate kinds of data, the development of suitably ingenious experiments, and the development of new theoretical constructs.

Pure ecological research will eventually provide the information needed for development of an ecological technology. At the moment, such research suffers from a lack of financial support and from weaknesses in training programs throughout the world. While financial support will probably increase as the pressures become greater, the basic intellectual quality of the training programs and research will probably not improve very much in the near future unless strenuous efforts are made. This is because of the fact that (a) the availability of money attracts research proposals which tend toward self-perpetuation almost regardless of quality, and (b) there is a shortage of intellectual personnel to even evaluate these proposals, let alone carry them out.

Unfortunately, while intellectual problems may best be handled at leisure, the practical problems are such as to encourage haste.

It is categorically impossible to solve the problems associated with human population increase by adoption of any one single modification of attitude or behavior (i.e., "unitary or simplistic solutions") since all such proposed modifications of behavior and attitude generate moral, political, technological, and scientific problems of major proportions. To teach or advocate unitary solutions is a cynical and amoral activity in the strictest sense of these words, generating present dangers and obscuring the search for future solutions, both effects being literally murderous.

The problems associated with human population increase exist on many levels, and may be outlined as follows:

An Outline of the Levels of Problems Associated with Human Increase—

I. Practical problems
  A. Starvation
  B. Pollution and illness (including problems of mental health)
  C. Political disintegration

These problems require for their solution answers to:

II. Scientific problems, of an applied kind, through:
  A. Applied technologies such as
    1. Fish and game management
    2. Pest control, both biological and chemical
    3. Air purification and water quality maintenance
    4. Waste disposal
    5. Ecological system management and zoning.

Which in turn depend on information and procedures derived from:

  B. Monitoring and data collection, including the problems of sampling theory, design of sampling gear, and information processing devices.

Which can be used for:

  C. Predictive regression equations and sensitivity tests.

All of the practical procedures listed above depend for their safe and effective use on the solution and formulation of:

III. Problems of pure ecology, for example:
  A. The theory of stability conditions in nonlinear, evolving, feedback systems
  B. The theory of ecological diversity—why are certain regions characterized by more resident species than others?

C. The theory of ecological energy transfers—what stabilizes the interaction between predators and prey in nature?

D. The development of a predictive evolutionary theory.

The major problems have been listed in such a way that the earlier listed depend in part on the latter to provide information needed for solutions. Simultaneously, financial and other support for the latter problems may, and perhaps must, be justified in terms of their importance to the earlier.

The eventual solution to the underlying problem of man's survival depends on *simultaneous* solutions of the whole spectrum of problems listed.

Recommendations

Having stated the weakness of many of the proposed solutions to the practical and urgent questions of ecology, I am required to commit myself to specific recommendations, lest I be considered an anti-intellectual prophet of doom.

I hope I've made it clear that there is no single "correct" ecological viewpoint, except perhaps for a certain degree of open-mindedness and intelligence. This is operationally significant in that an ecologist cannot claim to be fulfilling his full professional function by merely "making people aware of the ecological viewpoint."

I do not believe that any man can acquire full professional competence in all of the areas relevant to ecology. A choice is required between attempting to be a professional in one of the relevant disciplines and of being a generalist. While I cannot rigorously demonstrate the lack of utility of pure generalists, I am convinced that the dangers of producing wrong solutions and the magnitude of their consequences make it vital that the decisions be made by a concordance of specialists representing the different relevant areas. For this purpose, rather than produce generalists it is necessary that we produce men equal to the best in their own areas but also capable of appreciating, evaluating, and communicating with other specialists in at least two areas other than their own. For example, a pure ecologist ought to be able to communicate with a mathematician and a sewage engineer in some mutually effective way. We cannot afford the obfuscatory jargonal mysteries which in the past have protected incompetence in the various academic disciplines. The problems associated with the production of such broad experts had best be handled by each of the relevant disciplines each in its own way.

We must avoid at all costs confusing glibness with logic and personal charisma with professional authority. It must be recognized at the outset that conflicts of interest do exist with reference to almost all ecological decisions, that, for example, not all species can be saved from extinction but at the same time destruction of natural areas is dangerous and may have practical as well as aesthetic consequences.

The immediate practical problem is that the different, highly competent experts dealing with specific subproblems of the general problem are honestly not aware of the full ramifications of their own work, and therefore may find themselves acting at cross-purposes to each other. I suggest that this situation is dangerous and that universities are in a strategic position to help alleviate this danger.

The following scheme was developed with the University of Michigan in mind, due to my own affiliation and to the long history of ecological research on many levels at Michigan. I believe, however, that the idea is generalizable to other public universities and to some private ones.

I suggest that the immediate practical next step is an educational one. The presently active politicians, economists, engineers, and scientists now working on ecological problems are generally not mutually conversant. The problems at issue are multileveled. While there is a limit to the expertise that can be expected of one man, the ability of experts to communicate with each other can, I believe, be considerably improved. This communication or even an attempt at this kind of communication must result in an improvement of our ability to deal with ecological problems.

As I have indicated, strictly practical problems require that free communication between workers at all levels be permanently maintained, not just in conferences, symposia, and pronouncements, but on a day-to-day working basis. I therefore recommend that the universities invite governors, state legislators, heads of state planning and conservation and game management offices together with sanitary engineers and public health officials to meet with their faculties either for an extended time or at an extended series of one-day meetings with the express purpose of all participants acquainting each other, in as complete and informal way as possible, with their goals for the ecological health of their regions, with the programs they are at present considering to bring about these goals, and most significantly with their own reservations and questions about these goals. *This must be done without any sense of attacking a hypothetical villain, and with a minimum of premature publicity*. It may be possible to actually find either that real solutions now exist to various apparently unsolvable problems or that, at the very least, there exist rational paths that might well be followed in trying to find solutions once the problems are understood by the appropriate people.

Many of the public pronouncements made by scientists, interested citizens, and politicians about ecological problems have the effect of "substituting purpose for action." They tend to provide for their promulgators and for their supporters among the public, the satisfying sense of being unable to take specific action because of a malicious, or at least uninformed, opponent or class of opponents. Other producers of hortatory and homiletic pronouncements take refuge from the necessity for action in a presumed public apathy.

I hope that I have demonstrated that there are, in fact, gaps in necessary information. There are legitimate differences of opinion on all levels from the form ecologically significant legislation ought to take to how funds for ecological research ought to be distributed, to the degree that interspecific competition occurs in nature. *These gaps and differences arise from a multiplicity of sources and are not legitimately the "fault" of any one particular person or class of persons. Without this realization further attempts at finding real solutions are almost impossible.*

While federal funds may prove helpful in both research and the activation of legislation, the entire country is simply too big a unit, with too many real disparate interests, to permit the development of practical avenues for solutions or of free effective communication between the various men involved in looking for solutions. At the other extreme, a town or country is too small to permit effective action on any level. A state is of reasonable size for this kind of thing.

An ongoing study session of the sort I have in mind is something new in this field. I would suggest that the meetings be conducted as closed seminars, without the press or public at large in attendance. This would prevent people from using the meetings as soap boxes from which to defeat their opponents. Defeating opponents is not our concern. We must initially stipulate that honest disagreement is necessary. The disagreements are absolutely valid in the sense that, given present information and lack of information, alternative, equally logical conclusions are possible. To settle such disagreements by attempting to put one's opponent in a poor light may be proper for political battles of most kinds but would not be appropriate on matters of as much practical significance as these. The spokesmen for commercial fishermen have real areas of potential disagreement with the spokesman for sport fishermen. Scientists trying to get money for one kind of research are in direct competition for funds with scientists working on other problems. Legislators from urban districts have real differences with legislators from rural districts. I would hope that these meetings would permit completely candid exchange among these men, without fear that their candor would be unfairly used to their disadvantage. The purpose is not to negotiate but to gain information and to give information.

Hopefully, the quality of public disagreement between proponents of two opposing viewpoints will be different if the antagonists are well informed. If this is not so, we must resign ourselves to perpeutal demagoguery.

The areas of mutual ignorance are great enough to require more than a one-day or even one-week meeting. At the same time, all of the persons involved will, we hope, be men actively concerned with important work that will not permit them to take any longer than a week to attend a conference. I suggest that either one week every four or six months for as long a period as the participants think that they are profiting from the discussions. Alternatively, one long weekend each month or six weeks might be used. I suggest that half the time at least of each meeting day be spent listening to formal, classroom style presentations of facts and theories of one or two of the relevant subareas of ecology (including its engineering and political aspects) and that the remainder of the time be spent in free discussion of the implications of what has been presented and in criticism (as hard-headed and impolite as necessary) of the material presented. I hope that these meetings would become an almost permanent part of the professional life of the participants, thereby aiding them in directing their research, engineering, or public administration activities along more realistic channels.

It is better for the universities to initiate this project, with a minimum of fanfare and money, than to wait for the government to request expert advice. This is true for two reasons:

1. The branches of the government are not, in fact, aware of either the range of expertise available at the university or of the relevance of this expertise to their problem.

2. A committee of experts called in to advise government agencies tends to provide unrealistic "pseudosolutions" to problems at issue since while, with luck, the various experts can communicate with each other, the representatives of government at the legislative level are typically not involved in the communication process.

Since these meetings are in no sense conventions, I would suggest meeting at relatively isolated places with living and drinking and talking facilities available in a single building and with very little opportunity to leave the building, but these are details.

I believe that universities can make themselves extremely valuable to the states and the nation by initiating a program for the honest and complete exchange of ecological information between people, each of whom is now dealing with ecological problems from some particular level or viewpoint without proper appreciation of the full ramifications of his own problem. Further, such exchange of information is vital if practical solutions to ecological problems are to be developed. Obviously, problems are becoming more difficult and more threatening. The time to begin is now.

The future of ecology is intimately associated with practical problems.

There exist ecological problems of considerable practical significance which necessarily have political, social, engineering, and scientific ramifications. They are not amenable to satisfactory solution by any one field of expertise. It seems of utmost practical value that free communication begin immediately between the experts dealing with these different aspects of ecological problems. The universities may be the ideal starting place for this communication.

Lewis Mumford

"closing statement"

. . . A deep respect for physical processes, particularly for mechanical processes, dominates our mind, because it's associated with our superb achievements in the physical sciences and technics. Hence, the physical sciences have set the pattern of all the other sciences. Accurate observation and statistical prediction prevail here.

Then there is the fact of the organic world. The organic world can't be interpreted solely in terms of physical process. It must be interpreted in terms of organic functions, of modes of growth, of prospective transformations, sometimes not yet visible in the present state of an organism. Here we rise beyond mere external process toward autonomy and inner control. Physical energies are used by organisms in order to sustain their existence and interact with their environment and fulfill their life pattern.

That takes us a step away from the inevitable future. As soon as you are dealing with an organism, you're dealing with an autonomous creature, who has more than one answer to any given situation: more than one niche open. Even the lowly amoeba has a mind of its own, as Jennings long ago showed. Robert Frost wrote a touching poem about a little mite walking over his writing paper which he was tempted to squash. When he recognized that the tiny insect was running away from his finger, he perceived in that little mite a mind like his own and decided to let it live.

The reactions of both the mite and the man lie outside the world of physics. For human sentiment was brought into play here, which inhibited the first automatic reaction. If we want to preserve the environment, we will have to rely upon getting aid from people who are still capable of having human sentiments.

From F. Fraser Darling and John P. Milton, eds., Future Environments of North America. *Copyright © 1966 by The Conservation Foundation. Reprinted by permission of the publishers, Doubleday & Company, Inc., and Natural History Press. Lewis Mumford delivered this address as the closing statement at a conference of The Conservation Foundation in April, 1965, at Warrenton, Virginia.*

On that topic we may well be warned by a little essay that Joseph Wood Krutch recently contributed to the *Saturday Review*.[1] He pointed out that students of biology, in the interest of an austere experimental science, are trained to kill creatures and to preside over their death but never to love them or make pets of them. Similarly Dr. [Seymour M.] Farber told me about his daughter's high school biology class in which the students were trained to insert a needle into the skull of a live frog and carry on that humanly repulsive experiment to the end, without the even dubious justification offered for medical vivisection.

Thus we are training, in the name of experimental science, a race of young exterminators. They are not likely to be more tender toward the organic habitat than they are to a single living frog.

If this is the way we are educating our children—training them to be callous toward, if not hostile to, living organisms—we are not going to save or improve the environment. We may not even be able to save any other form of human life. It is an offense against both life and morals to treat a high-level organism as though it were something insensate. It doesn't matter very much to iron or copper or molybdenum what you do to it, but it does matter even to the lowliest organism when you interfere with its course of life.

Then, finally, of course, we come to another realm, the realm of human society. While based upon physical process and biological function, this area is specifically the realm of purpose, meaning, and value. Physical processes go on all the time in every organism. And we function like other animals, of course; but meaning and value and purpose are what dominate a truly human existence; and when they are absent, even purely organic functions deteriorate.

Now, it's obvious this is a subject for a whole talk, and in the course of the next few minutes I haven't time to explain how it is that the physical sciences, through their very mode of origin in the seventeenth century, displaced man and looked down upon organic processes as somehow inferior, because they don't lend themselves to exact analysis, the kind of analysis that can only take place with a living organism after you have killed it.

There is always something that eludes you when you examine a living organism by the methods of the physical sciences. What eludes you, of course, is life. Life is the factor that you can't understand or control, ultimately, except from within.

The result is that science in the strict sense doesn't really like to deal with organisms as living wholes and isn't at home in the world of the personality, the world of values and purposes and meanings. Even the

[1] Joseph Wood Krutch, "What Does Violence Say About Man?" *Saturday Review*, LIXVIII (March 27, 1965), 18–19.

biological sciences prefer to deal with the genes or with DNA. There is an enormous amount of fascinating activity in both these departments. But the organism and its living environment have dropped out of the picture, since the organism can't be reduced to a tissue of measurable abstractions.

Now, this has a curious practical result. You can't get rid of purpose, but since the scientist has excluded the category of purpose, he is singularly unprepared to recognize or deal with the institutionalized purposes that are actually controlling our society: forces such as finance capitalism, bureaucratic organization, mechanization, and automation. All of these form part of the great technological apparatus of war. The sciences have passively accepted these purposes, as if they did no harm as long as they do not interfere with the pursuit of science and technology. Give the scientist his laboratory, give him his budget, give him his assistants, give him his honors, and he'll work for any government or corporation without challenging the objectives or questioning the social results.

The result is, therefore, that science has become embrangled with all sorts of negative purposes, like nuclear weapons and rockets. And even in the present stage of our ethics, the overexcitement about DNA shows suspicious symptom of a desire to exercise godlike power.

Recently I was frightened when I looked at the CIBA symposium on the "Future of Life" to read the things that Crick, the great exponent of DNA, was saying about what he would do to change the genetic structure of the human race by means of the knowledge and apparatus he might soon have at his command. He would be able to make different kinds of human beings. What examination did he pass to qualify for that task?

Just remember this little illustration. Is it wise to entrust even Nobel prizewinners with godlike powers? If you knew the history of the gods, you'd know that in the early days at least in Mesopotamia and in Egypt the gods were all mad—mad with the lust of power, the desire to control. And when scientists speak the same way as a Mesopotamian god does, we have reason to wonder whether they are speaking in the spirit of pure rationality and under an austere scientific discipline or whether some irrational factor that they have ignored isn't perhaps taking hold of them.

Now, I come back to the theme of this conference. What is the valid purpose of a conference like this?

We began, somewhat unfortunately perhaps, with the physical environment. And we might have got off to a surer start, I won't say a quicker start but a surer start, if we had dealt first of all with man himself, for man must first save himself from his own mischievous fantasies and machinations if he is to save the environment. Obviously the purpose of a conference like this is not just to promote ecology. Ecology is a well-established scientific discipline which by now is self-promoting. Nor can our primary aim be merely to preserve such residual near-primeval habitats as may still be in existence: even less can it be to "restore" them. Such restorations would produce only museum pieces, a sort of scientific Williamsburg.

But the real purpose of a conference like this—is it not?—is to insure the existence or the replenishment of a sufficiently varied environment to sustain all of life, including human life and thus to widen the ground for man's further conscious development. That ultimately, it seems to me, is what the whole business is about.

Man has developed in the past in a back-and-forth response to an extremely complex organic environment, which, beginning in paleolithic times, he has sampled, staked out, explored, and become increasingly conscious of in all its ramifications. If this planetary habitat had been as uniform, as fixed, as well controlled as a space capsule, man would have undergone no changes whatever. He would have had no incentive to change, no reason to develop, no possibilities beyond what the space capsule itself offered him.

Now, this man-sustaining environment can be variously interpreted.

One of the simplest interpretations is that of my old friend Benton MacKaye, he who conceived and planned the Appalachian Trail. He divided the human habitat into the primeval, the rural, and the communal. I find this a very useful classification, because the primeval is the paleolithic environment, the rural is neolithic, and the communal part became highly developed only with the emergence of urban civilizations.

Man became a moral animal in early paleolithic times, and he probably had more cooperative relations with the creatures who shared his habitat than he does today. It's the paleolithic hunter who begs forgiveness of the animal he has to kill for food. Our basic morality, of caring for and nurturing life, goes back even to the mammals, in the care and nurture of the young. That's the rock-bottom basis for all the morality worth calling such.

Then comes the great neolithic process of domestication, a great change that took place slowly, transforming the landscape and making over the whole mode of life. This change gave to sexuality a larger role than it could have had before. In neolithic life the culture of sex, in the domestication of plants and animals and man himself, pervades the whole habitat. "Home and mother" are written over the cultivated landscape. Man now has a fixed dwelling place, a secure food supply, and the prospect of both biological and cultural continuity.

Then on top of that came the environment of civilization, which is cosmic and urban. Civilization comes in at a time when man observes the stars and the planets long enough to see that his whole life is related not just to the local terrain but to the sun and moon, and to movements and energies that lie far beyond his own immediate habitat.

These are the three great habitats of man. And now we find that all three habitats are disappearing before our eyes. Some are severely threatened, some have already been obliterated. Now, the present danger is not just that a rare wild species or some precious natural feature like the Colorado River gorge may be obliterated. The great threat is to man's own existence.

And what has mainly brought about this danger? The fact that man has now committed himself to an expanding technology in which material processes override human meanings and purposes. This has led to some very curious paradoxes.

All of us in a way, vicariously or directly, are oversensitive about the disappearance of this or that zoological or botanical species. Yet this in itself is not necessarily an evil. Should we mourn the passing of the hairy mammoth or the saber-toothed tiger? Don't forget that some of our most important food plants have disappeared precisely because they have been domesticated. But there is in fact a reason for our overtenderness and apprehension. Because we know that all life is now threatened. In our concern with the whooping crane we are at once symbolizing and concealing a far deeper anxiety—namely, the prospective total extermination of all species. The general silence on this larger subject is strange, and our own silence is even stranger. We have been gathered here for four days and have discussed many things. But has anybody said a word about the fact that the leaders in the Pentagon, if they become even more unreasonable than now, may destroy the major habitats on the planet? That we have not said a word about this fact, that we act as though it were nonexistent, is fantastic.

I don't blame this particular group. I have been fighting this pathological inertia for fifteen years, and I know that it is such a deep-seated inertia, based on such a fundamental fear, that it is very hard to overcome. But man himself is the wild species that is threatened, and it's time we recognize where the threat comes from: not from our enemies but from ourselves.

We all know the patent signs of this threat. The wholesale "normal" pollution of the water and the air. Sewage; industrial waste; lead from gasoline; nuclear waste; herbicides and pesticides. Every habitat is being to one degree or another spoiled or befouled not so much by man's own presence as by the lethal products of his ever-expanding technology.

We are aware of the desiccation and erosion of the landscape through overpopulation, and I share to the full Mr. Vogt's anxiety about this. We all should be anxious about it. The planet will be a very unpleasant place if the present overproduction of human beings should be maintained. But this evil is magnified by the constant ingestion of chemical poisons which Rachel Carson pointed out. Our life is being poisoned at the source.

After all, one of man's greatest achievements was the invention of food, not just fodder. All animals eat fodder. Man invented food. Food is not merely something that you put in your stomach and digest. Food is an occasion for a social act. It's an occasion for meeting. It's an occasion for conversation. Food is something that stirs the senses. You are pleasantly titillated by good food, while you are disgusted by bad food and bored by mediocre food. The landscape in which a variety of good foods is grown is a healthy landscape for man and beast.

Now, instead of enriching agriculture and horticulture, we have scientists coming along saying, "Don't worry about overpopulation, my dear fellow. Look here: there are plenty of algae! We could even make them out of the sewage if you ask us to. We are already developing this new resource for space capsules. Mankind can learn to swallow this and go on living."

These examples that I am giving you are symptoms of a wider process that will be inevitably destructive of all that ecologists and conservationists are interested in. The result will be the replacement of the natural and human habitat, which is extremely complex, with a simplified, uniform overcontrolled technological environment, in which only equally simplified and underdimensioned human beings will be capable of existing.

Technology has become the Canada thistle of our culture. You remember W. H. Hudson's description of the Pampas in the Argentine when the Canada thistle took over, and overtopped a man riding on horseback, because there wasn't any other plant around or any creature capable of keeping the Canada thistle down.

Mind you, I'm no opponent of technology. I have written two books on technics and its relation to civilization, and I regard an advanced technology as a necessity. But ought we not to take another look at the consequences of this breakup of the ecological pattern by a single factor of our environment? Are we not already paying too high a price for technological and scientific progress?

The basic assumption behind modern technology is that organic functions, human purposes, and cultural values must be reduced to their lowest factor and brought under control. Whose control? The control of the people who are in charge of the technological process. Not a control achieved by a consensus of mankind or by reference to the accumulated values of human history. A control essentially on the basis of one-generation knowledge put together mainly with the aid of five-year-old minds.

You'll find in current literature that the people who are most eager to exercise control are proud of the fact that they are using only raw, recent knowledge, untested for even a generation; and they are prepared to dismiss anybody who hasn't got his five-year-old knowledge, even if he has 500,000 years of knowledge to weigh in the scales against it.

If you are interested in redeeming the human habitat you must deal with this pathological technical syndrome: one exhibits a barely concealed hostility to living organisms, vital functions, organic association. This technology is based on a desire to displace the organic with the synthetic and the prefabricated, the scientifically controlled, and to rule out every aspect of life that isn't amenable to this process.

Along with this goes a subjective tendency—compulsion, rather—to exercise control as though this were the final achievement of mankind, that man should control every aspect in the environment about him. That reminds me by contrast of a sentence Boris Pasternak drops in *Doctor Zhivago*. He says people talk about "controlling life." And he points out that anybody who talks about controlling life has never begun to understand what life is. Life is essentially an autonomous historic process, and the larger part of man's still-active history is beyond the reach of the controllers. Up to a point you can control organisms negatively, by conditioning or confinement, though if you press them too hard they will die. But you can't control them for any length of time positively, because you'll produce reactions of surprising kind, of which the violence we see in our cities today is perhaps one of the symptoms.

At present we are organizing all our activities on a totalitarian mechanical pattern and providing an "ideal" totalitarian habitat, the encapsulated environment—uniform, standardized, machine-fabricated, automatic, under strict control from the moment of birth to the moment of death, from incubator to incinerator, so to speak.

The models for this are all around us. They go from the commonplace chicken farm of today, where no human being dares to enter lest the poor birds panic at the unfamiliar human presence, to the underground rocket silos or to Glacken's transcontinental jet plane, where his contact with the outside environment by eye was denied him so that television or motion pictures could supply a controllable substitute. This is fast becoming the universal environment of our culture.

The natural and the humanized habitat, as a result of the overuse of technological equipment, then becomes either physically unusable or psychologically invisible. People don't see it. They're not aware of the thousand things that we who know something about nature are aware of when we're holding conversation with the environment.

Anybody who is fully alive and who has even a small store of the available scientific knowledge can't be in any kind of environment without engaging in a kind of dialogue, without asking questions and responding to it. The technological environment is by intention a "one-way system." No conversations may take place without permission from the control center. People have begun to accept this as the ideal environment.

One of Loren Eiselely's students said to him: "Why not destroy all organisms and clear the ground for man? Man can make synthetic substitutes for everything the organic world does."

That student curiously forgot in destroying all other organisms he was destroying the possibility of continuing human life. Of course he didn't have enough biological knowledge to realize that. But also he was destroying man's history, without which man cannot make himself fully human. Man's history is associated with the entire organic world. He hasn't been alone. He has had companions: he has had helpers: he has had cooperators. They have taught him many things, more than he has ever up to now been able to teach them.

Wipe this all out and what happens? What happens, of course, is that you lose contact with the real world. Wipe out nature, wipe out human purposes, memories, and expectancies, and the real world disappears. And what's the result of that loss of contact with the real world? The name for it is insanity. Alienation, loss of identity, suicidal depression, irrational hostility, moral insensibility are some of the current symptoms.

The "brave new world" of our totalitarian technics and our machine-made totalitarian habitat lacks essential human dimensions. And one of the things it lacks is sixty million years or so of mammalian experience, and a million or five hundred thousand years of human experience and memory. We are now busily wiping out every manner of botanical and zoological variety, in order that the machine, or some plastic substitute for a natural species, may flourish.

Fortunately, there is something self-defeating about our technological dynamism: it is unstable almost by definition, because those who further it believe in instability, and do not realize that without continuity nothing that can be called progress is possible. In economic terms, our dominant system calls for constant turnover and constant expansion, whereas organic changes are changes that tend to promote equilibrium and regulate orderly growth. Those who are now making critical decisions for us, in both industry or government, make the mistake of equating power with life, and under this delusion they have been countenancing the mass production of pesticides and the production of nuclear weapons, which may permanently wreck the habitability of the planet—and, ironically, but fatally, bring technology itself to an end.

So now I come back to our central theme. By what means can we pre-

serve and develop the great variety of habitats, primeval, communal, domesticated, and urbane, which modern man needs, now more than ever,
to maximize his potentialities for living? We do well to begin with the
primaeval habitat, the ancestral habit of paleolithic man. For it was in
that habitat that *Homo sapiens* developed speech and ritual and art and
morals: the foundation of all that can be properly called human.

The purpose we should keep steadfastly in mind, it seems to me, is the
maintenance and the furtherance of all these potentialities. Our concern
for preserving this or that threatened species, this or that invaded wilderness area, is primarily symbolic. If we say with the poet, Gerard Manley
Hopkins, "Wet and wildness, let them be left, let them be left," it is
because this wildness remains a precious ingredient in the human
soul: not to be surrendered without question to someone with a bulldozer who wants to promote a land development, or stake out a hydroelectric power site.

When we rally to preserve the remaining redwood forests or to protect
the whooping crane, we are rallying to preserve ourselves, we are trying
to keep in existence the organic variety, the whole span of natural resources, upon which our own further development will be based. If we
surrender this variety too easily in one place, we shall lose it everywhere;
and we shall find ourselves enclosed in a technological prison, without
even the hope that sustains a prisoner in jail—that someday we may
get out. Should organic variety disappear, there will be no "out."

Once we define these broad purposes of conservation, we can assign
positive values and a positive place to technical improvements. Just as
we know now that even in paleolithic times, man's bow and arrow made
a necessary contribution toward preserving the balance of species in a
habitat favorable for wild creatures, so man's other technical needs have
enriched our intercourse with the environment. The question always
must be: What essential human need, viewed in historic perspective, is
being fulfilled or is being sacrificed?

But we have to challenge the notion that there is something sacred
in large-scale technological operations, whether they are for a new super-
highway, a new power station, or a new nuclear power plant. There is no
wealth, as Ruskin observed, but Life is what gives reason and purpose
to technology—not the other way around. We can cordially welcome
the machine, so long as it does not dominate us, does not seek to over-
whelm us, does not give us instructions how to live.

Too many people today have shown they are ready to submit to
having their soil, water, and food polluted, to having the air as choked
with noise as their scenery is with motorcar cemeteries, to committing
any personal sacrifice of their own life in order to advance the machine.
We have taken every technological permission to be a command. Because scientific advances have given us the power to send a rocket to the

moon, we are now wasting exorbitant sums on that barren adventure: sums we could use to much better purpose on earth.

One of the best reasons for our conservation movement, with its broad foundations, ever since George Perkins Marsh, in both natural and human history, is that it demonstrates the irrationality of allowing any single factor to dominate the rest of the environment. Our technology has overemphasized, in every sphere of life, the factor of power, of mass production and standardization; it seeks to decrease variety in order to promote quantity. Our aim rather should be to promote variety in order to curb this monotonous quantification.

This brings me back to the theme on which Mr. Brandwein held forth this morning. The need for re-education of ourselves so as to get on top of a technological system that is destroying both organic variety and human choice. And if this is our task, we must perhaps begin to effect a transformation not in wild nature alone, but in the city; for this is where the forces that have undermined both the natural and the historic habitat have assembled. The replenishment of life in our cities and the replenishment of our larger habitat will prosper if these two movements go hand in hand, and interact. But in educational terms, this means that we must provide a curriculum aimed not at producing more technicians, more engineers, more mathematicians, more scientists, but at producing more whole men and women, at home in every part of the environment.

In a word, the conservation of natural resources means nothing less than the conservation of human potentialities. And in that setting, all our present interests take on a wider meaning and open up a larger purpose.

We need to distrust a system of thought that has cut itself off deliberately from the culture and the cultivation of the whole organism and that has acquired an exaggerated respect for the abstract intelligence, even though that intelligence is capable of a more sophisticated kind of thinking than man has ever achieved before.

Don't think I don't admire my superiors when I see them at work, the great mathematicians, the great physical scientists, all those who are capable of this degree of abstraction! I find deficiencies, though, very often, in other parts of their life, and I recognize that the really great ones—the Faradays, the Einsteins, the Clerk Maxwells—bring to their science their whole personality and this is what saves them, and perhaps also adds to their greatness.

Great minds utilize more of their own organism, and have more of the environment at their command than the people who have only learned to live a segmented life and to think in terms of segmented knowledge.

So I now come back to our theme. Our theme is how to preserve and develop a variety of habitats, primitive, domesticated, urbane, how to keep going all that we have acquired from paleolithic man.

Don't forget that we can't leave paleolithic man behind us, because he invented the symbols of language, and if we turn our backs on the paleolithic man and his environment, we are turning our backs upon the possibility of speech, upon the possibility of everything that is derived from his fundamental discoveries of symbols and of morals. . . .

The purpose that we should have in mind, it seems to me, the purpose which we must cling to when we consider the improvement of habitat, is to become more conscious through thought and action and all the works of human art of the possibilities for further human development. It's not just to save the grasslands or the primeval forest, or to save the whooping crane.

Once we accept this premise, we can assign positive human values to technics. Technics itself, of course, has a place to play in every habitat—but not by itself, not to dominate us, not to give us orders as to how to live. It's we, the living, who must tell our technology how much of it is tolerable and how much of it we will put to one side even if it exists. We must take our instructions from human history and the human prospect, which is always centered in human beings and has reference to man's whole future development.

So to re-establish a life-favoring environment we must take up the theme [Paul F.] Brandwein[2] amplified this morning. Unless we can re-educate ourselves so as to get on top of this technological system, we shall probably find it impossible to go on for any great length of time in the wasteful, destructive, dehumanized way we are now pursuing. Our habitats will become insignificant and will disappear—and we ourselves along with them.

That means we must begin from the opposite direction. If we want to preserve nature, let's get back to the city and see what makes a man, a man in a human environment. The city as a human environment has been spoiled as badly as the primeval environment by forces that have been acting without our sufficient understanding or control during the last fifty or hundred years. Yet it is in and through the city, with all the resources it offers for the mind that man has created a symbolic counterpart to nature's creativity, variety, and exuberance.

We need the cooperation of all organisms, we need a sense of entire human history in order to root our life once more in realities, not in our abstractions, fantasies, and hallucinations. We mustn't retire into our

[2] [See Paul F. Brandwein, "Origins of Public Policy and Practice in Conservation: Early Education and the Conservation of Sanative Environments," *Future Environments of North America*, pp. 628–47 and the discussion of his paper on pp. 698–718.]

mind, even the highest kind of mind. We must be able to have intercourse with our fellows, intercourse with the entire environment around
us in all their concrete richness.

Man needs the whole cosmos to sustain him. The knowldege of this
cosmos and every living part of it enriches him, enables him to know
himself for the first time, to have some sense of the further advantages
and the further fulfillments that lie ahead of him if once he gets on top
of the forces that now threaten his life.

There, I think, are the conditions under which it will be profitable to
examine the future of human environments on the North American
continent.

Paul Goodman

can technology be humane?

On March 4, 1969, there was a work stopage and teach-in initiated by dissenting professors at the Massachusetts Institute of Technology, and followed at thirty other major universities and technical schools across the country, against misdirected scientific research and the abuse of scientific technology. Here I want to consider this event in a broader context than the professors did, indeed as part of a religious crisis. For an attack on the American scientific establishment is an attack on the world-wide system of belief. I think we are on the eve of a new Protestant Reformation, and no institution or status will go unaffected.

March 4 was, of course, only the latest of a series of protests in the twenty-five years since the Manhattan Project to build the atom bomb, during which time the central funding of research and innovation has grown so enormously and its purposes have become so unpalatable. In 1940 the federal budget for research and development was less than 100 million dollars, in 1967 17 billion. Hitler's war was a watershed of modern times. We are accustomed, as H. R. Trevor-Roper has pointed out, to write Hitler off as an aberration, of little political significance. But, in fact, the military emergency that he and his Japanese allies created confirmed the worst tendencies of the giant states, till now they are probably irreversible by ordinary political means.

After Hiroshima, there was the conscience-stricken movement of the Atomic Scientists and the founding of their *Bulletin*. The American Association for the Advancement of Science pledged itself to keep the public informed about the dangerous bearings of new developments. There was the Oppenheimer incident. Ads of the East Coast scientists successfully stopped the bomb shelters, warned about the fallout, and helped produce the test ban. There was a scandal about the bombardment of the Van Allen belt. Scientists and technologists formed a power-

Reprinted, by permission, from the November 22, 1969, issue of The New York Review of Books. *Copyright © 1969 by The New York Review.*

ful (and misguided) *ad hoc* group for Johnson in the 1964 election. In some universities, sometimes with bitter struggle, classified contracts have been excluded. There is a Society for Social Responsibility in Science. Rachel Carson's book on the pesticides caused a stir, until the Department of Agriculture rescued the manufacturers and plantation-owners. Ralph Nader has been on his rampage. Thanks to spectacular abuses like smog, strip-mining, asphalting, pesticides, and oil pollution, even ecologists and conservationists have been getting a hearing. Protest against the boom has slowed up the development of the supersonic transport. Most recent has been the concerted outcry against the anti-ballistic missiles.

The target of protest has become broader and the grounds of complaint deeper. The target is now not merely the military, but the universities, commercial corporations, and government. It is said that money is being given by the wrong sponsors to the wrong people for the wrong purposes. In some of the great schools, such funding is the main support, e.g., at MIT, 90 percent of the research budget is from the government, and 65 percent of that is military.

Inevitably, such funding channels the brainpower of most of the brightest science students, who go where the action is, and this predetermines the course of American science and technology for the foreseeable future. At present nearly 200,000 American engineers and scientists spend all their time making weapons, which is a comment on, and perhaps explanation for, the usual statement that more scientists are now alive than since Adam and Eve. And the style of such research and development is not good. It is dominated by producing hardware, figuring logistics, and devising salable novelties. Often there is secrecy, always nationalism. Since the grants go overwhelmingly through a very few corporations and universities, they favor a limited number of scientific attitudes and preconceptions, with incestuous staffing. There is a premium on "positive results"; surprising "failures" cannot be pursued, so that science ceases to be a wandering dialogue with the unknown.

The policy is economically wasteful. A vast amount of brains and money is spent on crash programs to solve often essentially petty problems, and the claim that there is a spin-off of useful discoveries is derisory, if we consider the sums involved. The claim that research is neutral, and it doesn't matter what one works on, is shabby, if we consider the heavy funding in certain directions. Social priorities are scandalous: money is spent on overkill, supersonic planes, brand-name identical drugs, annual model changes of cars, new detergents, and color television, whereas water, air, space, food, health, and foreign aid are neglected. And much research is morally so repugnant, e.g., chemical and biological weapons, that one dares not humanly continue it.

The state of the behavioral sciences is, if anything, worse. Their claim to moral and political neutrality becomes, in effect, a means of diverting attention from glaring social evils, and they are in fact used—or would be if they worked—for warfare and social engineering, manipulation of people for the political and economic purposes of the powers that be. This is an especially sad betrayal since, in the not-too-distant past, the objective social sciences were developed largely to dissolve orthodoxy, irrational authority, and taboo. They were heretical and intellectually revolutionary, as the physical sciences had been in their own Heroic Age, and they weren't getting government grants.

This is a grim indictment. Even so, I do not think the dissenting scientists understand how deep their trouble is. They still take themselves too much for granted. Indeed, a repeated theme of the March 4 complaints was that the science budget was being cut back, especially in basic research. The assumption was that though the sciences are abused, Science would rightly maintain and increase its expensive preeminence among social institutions. Only Science could find the answers.

But underlying the growing dissent there is an historical crisis. There has been a profound change in popular feeling, more than among the professors. Put it this way: Modern societies have been operating as if religion were a minor and moribund part of the scheme of things. But this is unlikely. Men do not do without a system of "meanings" that everybody believes and puts his hope in even if, or especially if, he doesn't know anything about it; what Freud called a "shared psychosis," meaningful because shared, and with the power that resides in dream and longing. In fact, in advanced countries it is science and technology themselves that have gradually and finally triumphantly become the system of mass faith, not disputed by various political ideologies and nationalisms that have also been mass religions. Marxism called itself "scientific socialism" as against moral and utopian socialisms; and movements of national liberation have especially promised to open the benefits of industrialization and technological progress when once they have gotten rid of the imperialists.

For three hundred years, science and scientific technology had an unblemished and justified reputation as a wonderful adventure, pouring out practical benefits, and liberating the spirit from the errors of superstition and traditional faith. During this century they have finally been the only generally credited system of explanation and problem-solving. Yet in our generation they have come to seem to many, and to very many of the best of the young, as essentially inhuman, abstract, regimenting, hand-in-glove with Power, and even diabolical. Young people say that science is antilife, it is a Calvinist obsession, it has been a weapon of white Europe to subjugate colored races, and manifestly—in view of recent scientific technology—people who think that way become insane. With science, the other professions are discredited; and the academic "disciplines" are discredited.

The immediate reasons for this shattering reversal of values are fairly obvious. Hitler's ovens and his other experiments in eugenics, the first atom bombs and their frenzied subsequent developments, the deterioration of the physical environment and the destruction of the biosphere, the catastrophes impending over the cities because of technological failures and psychological stress, the prospect of a brainwashed and drugged 1984. Innovations yield diminishing returns in enhancing life. And instead of rejoicing, there is now widespread conviction that beautiful advances in genetics, surgery, computers, rocketry, or atomic energy will surely only increase human woe.

In such a crisis, in my opinion, it will not be sufficient to ban the military from the universities; and it will not even be sufficient, as liberal statesmen and many of the big corporations envisage, to beat the swords into ploughshares and turn to solving problems of transportation, desalinization, urban renewal, garbage disposal, and cleaning up the air and water. If the present difficulty is religious and historical, it is necessary to alter the entire relationship of science, technology, and social needs both in men's minds and in fact. This involves changes in the organization of science, in scientific education, and in the kinds of men who make scientific decisions.

In spite of the fantasies of hippies, we are certainly going to continue to live in a technological world. The question is a different one: is that workable?

Prudence

Whether or not it draws on new scientific research, technology is a branch of moral philosophy, not of science. It aims at prudent goods for the commonweal and to provide efficient means for these goods. At present, however, "scientific technology" occupies a bastard position in the universities, in funding, and in the public mind. It is half tied to the theoretical sciences and half treated as mere know-how for political and commercial purposes. It has no principles of its own. To remedy this— so Karl Jaspers in Europe and Robert Hutchins in America have urged —technology must have its proper place on the faculty as a learned profession important in modern society, along with medicine, law, the humanities, and natural philosophy, learning from them and having something to teach them. As a moral philosopher, a technician should be able to criticize the programs given him to implement. As a professional in a community of learned professionals, a technologist must have a different kind of training and develop a different character than we see at present among technicians and engineers. He should know something of the social sciences, law, the fine arts, and medicine, as well as relevant natural sciences.

Prudence is foresight, caution, utility. Thus it is up to the technologists, not to regulatory agencies of the government, to provide for safety and to think about remote effects. This is what Ralph Nader is saying and Rachel Carson used to ask. An important aspect of caution is flexibility, to avoid the pyramiding catastrophe that occurs when something goes wrong in interlocking technologies, as in urban power failures. Naturally, to take responsibility for such things often requires standing up to the front office and urban politicians, and technologists must organize themselves in order to have power to do it.

Often it is clear that a technology has been oversold, like the cars. Then even though the public, seduced by advertising, wants more, technologists must balk, as any professional does when his client wants what isn't good for him. We are now repeating the same self-defeating congestion with the planes and airports: the more the technology is oversold, the less immediate utility it provides, the greater the costs, and the more damaging the remote effects. As this becomes evident, it is time for technologists to confer with sociologists and economists and ask deeper questions. Is so much travel necessary? Are there ways to diminish it? Instead, the recent history of technology has consisted largely of a desperate effort to remedy situations caused by previous overapplication of technology.

Technologists should certainly have a say about simple waste, for even in an affluent society there are priorities—consider the supersonic transport, which has little to recommend it. But the moon shot has presented the more usual dilemma of authentic conflicting claims. I myself believe that space exploration is a great human adventure, with immense aesthetic and moral benefits, whatever the scientific or utilitarian uses. Yet it is amazing to me that the scientists and technologists involved have not spoken more insistently for international cooperation instead of a puerile race. But I have heard some say that except for this chauvinist competition, Congress would not vote any money at all.

Currently, perhaps the chief moral criterion of a philosophic technology is modesty, having a sense of the whole and not obtruding more than a particular function warrants. Immodesty is always a danger of free enterprise, but when the same disposition is financed by big corporations, technologists rush into production with neat solutions that swamp the environment. This applies to packaging products and disposing of garbage, to freeways that bulldoze neighborhoods, highrises that destroy landscape, wiping out a species for a passing fashion, strip mining, scrapping an expensive machine rather than making a minor repair, draining a watershed for irrigation because (as in Southern Califonia) the cultivable land has been covered by asphalt. Given this disposition, it is not surprising that we defoliate a forest in order to expose a guerrilla and spray teargas from a helicopter on a crowded compus.

Since we are technologically overcommitted, a good general maxim in advanced countriès at present is to innovate in order to simplify the technical system, but otherwise to innovate as sparingly as possible. Every advanced country is overtechnologized; past a certain point, the quality of life diminishes with new "improvements." Yet no country is rightly techologized, making efficient use of available techniques. There are ingenious devices for unimportant functions, stressful mazes for essential functions, and drastic dislocation when anything goes wrong, which happens with increasing frequency. To add to the complexity, the mass of people tend to become incompetent and dependent on repairmen—indeed, unrepairability except by experts has become a desideratum of industrial design.

When I speak of slowing down or cutting back, the issue is not whether research and making working models should be encouraged or not. They should be, in every direction, and given a blank check. The point is to resist the temptation to apply every new device without a second thought. But the big corporate organization of research and development makes prudence and modesty very difficult; it is necessary to get big contracts and rush into production in order to pay the salaries of the big team. Like other bureaucracies, technological organizations are run to maintain themselves but they are more dangerous because, in capitalist countries, they are in a competitive arena.

I mean simplification quite strictly, to simplify the *technical* system. I am unimpressed by the argument that what is technically more complicated is really economically or politically simpler, e.g., by complicating the packaging we improve the supermarkets; by throwing away the machine rather than repairing it, we give cheaper and faster service all around; or even by expanding the economy with trivial innovations, we increase employment, allay discontent, save on welfare. Such ideas may be profitable for private companies or political parties, but for society they have proved to be an accelerating rat race. The technical structure of the environment is too important to be a political or economic pawn; the effect on the quality of life is too disastrous; and the hidden social costs are not calculated, the auto graveyards, the torn-up streets, the longer miles of commuting, the advertising, the inflation, etc.

As I pointed out in *People or Personnel*, a country with a fourth of our per capita income, like Ireland, is not necessarily less well off; in some respects it is much richer, in some respects a little poorer. If possible, it is better to solve political problems by political means. For instance, if teaching machines and audio-visual aids are indeed educative, well and good; but if they are used just to save money on teachers, then not good at all—nor do they save money.

Of course, the goals of right technology must come to terms with other values of society. I am not a technocrat. But the advantage of raising technology to be a responsible learned profession with its own principles is that it can have a voice in the debate and argue for *its* proper contribution to the community. Consider the important case of modular sizes in building, or prefabrication of a unit bathroom: these conflict with the short-run interests of manufacturers and craft unions, yet to deny them is technically an abomination. The usual recourse is for a government agency to set standards; such agencies accommodate to interests that have a strong voice, and at present technologists have no voice.

The crucial need for technological simplification, however, is not in the advanced countries—which can afford their clutter and probably deserve it—but in underdeveloped countries which must rapidly innovate in order to diminish disease, drudgery, and deepening starvation. They cannot afford to make mistakes. It is now widely conceded that the technological aid we have given to such areas according to our own high style—a style usually demanded by the native ruling groups—has done more harm than good. Even when, as frequently if not usually, aid has been benevolent, without strings attached, not military, and not dumping, it has nevertheless disrupted ways of life, fomented tribal wars, accelerated urbanization, decreased the food supply, gone wasted for lack of skills to use it, developed a do-nothing élite.

By contrast, a group of international scientists called Intermediate Technology argue that what is needed is techniques that use only native labor, resources, traditional customs, and teachable know-how, with the simple aim of remedying drudgery, disease, and hunger, so that people can then develop further in their own style. This avoids cultural imperialism. Such intermediate techniques may be quite primitive, on a level unknown among us for a couple of centuries, and yet they may pose extremely subtle problems, requiring exquisite scientific research and political and human understanding, to devise a very simple technology. Here is a reported case (which I trust I remember accurately): In Botswana, a very poor country, pasture was overgrazed, but the economy could be salvaged if the land were fenced. There was no local material for fencing, and imported fencing was prohibitively expensive. The solution was to find the formula and technique to make posts out of mud, and a pedagogic method to teach people how to do it.

In *The Two Cultures*, C. P. Snow berated the humanists for their irrelevance when two-thirds of mankind are starving and what is needed is science and technology. They have perhaps been irrelevant; but unless technology is itself more humanistic and philosophical, it is of no use. There is only one culture.

Finally, let me make a remark about amenity as a technical criterion. It is discouraging to see the concern about beautifying a highway and banning billboards, and about the cosmetic appearance of the cars, when there is no regard for the ugliness of bumper-to-bumper traffic and the suffering of the drivers. Or the concern for preserving an historical landmark while the neighborhood is torn up and the city has no shape. Without moral philosophy, people have nothing but sentiments.

Ecology

The complement to prudent technology is the ecological approach to science. To simplify the technical system and modestly pinpoint our artificial intervention in the environment makes it possible for the environment to survive in its complexity evolved for a billion years, whereas the overwhelming instant intervention of tightly interlocked and bulldozing technology has already disrupted many of the delicate sequences and balances. The calculable consequences are already frightening, but of course we don't know enough, and won't in the foreseeable future, to predict the remote effects of much of what we have done. The only possible conclusion is to be prudent; when there is serious doubt, to do nothing.

Cyberneticists—I am thinking of Gregory Bateson—come to the same cautious conclusion. The use of computers has enabled us to carry out crashingly inept programs on the bases of willful analyses. But we have also become increasingly alert to the fact that things respond, systematically, continually, cumulatively; they cannot simply be manipulated or pushed around. Whether bacteria or weeds or bugs or the technologically unemployed or unpleasant thoughts, they cannot be eliminated and forgotten; repressed, the nuisances return in new forms. A complicated system works most efficiently if its parts readjust themselves decentrally, with a minimum of central intervention or control, except in case of breakdown. Usually there is an advantage in a central clearinghouse of information about the gross total situation, but decision and execution require more minute local information. The fantastically simulated moon landing hung on a last split-second correction on the spot. In social organization, deciding in headquarters means relying on information that is cumulatively abstract and irrelevant, and chain-of-command execution applies standards that cumulatively do not fit the concrete situation. By and large it is better, given a sense of the whole picture, for those in the field to decide what to do and do it (cf. *People or Personnel*, Chapter III).

But with organisms too, this has long been the bias of psychosomatic medicine, the Wisdom of the Body, as Cannon called it. To cite a classical experiment of Ralph Hefferline of Columbia: a subject is wired to suffer an annoying regular buzz, which can be delayed and finally eliminated if he makes a precise but unlikely gesture, say by twisting his ankle in a certain way; then it is found that he adjusts quicker if he is *not* told the method and it is left to his spontaneous twitching than if he is told and tries deliberately to help himself. He adjusts better without conscious control, his own or the experimenter's.

Technological modesty, fittingness, is not negative. It is the ecological wisdom of cooperating with Nature rather than trying to master her. (The personification of "Nature" is linguistic wisdom.) A well-known example is the long-run superiority of partial pest-control in farming by using biological deterrents rather than chemical ones. The living defenders work harder, at the right moment, and with more pin-pointed targets. But let me give another example because it is so lovely—though I have forgotten the name of my informant: A tribe in Yucatan educates its children to identify and pull up all weeds in the region; then what is left is a garden of useful plants that have chosen to be there and now thrive.

In the life sciences there is at present a suggestive bifurcation in methodology. The rule is still to increase experimental intervention, but there is also a considerable revival of old-fashioned naturalism, mainly watching and thinking, with very modest intervention. Thus, in medicine, there is new diagnostic machinery, new drugs, spectacular surgery; but there is also a new respect for family practice with a psychosomatic background, and a strong push, among young doctors and students, for a social-psychological and sociological approach, aimed at preventing disease and building up resistance. In psychology, the operant conditioners multiply and refine their machinery to give maximum control of the organism and the environment (I have not heard of any dramatic discoveries, but perhaps they have escaped me). On the other hand, the most interesting psychology in recent years has certainly come from animal naturalists, e.g., pecking order, territoriality, learning to control aggression, language of the bees, overcrowding among rats, trying to talk to dolphins.

On a fair judgment, both contrasting approaches give positive results. The logical scientific problem that arises is, What is there in the nature of things that makes a certain method, or even moral attitude, work well or poorly in a given case? This question is not much studied. Every scientist seems to know what "the" scientific method is.

Another contrast of style, extremely relevant at present, is that between Big Science and old-fashioned shoestring science. There is plenty of research, with corresponding technology, that can be done only by Big Science; yet much, and perhaps most, of science will always be shoestring science, for which it is absurd to use the fancy and expensive equipment that has gotten to be the fashion.

Consider urban medicine. The problem, given a shortage of doctors and facilities, is how to improve the level of mass health, the vital statistics, and yet to practice medicine, which aims at the maximum possible health for each person. Perhaps the most efficient use of Big Science technology for the general health would be compulsory biennial checkups, as we inspect cars, for early diagnosis and to forestall chronic conditions with accumulating costs. Then an excellent machine would be a total diagnostic bus to visit the neighborhoods, as we do chest X-rays. On the other hand, for actual treatment and especially for convalescence, the evidence seems to be that small personalized hospitals are best. And to revive family practice, maybe the right idea is to offer a doctor a splendid suite in a public housing project.

Our contemporary practice makes little sense. We have expensive technology stored in specialists' offices and big hospitals, really unavailable for mass use in the neighborhoods; yet every individual, even if he is quite rich, finds it almost impossible to get attention to himself as an individual whole organism in his setting. He is sent from specialist to specialist and exists as a bag of symptoms and a file of test scores.

In automating there is an analogous dilemma of how to cope with masses of people and get economies of scale, without losing the individual at great consequent human and economic cost. A question of immense importance for the immediate future is, Which functions should be automated or organized to use business machines, and which should not? This question also is not getting asked, and the present disposition is that the sky is the limit for extraction, refining, manufacturing, processing, packaging, transportation, clerical work, ticketing, transactions, information retrieval, recruitment, middle management, evaluation, diagnosis, instruction, and even research and invention. Whether the machines can do all these kinds of jobs and more is partly an empirical question, but it also partly depends on what is meant by doing a job. Very often, e.g., in college admissions, machines are acquired for putative economies (which do not eventuate); but the true reason is that an overgrown and overcentralized organization cannot be administered without them. The technology conceals the essential trouble, e.g., that there is no community of scholars and students are treated like things. The function is badly performed, and finally the system breaks down anyway. I doubt that enterprises in which interpersonal relations are important are suited to much programming.

But worse, what can happen is that the real function of the enterprise is subtly altered so that it is suitable for the mechanical system. (E.g., "information retrieval" is taken as an adequate replacement for critical scholarship.) Incommensurable factors, individual differences, the local context, the weighting of evidence are quietly overlooked though they may be of the essence. The system, with its subtly transformed purposes, seems to run very smoothly; it is productive, and it is more and more out of line with the nature of things and the real problems. Meantime it is geared in with other enterprises of society, e.g., major public policy may depend on welfare or unemployment statistics which, as they are tabulated, are blind to the actual lives of poor families. In such a case, the particular system may not break down, the whole society may explode.

I need hardly point out that American society is peculiarly liable to the corruption of inauthenticity, busily producing phony products. It lives by public relations, abstract ideals, front politics, show-business communications, mandarin credentials. It is preeminently overtechnologized. And computer technologists especially suffer the euphoria of being in a new and rapidly expanding field. It is so astonishing that the robot can do the job at all or seem to do it, that it is easy to blink at the fact that he is doing it badly or isn't really doing quite that job.

Decentralization

The current political assumption is that scientists and inventors, and even social scientists, are "value-neutral," but their discoveries are "applied" by those who make decisions for the nation. Counter to this, I have been insinuating a kind of Jeffersonian democracy or guild socialism, that scientists and inventors and other workmen are responsible for the uses of the work they do, and ought to be competent to judge these uses and have a say in deciding them. They usually are competent. To give a striking example, Ford assembly line workers, according to Harvey Swados, who worked with them, are accurately critical of the glut of cars, but they have no way to vent their dissatisfactions with their useless occupation except to leave nuts and bolts to rattle in the body.

My bias is also pluralistic. Instead of the few national goals of a few decision-makers, I propose that there are many goods of many activities of life, and many professions and other interest groups each with its own criteria and goals that must be taken into account. A society that distributes power widely is superficially conflictful but fundamentally stable.

Research and development ought to be widely decentralized, the national fund for them being distributed through thousands of centers of initiative and decision. This would not be chaotic. We seem to have forgotten that for four hundred years Western science majestically progressed with no central direction whatever, yet with exquisite international coordination, little duplication, almost nothing getting lost, in constant communication despite slow facilities. The reason was simply that all scientists wanted to get on with the same enterprise of testing the boundaries of knowledge, and they relied on one another.

What is as noteworthy is that something similar holds also in invention and innovation, even in recent decades when there has been such a concentration of funding and apparent concentration of opportunity. The majority of big advances have still come from independents, partnerships, and tiny companies. (Evidence published by the Senate Sub-Committee on Antitrust and Monopoly, May 1965.) To name a few, jet engines, xerography, automatic transmission, cellophane, air-conditioning, quick freeze, antibiotics, and tranquilizers. The big technological teams must have disadvantages that outweigh their advantages, like lack of single-mindedness, poor communications, awkward scheduling. Naturally, big corporations have taken over the innovations, but the Senate evidence is that 90 percent of the government subsidy has gone for last-stage development for production, which they ought to have paid out of their own pockets.

We now have a theory that we have learned to learn, and that we can program technical progress, directed by a central planning board. But this doesn't make it so. The essence of the new still seems to be that nobody has thought of it, and the ones who get ideas are those in direct contact with the work. *Too precise* a preconception of what is wanted discourages creativity more than it channels it; and bureaucratic memoranda from distant directors don't help. This is especially true when, as at present, so much of the preconception of what is wanted comes from desperate political anxiety in emergencies. Solutions that emerge from such an attitude rarely strike out on new paths, but rather repeat traditional thinking with new gimmicks; they tend to compound the problem. A priceless advantage of widespread decentralization is that it engages more minds, and more mind, instead of a few panicky (or greedy) corporate minds.

A homespun advantage of small groups, according to the Senate testimony, is that co-workers can talk to one another, without schedules, reports, clock-watching, and face-saving.

An important hope from decentralizing science is to develop knowledgeable citizens, and provide not only a bigger pool of scientists and inventors but also a public better able to protect itself and know how to judge the enormous budgets asked for. The safety of the environment is too important to be left to scientists, even ecologists. During the last decades of the nineteenth century and the first decade of the twentieth, the heyday of public faith in the beneficent religion of science and invention, say from Pasteur and Huxley to Edison and the Wright Brothers, philosophers of science had a vision of a "scientific way of life," one in which people would be objective, respectful of evidence, accurate, free of superstition and taboo, immune to irrational authority, experimental. All would be well, is the impression one gets from Thomas Huxley, if everybody knew the splendid Ninth Edition of the *Encyclopaedia Britannica* with its articles by Darwin and Clerk Maxwell. Veblen put his faith in the modesty and matter-of-factness of engineers to govern. Sullivan and Frank Lloyd Wright spoke for an austere functionalism and respect for the nature of materials and industrial processes. Patrick Geddes thought that new technology would finally get us out of the horrors of the Industrial Revolution and produce good communities. John Dewey devised a system of education to rear pragmatic and experimental citizens to be at home in the new technological world rather than estranged from it. Now fifty years later, we are in the swamp of a scientific and technological environment and there are more scientists alive, etc., etc. But the mention of the "scientific way of life" seems like black humor.

Many of those who have grown up since 1945 and have never seen any other state of science and technology assume that rationalism itself is totally evil and dehumanizing. It is probably more significant than we like to think that they go in for astrology and the Book of Changes, as well as inducing psychedelic dreams by technological means. Jacques Ellul, a more philosophic critic, tries to show that technology is necessarily over-controlling, standardizing, and voraciously inclusive, so that there is no place for freedom. But I doubt that any of this is intrinsic to science and technology. The crude history has been, rather, that they have fallen willingly under the dominion of money and power. Like Christianity or communism, the scientific way of life has never been tried.

To satisfy the March 4 dissenters, to break the military-industrial corporations and alter the priorities of the budget, would be to restructure the American economy almost to a revolutionary extent. But to meet the historical crisis of science at present, for science and technology to become prudent, ecological, and decentralized requires a change that is even more profound, a kind of religious transformation. Yet there is nothing untraditional in what I have proposed; prudence, ecology, and decentralization are indeed the high tradition of science and technology. Thus the closest analogy I can think of is the Protestant Reformation, a change of moral allegiance, liberation from the Whore of Babylon, return to the pure faith.

Science has long been the chief orthodoxy of modern times and has certainly been badly corrupted, but the deepest flaw of the affluent societies that has alienated the young is not, finally, their imperialism, economic injustice, or racism, bad as these are, but their nauseating phoniness, triviality, and wastefulness, the cultural and moral scandal that Luther found when he went to Rome in 1510. And precisely science, which should have been the wind of truth to clear the air, has polluted the air, helped to brainwash, and provided weapons for war. I doubt that most young people today have even heard of the ideal of the dedicated researcher, truculent and incorruptible, and unrewarded, for instance the "German scientist" that Sinclair Lewis described in *Arrowsmith*. Such a figure is no longer believable. I don't mean, of course, that he doesn't exist; there must be thousands of him, just as there were good priests in 1510.

The analogy to the Reformation is even more exact if we consider the school system, from educational toys and Head Start up through the universities. This system is manned by the biggest horde of monks since the time of Henry VIII. It is the biggest industry in the country. I have heard the estimate that 40 percent of the national product is in the Knowledge Business. It is mostly hocus-pocus. Yet the belief of parents in this institution is quite delusional and school diplomas are in fact the only entry to licensing and hiring in every kind of job. The abbots of this system are the chiefs of science, e.g., the National Science Foundation, who talk about reform but work to expand the school budgets, step up the curriculum, and inspire the endless catechism of tests.

These abuses are international, as the faith is. For instance, there is no essential difference between the military-industrial or the school system, of the Soviet Union and the United States. There are important differences in way of life and standard of living, but the abuses of technology are very similar: pollution, excessive urbanization, destruction of the biosphere, weaponry, and disastrous foreign aid. Our protesters naturally single out our own country, and the United States is the most powerful country, but the corruption we are speaking of is not specifically American nor even capitalist; it is a disease of modern times.

But the analogy is to the Reformation, it is not to primitive Christianity or some other primitivism, the abandonment of technological civilization. There is indeed much talk about the doom of Western civilization, and a few Adamites actually do retire into the hills; but for the great mass of mankind, and myself, that's not where it's at. There is not the slightest interruption to the universalizing of Western civilization, including most of its delusions, into the so-called Third World. (If the atom bombs go off, however?)

Naturally the exquisitely interesting question is whether or not this Reformation will occur, how to make it occur, against the entrenched world-wide system of corrupt power that is continually aggrandizing itself. I don't know. In my analogy I have deliberately been choosing the date 1510, Luther in Rome, rather than 1517 when, in the popular story, he nailed his Theses on the cathedral door. There are everywhere contradictory signs and dilemmas. The new professional and technological class is more and more entangled in the work, statuses, and rewards of the system, and yet this same class, often the very same people, are more and more protestant. On the other hand, the dissident young, who are unequivocally for radical change, are so alienated from occupation, function, knowledge, or even concern, that they often seem to be simply irrelevant to the underlying issues of modern times. The monks keep "improving" the schools and getting bigger budgets to do so, yet it is clear that high schools will be burned down, twelve-year-olds will play truant in droves, and the taxpayers are already asking what goes on and voting down the bonds.

The interlocking of technologies and all other institutions makes it almost impossible to reform policy in any part; yet this very interlocking that renders people powerless, including the decision-makers, creates a remarkable resonance and chain reaction if any determined group, or even determined individual, exerts force. In the face of overwhelmingly collective operations like the space exploration, the average man must feel that local or grassroots efforts are worthless, there is no science but Big Science, and no administration but the State. And yet there is a powerful surge of localism, populism, and community action, as if people were determined to be free even if it makes no sense. A mighty empire is stood off by a band of peasants, and *neither* can win—this is even more remarkable than if David beats Goliath; it means that neither principle is historically adequate. In my opinion, these dilemmas and impasses show that we are on the eve of a transformation of conscience.

Barry Commoner

to survive on the earth

. . . What actions can be taken to avoid the calamities that seem to follow so closely on the heels of modern technological progress? I have tried to show that science offers no "objective" answer to this question. There is a price attached to every solution; any judgment will necessarily reflect the value we place on the benefits yielded by a given technological advance and the harm we associate with its hazards. The benefits and the hazards can be described by scientific means, but each of us must choose that balance between them which best accords with our own belief of what is good—for ourselves, for society, and for humanity as a whole.

In discussing what ought to be done about these problems, I can speak only for myself. As a scientist, I can arrive at my own judgments— subject to the open criticism which is so essential to scientific discourse —about the scientific and technological issues. As a citizen, I can decide which of the alternative solutions my government ought to pursue, and, using the instruments of politics, act for the adoption of this course. As a human being, I can express in this action my own moral convictions.

As a biologist, I have reached this conclusion: we have come to a turning point in the human habitation of the earth. The environment is a complex, subtly balanced system, and it is this integrated whole which receives the impact of all the separate insults inflicted by pollutants. Never before in the history of this planet has its thin life supporting surface been subjected to such diverse, novel, and potent agents. I believe that the cumulative effects of these pollutants, their interactions and amplification, can be fatal to the complex fabric of the biosphere. And, because man is, after all, a dependent part of this system, I believe that continued pollution of the earth, if unchecked, will eventually destroy the fitness of this planet as a place for human life.

My judgment of the possible effects of the most extreme assault on the biosphere—nuclear war—has already been expressed. Nuclear war would, I believe, inevitably destroy the economic, social, and political structure of the combatant nations; it would reduce their populations, industry and agriculture to chaotic remnants, incapable of supporting an organized effort for recovery. I believe that world-wide radioactive contamination, epidemics, ecological disasters, and possibly climatic changes would so gravely affect the stability of the biosphere as to threaten human survival everywhere on the earth.

If we are to survive, we need to become aware of the damaging effects of technological innovations, determine their economic and social costs, balance these against the expected benefits, make the facts broadly available to the public, and take the action needed to achieve an acceptable balance of benefits and hazards. Obviously, all this should be done *before* we become massively committed to a new technology. One of our most urgent needs is to establish within the scientific community some means of estimating and reporting on the expected benefits and hazards of proposed environmental interventions *in advance*. Such advance consideration could have averted many of our present difficulties with detergents, insecticides, and radioactive contaminants. It could have warned us of the tragic futility of attempting to defend the nation's security by a means that can only lead to the nation's destruction.

We have not yet learned this lesson. Despite our earlier experience with nondegradable detergents, the degradable detergents which replaced them were massively marketed, by joint action of the industry in 1965, without any pilot study of their ecological effects. The phosphates which even the new detergents introduce into surface waters may force their eventual withdrawal. The United States, Great Britain, and France are already committed to costly programs for supersonic transport planes but have thus far failed to produce a comprehensive evaluation of the hazards from sonic boom, from cosmic radioactivity, and from the physiological effects of rapid transport from one time zone to another. The security of every nation in the world remains tied to nuclear armaments, and we continue to evade an open public discussion of the basic question: do we wish to commit the security of nations to a military system which is likely to destroy them?

It is urgent that we face this issue openly, now, before by accident or design we are overtaken by nuclear catastrophe. U Thant has proposed that the United Nations prepare a report on the effects of nuclear war and disseminate it throughout the world. Such a report could become the cornerstone of world peace. For the world would then know that, so long as nuclear war remains possible, we are all counters in a colossal gamble with the survival of civilization.

The costs of correcting past mistakes and preventing the threatened ones are already staggering, for the technologies which have produced them are now deeply embedded in our economic, social, and political structure. From what is now known about the smog problem, I think it unlikely that gasoline-driven automobiles can long continue to serve as the chief vehicle of urban and suburban transportation without imposing a health hazard which most of us would be unwilling to accept. Some improvement will probably result from the use of new devices to reduce emission of waste gasoline. But in view of the increasing demand for urban transportation any really effective effort to reduce the emission of waste fuel, carbon monoxide, and lead will probably require electric-powered vehicles and the replacement of urban highway systems by rapid transit lines. Added to current demands for highway-safe cars, the demand for smog-free transportation is certain to have an important impact on the powerful and deeply entrenched automobile industry.

The rapidly accelerating pollution of our surface waters with excessive phosphate and nitrate from sewage and detergents will, I believe, necessitate a drastic revision of urban waste systems. It may be possible to remove phosphates effectively by major modifications of sewage and water treatment plants, but there are no methods in sight that might counter the accumulation of nitrate. Hence, control will probably need to be based chiefly on preventing the entry of these pollutants into surface waters.

According to a report by the Committee on Pollution, National Academy of Sciences, we need to plan for a complete transformation of urban waste-removal systems, in particular to end the present practice of using water to get rid of solid wastes. The technological problems involved are so complex that the report recommends, as an initial step, the construction of a small pilot city to try out the new approach.

The high productivity of American agriculture, and therefore its economic structure, is based on the use of large amounts of mineral fertilizer in which phosphate and nitrate are major components. This fertilizer is not entirely absorbed by the crops and the remainder runs off into streams and lakes. As a result, by nourishing our crops and raising agricultural production, we help to kill off our lakes and rivers. Since there is no foreseeable means of removing fertilizer runoff from surface waters, it will become necessary, it seems to me, to impose severe restrictions on the present unlimited use of mineral fertilizers in agriculture. Proposed restraints on the use of synthetic pesticides have already aroused a great deal of opposition from the chemical industry and from agriculture. Judged by this response, an attempt to regulate the use of mineral fertilizers will confront us with an explosive economic and political problem.

And suppose that, as it may, the accumulation of carbon dioxide begins to threaten the entire globe with catastrophic floods. Control of this danger would require the modification, throughout the world, of domestic furnaces and industrial combustion plants—for example, by the addition of devices to absorb carbon dioxide from flue gases. Combustion-driven power plants could perhaps be replaced with nuclear ones, but this would pose the problem of safely disposing of massive amounts of radioactive wastes and create the hazard of reactor accidents near centers of population. Solar power, and other techniques for the production of electrical power which do not require either combustion or nuclear reactors, may be the best solution. But here too massive technological changes will be needed in all industrial nations.

The problems of industrial and agricultural pollution, while exceedingly large, complex, and costly, are nevertheless capable of correction by the proper technological means. We are still in a period of grace, and if we are willing to pay the price, as large as it is, there is yet time to restore and preserve the biological quality of the environment. But the most immediate threat to survival—nuclear war—would be a blunder from which there would be no return. I know of no technological means, no form of civil defense or counteroffensive warfare, which could reliably protect the biosphere from the catastrophic effects of a major nuclear war. There is, in my opinion, only one way to survive the threats of nuclear war—and that is to insure that it never happens. And because of the appreciable chance of an accidental nuclear war, I believe that the only way to do so is to destroy the world's stock of nuclear weapons and to develop less self-defeating means of protecting national security. Needless to say, the political difficulties involved in international nuclear disarmament are monumental.

Despite the dazzling successes of modern technology and the unprecedented power of modern military systems, they suffer from a common and catastrophic fault. While providing us with a bountiful supply of food, with great industrial plants, with high-speed transportation, and with military weapons of unprecedented power, they threaten our very survival. Technology has not only built the magnificent material base of modern society, but also confronts us with threats to survival which cannot be corrected unless we solve very grave economic, social, and political problems.

How can we explain this paradox? The answer is, I believe, that our technological society has committed a blunder familiar to us from the nineteenth century, when the dominant industries of the day, especially lumbering and mining, were successfully developed—by plundering the earth's natural resources. These industries provided cheap materials for constructing a new industrial society, but they accumulated a huge debt in destroyed and depleted resources, which had to be paid by later generations. The conservation movement was created in the United States to control these greedy assaults on our resources. The same thing is happening today, but now we are stealing from future generations not just their lumber or their coal, but the basic necessities of life: air, water, and soil. A new conservation movement is needed to preserve life itself.

The earlier ravages of our resources made very visible marks, but the new attacks are largely hidden. Thoughtless lumbering practices left vast scars on the land, but thoughtless development of modern industrial, agricultural, and military methods only gradually poison the air and water. Many of the pollutants—carbon dioxide, radioisotopes, pesticides, and excess nitrate—are invisible and go largely unnoticed until a lake dies, a river becomes foul, or children sicken. This time the world is being plundered in secret.

The earlier depredations on our resources were usually made with a fair knowledge of the harmful consequences, for it is difficult to escape the fact that erosion quickly follows the deforestation of a hillside. The difficulty lay not in scientific ignorance, but in willful greed. In the present situation, the hazards of modern pollutants are generally not appreciated until after the technologies which produce them are well established in the economy. While this ignorance absolves us from the immorality of the knowingly destructive acts that characterized the nineteenth century raids on our resources, the present fault is more serious. It signifies that the capability of science to guide us in our interventions into nature has been seriously eroded—that science has, indeed, got out of hand.

In this situation, scientists bear a very grave responsibility, for they are the guardians of the integrity of science. In the last few decades serious weaknesses in this system of principles have begun to appear. Secrecy has hampered free discourse. Major scientific enterprises have been governed by narrow national aims. In some cases, especially in the exploration of space, scientists have become so closely tied to basically political aims as to relinquish their traditional devotion to open discussion of conflicting views on what are often doubtful scientific conclusions.

What can scientists do to restore the integrity of science and to provide the kind of careful guidance to technology that is essential if we are to avoid catastrophic mistakes? No new principles are needed; instead, scientists need to find new ways to protect science itself from the encroachment of political pressures. This is not a new problem, for science and scholarship have often been under assault when their freedom to seek and to discuss the truth becomes a threat to existing economic or political power. The internal strength of science and its capability to understand nature have been weakened whenever the principles of scientific discourse were compromised, and restored when these principles were defended. The medieval suppressions of natural science, the perversion of science by Nazi racial theories, Soviet restraints on theories of genetics, and the suppression by United States military secrecy of open discussion of the Starfish project, have all been paid for in the most costly coin—knowledge. The lesson of all these experiences is the same. If science is to perform its duty to society, which is to guide, by objective knowledge, human interactions with the rest of nature, its integrity must be defended. Scientists must find ways to remove the restraints of secrecy, to insist on open discussion of the possible consequences of large-scale experiments *before* they are undertaken, to resist the hasty and unconditional support of conclusions that conform to the demands of current political or economic policy.

Apart from these duties toward science, I believe that scientists have a responsibility in relation to the technological uses which are made of scientific developments. In my opinion, the proper duty of the scientist to the social consequence of his work cannot be fulfilled by aloofness or by an approach which arrogates to scientists alone the social and moral judgments which are the right of every citizen. I propose that scientists are now bound by a new duty which adds to and extends their older responsibility for scholarship and teaching. We have the duty to inform, and to inform in keeping with the traditional principles of science, taking into account all relevant data and interpretations. This is an involuntary obligation to society; we have no right to withhold information from our fellow citizens, or to color its meaning with our own social judgments.

Scientists alone cannot accomplish these aims, for despite its tradition of independent scholarship, science is a dependent segment of society. In this sense defense of the integrity of science is a task for every citizen. And in this sense, too, the fate of science as a system of objective inquiry, and therefore its ability safely to guide the life of man on earth, will be determined by social intent. Both awareness of the grave social issues generated by new scientific knowledge, and the policy choices which these issues require, therefore become matters of public morality. Public morality will determine whether scientific inquiry remains free. Public morality will determine at what cost we shall enjoy freedom from insect pests, the convenience of automobiles, or the high productivity of agriculture. Only public morality can determine whether we ought to intrust our national security to the catastrophic potential of nuclear war.

There is a unique relationship between the scientist's social responsibilities and the general duties of citizenship. If the scientist, directly or by inferences from his actions, lays claim to a special responsibility for the resolution of the policy issues which relate to technology, he may, in effect, prevent others from performing their own political duties. If the scientist fails in his duty to inform citizens, they are precluded from the gravest acts of citizenship and lose their right of conscience.

We have been accustomed, in the past, especially in our organized systems of morality—religion—to exemplify the principles of moral life in terms which relate to Egypt under the pharaohs or Rome under the emperors. Since the establishment of Western religions, their custodians have, of course, labored to achieve a relevance to the changing states of society. In recent times the gap between traditional moral principles and the realities of modern life has become so large as to precipitate, beginning in the Catholic church, and less spectacularly in other religious denominations, urgent demands for renewal—for the development of statements of moral purpose which are directly relevant to the modern world. But in the modern world the substance of moral issues cannot be perceived in terms of the casting of stones or the theft of a neighbor's ox. The moral issues of the modern world are embedded in the complex substance of science and technology. The exercise of morality now requires the determination of right between the farmers whose pesticides poison the water and the fishermen whose livelihood may thereby be destroyed. It calls for a judgment between the advantages of replacing a smoky urban power generator with a smoke-free nuclear one which carries with it some hazard of a catastrophic accident. The ethical principles involved are no different from those invoked in earlier times, but the moral issues cannot be discerned unless the new substance in which they are expressed is understood. And since the substance of science is still often poorly perceived by most citizens, the technical content of the issues of the modern world shields them from moral judgment.

Nowhere is this more evident than in the case of nuclear war. The horrible face of nuclear war can only be described in scientific terms. It can be pictured only in the language of roentgens and megatonnage; it can be understood only by those who have some appreciation of industrial organization, of human biology, of the intricacies of world-wide ecology. The self-destructiveness of nuclear war lies hidden behind a mask of science and technology. It is this shield, I believe, which has protected this most fateful moral issue in the history of man from the judgment of human morality. The greatest moral crime of our time is the concealment of the nature of nuclear war, for it deprives humanity of the solemn right to sit in judgment on its own fate; it condemns us all, unwittingly, to the greatest dereliction of conscience.

The obligation which our technological society forces upon all of us, scientist and citizen alike, is to discover how humanity can survive the new power which science has given it. It is already clear that even our present difficulties demand far-reaching social and political actions. Solution of our pollution problems will drastically affect the economic structure of the automobile industry, the power industry, and agriculture and will require basic changes in urban organization. To remove the threat of nuclear catastrophe we will be forced at last to resolve the pervasive international conflicts that have bloodied nearly every generation with war.

Every major advance in the technological competence of man has enforced revolutionary changes in the economic and political structure of society. The present age of technology is no exception to this rule of history. We already know the enormous benefits it can bestow; we have begun to perceive its frightful threats. The political crisis generated by this knowledge is upon us.

Science can reveal the depth of this crisis, but only social action can resolve it. Science can now serve society by exposing the crisis of modern technology to the judgment of all mankind. Only this judgment can determine whether the knowledge that science has given us shall destroy humanity or advance the welfare of man.

ECOLOGY AND SOCIAL INSTITUTIONS

Is ecology a phase of science of limited interest and utility? Or, if taken seriously as an instrument for the long-run welfare of mankind, would it endanger the assumptions and practices accepted by modern societies, whatever their doctrinal commitments? [1]

As the ecological crisis develops, the necessity to control the undesirable side effects of technology will—inexorably—demand that industrialized nations modify or radically alter their political and economic systems to accommodate the facts of ecology and the values that emerge from those facts. Not to adopt this policy is simply to guarantee that the prophecies of scientific Cassandras will be fulfilled and that avoidable catastrophes will in fact occur. Despite this certainty, no available evidence indicates that industrialized nations are now engaged in planning those crucial institutional changes that will permit the continuation of an ecologically sound biosphere. Instead, business and government have substituted rhetoric for action, planned more tedious symposia, and spent minuscule sums of money for programs that in themselves may be either futile or, worse, actual causes of pollution.

The institutional crises that this intransigence will precipitate, and that the industrialized nations are just now beginning to confront, result partially from the historical alienation of Western religious and humanistic traditions from ecological wisdom; but the problem is also a consequence of the void that exists between the brilliant insights of ecologically oriented scientists, scholars, journalists, and men of letters, and the social, political, and economic conclusions implicit in their studies.

In fact, the same group of outstanding (and literate) scientists—

[1] Paul B. Sears, "Ecology—A Subversive Subject," *BioScience*, 14 (7): 11 July 1964.

Leopold, Rachel Carson, Darling, Vogt, Osborn, Commoner, Ehrlich, Dubos, Cole, Slobodkin to name a few—who have alerted the United States to the dangers of environmental deterioration have—without exception—ignored, or hedged on, the political and societal implications of ecology.

Dr. Commoner, for example, points out that "science can reveal the depth of this crisis, but only social action can resolve it"; he nevertheless fails to indicate how "social action" can be meaningful when business decisions are dictated by the profit motive, economic policies reflect cornucopian fantasies of endless cancerlike expansion of GNP, and advertising spends $23 billion annually to convert human beings into moronic "consumers," programmed from childhood to devour mountains of "products" they neither need nor really want.

Although Lawrence Slobodkin argues intelligently for the ecological sophistication of science and technology, he avoids the problem of funding desired programs and the question of how industry would receive ecological knowledge if it were not easily exchanged for higher dividends. Slobodkin admits that there "are conflicts," but his reluctance to grasp the depth of those "conflicts" illustrates precisely what Lewis Mumford meant when he wrote that scientists are "singularly unprepared to recognize or deal with the institutionalized purposes that are actually controlling our society." Even hyper-astute Lewis Mumford, when he peers into the abyss separating ecological wisdom from current practice and sees "finance capitalism," backs off, ignoring the significance of his observation.

The refusal to confront the political implications of ecology is more conspicuous when government officials substitute fraudulent rhetoric for action, when cynical politicians try to co-opt the eco-activist youth movement, or when a major polluter decides to exploit "clean energy" as a profitable slogan.

In these respects, then, the new "war" to save the environment is already replete with the same devious rhetoric that has been used for centuries to hide chronic American failures behind a barrage of promises, platitudes, and phony "reforms." But the ecological crisis, unlike other issues, is immune to both rhetoric and tokenism; the ecological facts of life proceed toward doomsday conditions as though the latest politico, bureaucrat, or PR man had neglected to deliver up his box of soft soap. And, although insincere rhetoric spread through corrupt media channels can shore up rationalizations for racism, militarism, political repression and the demise of democracy, none of the standard tactics will reverse the deterioration of the biosphere. The ecological crisis is, by its nature, a problem which cannot be co-opted, bought off, deceived, jailed, or assassinated.

Although the political implications of ecology are difficult to predict, major environmental problems will never be diminished, much less eliminated, until the political system is capable at least of reallocating national wealth away from war machines, moondoggles, pork barrels, highways, and other wasteful, socially useless, or ecologically destructive expenditures. These resources must be directed against the multiple crises of racism, poverty, health, aging, urban blight, education, and social injustice, all of which are inextricably connected with the solution of ecological problems. A value system that could arrest environmental degradation would of necessity have to abolish many seemingly unrelated problems.[2]

Since the causes of the present crisis are related to wasteful consumption and increasing population, many commentators recommend mandatory birth control and economic austerity. But in order to expect the victims of poverty, racism, and class or ethnic bias to make great sacrifices for the sake of the nation, the power structure would first have to indicate that it was—at last—serious about redistributing income, abolishing racial discrimination, dismantling the social caste system, and decentralizing power. Certainly it is naive to insist that those who are victimized by society should make sacrifices similar in kind to those who possess and exploit the benefits society has to offer.[3]

Not only will the ecological crisis result in challenges to social injustice, it will also call into question the capitalist's dream of ever-expanding markets for investment, a condition that Marx felt was the élan vital of the system. In the words of Robert Heilbroner, Marx felt that "the essence of capitalism . . . is expansion," and that "the capitalist, as a historical 'type,' finds his raison d'être in the insatiable search for additional money-wealth gained through the constant growth of the economic system. The idea of a 'stationary' capitalism is, in Marxian eyes, a contradiction in terms, on a logical par with a democratic aristocracy or an industrial feudalism."[4] Yet ecological prudence allows for only the most scrupulously planned economic activity, designed to meet real human needs in an ecologically sound manner. To realize

[2] For example, it is impossible to imagine an ecologically committed society possessing doomsday weapons, using chemical defoliants, maintaining ecologically insane ghettos, and treating human fauna more barbarously than nonhuman fauna.

[3] Likewise, the wealthy nations recommend birth control and austerity to the Third World, ignoring "the role of external factors in creating Third World retardation—more pointedly, the connection between the imperial and cosmopolitan centers and the colonized peripheries." See "The Disappointing Decade of Development," by Denis Goulet, in *The Center Magazine* (September, 1969) and the rebuttal by Irving Louis Horowitz in the same periodical (November, 1970), partially quoted above.

[4] Robert L. Heilbroner, "Ecological Armageddon," in *The New York Review of Books* (April 23, 1970), p. 7.

these goals, Heilbroner writes, "the main avenue of traditional capitalist accumulation would have to be considerably constrained; . . . net investment in mining and manufacturing would effectively cease; . . . the rate and kind of technological change would need to be supervised and probably greatly reduced; and . . . as a consequence, the flow of profits would almost certainly fall." [5] To question the sacred assumptions of endless expansion of production, markets, and profits is, as the Wall Street Journal recently noted, "to threaten the American Dream itself."

What chances are there for preserving the basic structure of the American system and at the same time maintaining the integrity of the biosphere? Without doubt, this question is destined to take its place next to the other great issues that are challenging the established order in the United States. For the liberal critic, Frank Potter, the societal mechanisms available to cope with the complexities of unfamiliar environmental issues currently operate in sluggish, contradictory, and unenlightened ways; but they are capable of reform and effective action if the impetus for change derives from broad-based public support.

Whereas Potter believes that it is possible to correct the malfunctions of the system, Jon Margolis coldly delineates some of the obstacles that liberal reformers must necessarily encounter as they attempt to adjust political, economic, and social realities to square with ecological criteria. Among the many unavoidable conflicts is that between the aesthetic objectives of white, upper-class conservationists (both established organizations and grass-roots movements) and the economic requirements of the poor and impoverished.

The radical critics see Potter's hopes for "adjustment" politics as unrealizable because the obstacles blocking equitable reforms are integral parts of the system. To eliminate the obstacles, they feel, is to give rise to a new radicalism, to the reconstruction of society based on the insights of an ecological conscience.

[5] Ibid.

Frank M. Potter, Jr.

everyone wants to save
the environment

It is difficult to find a newspaper today that doesn't have at least one story on environmental problems. People who read these stories react to them and, with increasing frequency, their reaction is sympathetic. Environmental concerns are no longer the private preserve of the bird-watchers: the same bell tolls for us all.

In 1969, the National Wildlife Federation commissioned two polling organizations to investigate American attitudes on environment. The polls reached the conclusion that most people are actively concerned about environmental problems and would prefer that a greater proportion of their taxes be devoted to the costs of solving them. The level of concern here rose with income and varied inversely with age. Over 50 percent of those interviewed felt that the government was devoting insufficient attention to environmental problems and was providing insufficient funds to resolve them. Over 80 percent felt a personal concern, and most of these registered "deep concern." What, then, keeps them from the barricades?

Apathy, one might think, but the surveys rule that out. The most significant inhibitor of action may be that we are too easily convinced of our own political impotence. The larger the grouping, the more difficult it is for any person to make a significant impact upon social decisions.

On the other hand, when they are really aroused, people can take and have taken effective action. For example, a coalition of citizens joined forces in 1969 to require a reluctant U.S. government to quadruple the amount of funds to be used for waste-water facilities. They did so by informing their elected representatives that this was a matter of specific, personal, and urgent priority; their representatives listened and

Reprinted, by permission, from the March 1970 issue of The Center Magazine, *a publication of the Center for the Study of Democratic Institutions in Santa Barbara, California.*

130

responded. Again, a few years ago, a small group of citizens banded together against the largest utility in the United States, opposing plans to construct a major hydroelectric plant within fifty miles of New York City. They stopped the utility company in its tracks. That company was Consolidated Edison, the plant was the Storm King project. The Federal Power Commission, which must decide whether or not the plant should be built, has still not made its decision. The strong case made by the citizens depended in large measure on the fact that they were able to propose alternatives to the project and to support their case by a wealth of technical and engineering detail that showed New York's serious power problems could be met by less damaging methods. Although Con Edison has not yet given up the project, it has adopted the alternatives, and many sophisticated agency-watchers now consider it unlikely that the Storm King plant will ever be built.

Collective action, then, can make a difference. Individually or collectively, we are confronted with a clear option: Are we to live well only for a short period, or must we cut back economic growth in favor of long-term survival for the species? For the most part we appear to have adopted the former course of action, and it is by no means clear that we would act much differently if the choice were clearer. "*Après moi, le déluge*" is an attitude confined neither to France nor to the eighteenth century. As individuals, we tend to be somewhat ambivalent about the importance of what might be called an environmental conscience.

With very little effort, we could educate our children about the importance of environmental responsibility; yet it is the children who seem to be taking the lead in educating us. A national Environmental Teach-In is scheduled for April, 1970, in schools and colleges across the country, and there are signs that problems of pollution are occupying a rapidly increasing portion of the attention of young people.

It is important to distinguish between the actions and attitudes of individuals and those of the citizen groups organized to consider environmental problems. The biggest problem faced by such groups is seldom a lack of motivation; it is financial. It is still rare for anyone whose economic interests are involved to oppose a polluter; this means that concerned citizens must themselves assume these costs, although the financial burdens of speaking out and working against a powerful and well-financed industry or government agency may be great. The costs of carrying on a major controversy may exceed $500,000. We cannot reasonably expect any private group to bear such a burden, nor should we as long as the group is acting to protect assets that are common and valuable to all of us.

It is important to note, though, that even concerned citizens do not always organize themselves to protect the environmental system as a whole—one group may be interested only in visual pollution while another is interested in noise. It is an unfortunate fact of life that a normal resolution of a pollution problem often means pushing it into another area which may not be so vigorously defended. For example, the public concern with power-generation facilities producing air pollution in the form of coal dust, oil droplets, and increased sulphur dioxide emissions encouraged the building of nuclear plants, which involve none of these pollutants but may well present other problems in terms of radioactive and thermal pollution of cooling water.

To look to private business for solutions to pollution may be futile. Its horizons are deliberately limited to those factors which are considered to be of immediate importance, principally economic, and the hidden costs to the society at large tend to be ignored. These costs still exist, however, and they must be borne by everyone if not by the industry which creates them. A classic example would be a pulp processing plant which emits fumes of hydrogen sulphide, causing foul air and peeling paint for miles downwind. The resulting inconvenience, possible health hazards, and certain increases in maintenance costs have not traditionally been imposed upon the agency which created them. Instead, they have been borne by our whole society, regardless of the capability or willingness of individual members to bear them.

To be sure, some private companies have taken steps to limit the antisocial consequences of their operations and have done so at considerable cost, quite beyond what they have been required to assume by law. But a voluntary approach to reducing environmental problems, it is clear, is just not good enough. For one thing, the forces of competition tend to minimize such voluntary efforts. Few men or companies, however public-spirited they may be, are prepared to expend large sums on the internalization of indirect costs. Nor can they do so without incurring the wrath of profit-seeking stockholders, who are even further removed from the environmental mischief they have indirectly created.

Polluting industries have most often resisted pressure to clean up their operations by claiming that the measures proposed are unduly prohibitive or confiscatory. Their chief means of resistance has usually involved threats to pull up stakes and move elsewhere. This last resort has been adopted infrequently, if at all, and is only likely to occur where a producer has found himself impossibly squeezed between falling profits and rising costs. It has also been alleged that these are the marginal producers whom the next strong wind will blow away in any case, so that little lasting economic damage to the area ever occurs.

The mechanics for balancing social costs against economic values, then, must be found outside the private institutions themselves, and they are—this is a major function of government. The laissez-faire philosophy which at one time characterized the attitude of American government toward American industry won't work today. It is also apparent that the government is likely to expand its program in this area. Public attention has already been focused on air and water pollution. But there are other areas in which governmental action must be anticipated—among them, noise, solid-waste disposal, and the by-products of energy transfer are mentioned with increasing frequency.

Governmental overview, if impartially and reasonably imposed, need not be hostile to the private sector; it may even be in its interest, both short-termed and long-termed. The National Association of Manufacturers has never been known as a hotbed of social activists, yet members of N.A.M. operating committees have endorsed proposals for a strong federal body to oversee environmental issues. Businessmen have to breathe, too, and most of them are prepared to accommodate themselves to the ecological imperative—as long as their competitors are subject to the same rules. We cannot assume, however, that increased governmental concern will take place without some economic disruption. Marginal producers will feel the pinch most strongly, and some may not survive. Nevertheless, the important consideration is that the rules must be enforced fairly and impartially upon all parties.

It is important to bear in mind that the mass of government workers—the *Lumpenbürokratie*—marches to a drumbeat that only it can hear. Higher levels of government, presumably more responsive to broad social needs, generally find their choices so circumscribed by business-as-usual decisions farther down the line that their options are dissipated by the inertia of the machinery. This is by no means peculiar to the solution of environmental problems, though these tend to be somewhat more acute because of the high stakes involved and because the new issues do not fit easily into the existing bureaucratic patterns.

In practically every agency of government, at almost every level, strong pressures to maintain the status quo are built up. As one progresses from local to national bureaucracy the inertia increases. A random example: early in the 1950s the Eisenhower Administration stated a strong preference for private power development as against public power, but it was not until the Kennedy Administration took office eight years later that the direction of bureaucratic thinking had changed enough to give effective support to the idea of private power. Nor could the Democrats reverse the trend.

There are also powerful personal influences that, in current bureaucratese, are "counterproductive." As one observer put it, "the paramount objective of the permanent bureaucracy is permanence." This contributes directly to the institutional resistance to change. Agency employees tend to react self-protectively. This was probably the principal roadblock encountered by Ralph Nader's "Raiders" in their government agency investigations during the past two summers. They often ran up against a bureaucratic wall which blocked the publication of several unfavorable agency reports on the controversial supersonic transport until the reports were wrenched from unwilling bureaucratic hands by actively concerned congressmen. To combat this reaction Congress passed the Freedom of Information Act, requiring disclosure of all but certain specified documents—a public law which has been honored far more in the breach than in the observance.

This problem is compounded by a frequent lack of clear policy guidance from the upper levels of government to the lower. New policies may be found in new regulations and pronunciamentos which either go unheeded or trickle down by word of mouth. This communications system serves as an efficient filter for any content that may fortuitously have crept into the public statements of the man or men at the top.

Such difficulties should not be ascribed solely to bureaucracy. The problem for bureaucrats is essentially the same as that of the private citizen: they are unable to relate everyday decisions to any specific action of the government machinery. Moreover, the results of yesterday's decisions are rarely communicated to the decision-makers as a corrective for tomorrow's programs. To be sure, there is enough feedback for everyone to know when a dam doesn't hold water (which happens), but when a dam destroys a delicate ecological balance and wreaks havoc in the local community, the mischief is rarely perceived as a genuine problem.

Still another troublesome aspect is that government agencies compete with one another. For decades, to cite an example, the Departments of the Interior and Agriculture have carried on a polite war; its prime casualties have frequently turned out to be considerations of the environment. Countless examples of this competition have been observed: timber-cutting practices on public lands and in national forests, pesticide regulation (if that is the correct term for it), dam building, and soil conservation are just a few. The same kind of competition may occasionally be found between the public and private sectors of the economy; once again, concern for the environment usually loses out.

In some respects, such competition is healthy. Occasionally, the public may even benefit from it. Several years ago, for instance, the Army Corps of Engineers conceived a plan to build a high dam on Alaska's Yukon River which would flood hundreds of thousands of acres of land in the process. The dam was successfully opposed by the Fish and Wildlife Service of the Interior Department on the ground that it would do untold damage to the wildlife in the region. The operative word here is "untold"; no one knew just how much damage would have been done and the corps was not really interested in finding out.

There are other consequences of governmental competition. Although they operate with public funds, governmental agencies are under pressure to make the most of the funds they expend. The budgetary restrictions placed upon the head of a large operating government agency are no less severe than those upon the directors of a large corporation, and the body to which they report is no more aware of the importance of environmental factors than the average stockholder of American Telephone & Telegraph. This comparison ought not to be pressed, however, since while it will be difficult to improve the ecological understanding of the average citizen, it is not beyond our grasp to educate Congress.

The essential function of the legislative branch of government is to formulate and to review policy. In so doing, it operates under constitutional or other social restraints, and it must of necessity paint with a broad brush. Translating basic policy decisions into specific go and no-go decisions, never an easy task, is often complicated by pressures within the executive branch to change the policy decisions themselves. More important, policy is only as good as the information upon which it is based, and this information tends to be biased, conflicting, fragmentary, and/or out-of-date.

Consider the effect of the following factors upon the theoretical non-bias with which a congressional policy decision is supposed to be approached:

The nature of the proposal—Most legislation enacted by the Congress is originally proposed by agencies in the executive branch. (This, incidentally, may not be quite so common today; the legislative proposals of the present administration have been criticized as somewhat sporadic. Many of the bills now before the Congress, however, are holdovers from earlier years, and the basic pattern seems to have changed very little.) Support for these measures tends to be channeled well in advance of their consideration—facts are marshaled, charts are drawn up, witnesses are prepared. A frequent result of this process is that the Congress may focus on the wrong issues.

The congressional committee structure—Committees of the Congress, and especially their ranking members, are among the principal focal points of power in Washington. This apparatus determines which bills are considered, whether testimony in opposition will be considered, and if so, how it will be rebutted. Unless the issue is getting the attention of the press and the public, or unless a maverick congressman digs in his heels, those controlling the committee have a relatively free hand in developing the arguments for and against the bill; hence they control its future.

The bias of congressional leaders—The environmental crisis is a relatively new phenomenon, and the young are more concerned with the problems than their elders. This is as true in the Congress as elsewhere. The result is that many of the older members, who exercise greater control over legislative action than their younger colleagues, are less inclined to meet the new challenge. Exceptions can easily be found, but the general truth of this observation is not seriously questioned. There is, then, a bias favoring inaction. It ought not to be discounted.

The adequacy of the testimony itself—Assuming that the measure is reasonable and that the controlling committee is interested in developing the real issues, the witnesses called to testify may nonetheless not be the best available. Witnesses on environmental issues have tended to be the elder statesmen—established scientists and professionals whose views on new problems and on the need for new approaches have been colored by their own studies and viewpoints, which are frequently considerably out-of-date. A review of nongovernmental scientific testimony over the past few years shows that several names pop up again and again; these individuals (who may be spectacularly well qualified in their own areas of competence) occasionally edge into areas in which they are not well qualified to speak, and they often seem to be responding to the unspoken needs of some committee members to be reassured that things are not all that bad, and somehow technology will find a way. Although not every expert witness falls into this category, it happens often enough to constitute a real problem. There is, consequently, a need to develop a base of scientific testimony available to the Congress on environmental issues and to see that younger scientists, whose factual knowledge is more current, are heard.

The context of the legislative decision—Another conflict, not at all restricted to environmental issues, faces the legislator who must decide whether to favor the good of his own constituency over national interests. Thus congressmen and senators from the West are generally inclined to favor legislative proposals to open public lands for development (mining, grazing, lumbering, oil exploration, etc.), whereas the interests of the entire country might seem to favor retaining these lands in a less exploited condition. How to measure the interests of local areas against those of society is a serious question. Resolving the conflict may be one of the most significant functions of government.

The broad nature of the authority and responsibility of the legislature may prevent it from exercising effective control over the actions of the organizations theoretically under its direction. The policies the legislators are called upon to define are so broad they cannot possibly be spelled out in detail, and yet it is in such details that the actions of government become manifest.

The legislative mechanism may also be criticized for its slow reaction time. The Congress is a highly conservative body—deliberate in adopting new courses of action, and slower to change them once they are adopted. This is, of course, a source of strength, preventing today's fad from becoming tomorrow's straitjacket. But it is also a real source of danger to the system. Science and technology have transformed the world of the mid-twentieth century into something that was quite unimaginable fifty years ago. The rate of change is accelerating, and it is a brave man who will claim that he can predict the state of the world in the year 2000. Shrill voices may decry technology and demand that there be a halt to new technological development; they are no more likely to be heeded than were the machinery-wrecking Luddites of nineteenth-century England. Whether they are right or wrong is quite beside the point; barring massive catastrophe, technology will not be significantly curbed and the rate of technological change will almost certainly continue to speed up.

New technology creates new social conventions, which in turn affect legislative policy. Yet the mechanisms for determining that policy are keyed to technological considerations that may have already been out-of-date in 1800, and to decision-making processes that have remained essentially unchanged since the days of Roger Bacon.

Consider massive changes in climate. Scientists tell us that urban development and energy transfer now have a significant effect upon global weather patterns. We hear on the one hand of the "greenhouse effect," which tends to raise atmospheric temperature as a function of increased carbon dioxide production, and on the other of increased amounts of pollution in the air, which tend to lower atmospheric temperature by decreasing the amount of solar radiation reaching the earth's surface. Some scientists, extrapolating present activities, speculate that it would take ten years to decide which is the more powerful effect, and that by then large-scale climatic changes may be irreversible. This view is by no means commonly held, but it is under serious consideration by men whose voices ought to be heard. They are not given a hearing before Congress; if they were, they might well be outnumbered ten to one by men saying, "We are not certain, we do not know, and we should take no action until we do."

Our ecological problems, then, are not the exclusive province of the Congress; they are those of the scientific community and of all of us who have an interest in human survival. There seems as yet no way to force these problems to the forefront, conjoined as they are with an historically validated precedent for doing nothing—at least not yet.

Legislators tend to focus upon institutions rather than individuals— to see the needs of the larger groups whose existence depends upon traditional thought patterns and legal fictions. A water pollution problem is perceived as that of a municipality or an oil company, an air pollution problem as that of a manufacturer. Yet it is individual citizens whose favor the legislator must seek if he is to survive. This suggests in turn that if individuals can organize themselves to be heard as an institution concerned with environmental survival the legislators will respond. This has not yet happened generally. No significant environmental lobby has yet made its voice heard on the national level.

The courts exist to see that the written and unwritten rules of society are followed; that the policies formed by the people and their elected representatives are observed. Within narrow limits, the courts have been successful in this function. As a means of achieving rational decisions on environmental issues, however, the courts are usually ineffective. Their influence could increase, but this would require a significant departure from the usual legalistic approach. It would involve the recognition of a basic and inalienable human right to a livable environment. Such a decision appears to be a remote possibility. Without this new constitutional approach, the courts will almost certainly be hamstrung by inadequate policies adopted by the legislature and by common-law rights which were defined centuries before the current environmental problems appeared.

Only in rare instances can the courts make decisions with more than local force and effect. The U.S. court in southern New York may properly hold that the federal Department of Transportation must observe certain procedures specified by statute that may have escaped the department's notice, and for this reason a highway shall not be built over the Hudson River. At the same time, the same department favors the construction of longer runways into the Columbia River. Technically, the decision of the New York court is not binding in Oregon; the Oregon courts are free to disagree with their East Coast brethren and such disagreements are in no way uncommon. A means does exist for resolving interjudicial disputes—the Supreme Court of the United States. The Court, however, is already operating under a fearful load and can devote only a limited amount of its energies to environmental questions, however important they may appear to be.

The courts also lack the information upon which to base their decisions. The common-law system is grounded upon the adversary system, the theory being that each side will present the most favorable case it can and that the court will then resolve the dispute on the basis of the evidence before it. The environmental problems arising today are very complex—very different from the land disputes and tort actions of centuries ago. In theory, expert testimony ought to be available to both sides to support their cases; in practice, this simply does not work. Even if environmentalists can afford to hire experts (and often they cannot), experts cannot always be found. It is a rare electrical engineer who will agree to take the witness stand on behalf of opponents to a power plant or transmission line; he knows that other utilities may thereafter hesitate to contract with him for services even in circumstances that may be wholly unrelated to the present controversy. Conscientious men do exist and some may be found to testify, but it is not easy to find them. Cases have been lost and will continue to be lost for this reason alone. Without that interplay of expert testimony, the court is at a major disadvantage.

Even if experts can be found by all parties, the court's information problems are not thereby solved. Technical questions are already difficult, and they are growing more complex every day. Judges spring from different backgrounds, but the law operates according to the theory that their experience is essentially irrelevant to the issues that they must decide. Historically, ignorance has been a prime virtue, the court acting as the *tabula rasa* upon which the cases of the opposing parties may be written. This is a manifest absurdity, but it is the way the law grew, and it is a fact that lawyers with weak technical cases prefer judges with little technical competence.

Another weakness built into the judicial system is its tendency to delay decision. Combined judicial and administrative delays have postponed the Storm King decision by five years already. If the parties fight down to the wire, a longer delay is likely. In many respects this delay has worked in favor of the conservation group, but this happy state of affairs is not the rule. Citizens opposed to a particular proposal or project are usually forced to seek injunctive relief from the courts; they may and often do find that this relief cannot be obtained without their posting a substantial bond which is quite beyond their means. The result is that while they work their way through the courts, the opposition is busily building or digging or chopping down. By the time that the court is ready to decide, the essential question has become moot. Injunctive relief is typically the only possible hope for environmentalists, since the alternative is a damage suit, and it is a basic tenet of such organizations that money cannot replace what is threatened.

Constitutional revision has been proposed as a means of providing a clearer and more enforceable definition of our rights to a satisfactory environment. New York State has adopted such a program, and similar efforts have been mounted on a national level. An Environmental Bill of Rights would indeed be a valuable tool, but no such proposal has a chance of even being seriously considered without vastly increased pressure upon the Congress and upon the legislatures of the several states.

Pollution will be inevitable until we can develop adequate tools for dealing with it. The government will never do the job by itself. The solution seems to lie, rather, in putting stronger weapons into the hands of the public—helping it to bring about the necessary reforms through legislative and judicial channels.

Jon Margolis

land of ecology

Senator Ted Stevens first noticed them last September. Stevens is an Alaska Republican; as such he supports the right of every able man to get rich by building things. When he saw late last summer that this faith too had its heretics, Stevens could not keep silence. "All of a sudden all these conservationists are coming out of the woodwork to tell us how to save Alaska," he said. He did not approve.

The statement did wonders for Stevens politically. Alaskans don't like conservationists. Nearly everyone else does, though, and in the past few years they have been coming out of the woodwork more often. Going right back in, too, and staying out of sight once they have made their point. Conservation may be the first revolution led by unknowns.

And make no mistake, it is a revolution, very likely the most contentious and the most important of the rest of the century. The radicals know this now; the politics of confrontation has been used on conservation disputes, and the politics of ecology is now a frequent term in the underground press. If only the conservationists knew it. Conservation is in revolt against its own past as much as against the country's present. Like the unfettered technology it fears, the conservation movement may contain within itself the seeds of its own destruction.

There is little doubt that conservation is quite the vogue. Hardly a county lacks some sort of citizens' conservation group. Usually, they are formed not to protect the environment in general but to battle a specific threat to it, often a threat close to home. With increasing frequency, the battles are being won. Consolidated Edison has not been able to build its power plant on Storm King Mountain in New York State; Dade County and the U.S. Transportation Department may yet be prevented from building the world's largest jetport in the Big Cypress Swamp of Florida, and there are more nuclear power plants on the drawing boards than will ever be on the waterside killing fish.

So successful have the protectors been that the developers have begun to fight back. In 1967, naturalists found a covey of ivory-billed woodpeckers, then considered extinct, in the heart of the Texas Big Thicket. But they didn't say precisely where for fear that timber and real-estate interests would kill the lovely birds. The theory is that the fewer natural wonders there are in any plot of land, the less reason Congress will have to preserve it. Similar tactics were used by the California lumber companies which tried to cut down the best of the redwoods while a bill to protect them was being debated.

Not that business is unaware of the growing public concern with conservation. Advertising and public-relations departments across the country are hard at work telling us how much corporations care about the environment they are befouling. In full-color, two-page ads in fancy magazines, oil companies inform how the fish actually like detonations for underwater wells, or that their brand of gasoline will pollute the air just a bit less. Magazines and television networks are devoting unprecedented time and space to conservation, and even newspapers, usually the last to know what the public really cares about, are beginning to cover the subject. Possibly they noticed the appointment of a hard-line law-and-order attorney general did not create nearly as much fuss as the naming of an interior secretary who dared deride conservation for its own sake.

Conservation crosses party lines and even ideologies. John Birchers and Communists, *Ramparts* and *Reader's Digest*, the *New York Times* and the Los Angeles *Free Press*, Max Lerner and James Kilpatrick, Barry Goldwater and George McGovern. This may not last, for the New Conservationists are about to enter the political arena full force, perhaps even borrowing from older revolutions such tactics as the sit-in, the boycott, and, who knows, can the Molotov cocktail be far behind? This will make some enemies. Even now, not everyone is a conservationist, though opposition also is bipartisan. Ronald Reagan, Richard Daley and Nelson Rockefeller are among those uncommitted to the cause.

Nonetheless there are places where a man can get elected by being a good conservationist. Westchester County, New York, is full of old-fashioned Republicans, and Richard Ottinger is a liberal young Democrat. But because he has pledged to save the Hudson River, those Republicans keep sending him to Congress. Richard McCarthy, another liberal New York congressman, comes from a working-class backlash district in Buffalo. When he goes home he doesn't talk about race and welfare; he talks about how dirty Lake Erie is. Union men out collecting money for the Committee on Political Education likewise have learned to get a dollar out of right-wing workers by telling them the money will support candidates committed to clean streams and lakes. Some local unions have even taken to opposing industrial expansion which would increase their membership. The current members, lacking the money to move to the suburbs, have begun to notice something foul in the air they breathe, and they don't want it any dirtier. Rich or poor, most people are lining up on the conservationist side of any given dispute.

Yet few of these newly enlisted troops know who their generals are, or even their sergeants. Nearly everyone knows which senators are prominently for or against the war, civil rights, and unions. But how many know that were it not for Gaylord Nelson of Wisconsin every drop of fresh water in America would be too sudsy to drink? Nelson, a liberal, is the leading conservationist in the Senate. John Saylor of Pennsylvania, a friend of the American Medical Association and the Chamber of Commerce, is the leading conservationist in the House.

One reason conservationists remain unknown while their cause is embraced is that many of them are westerners, while the people who make people famous are in the East, meaning the Northeast. Conservation, after all, means the wise use or preservation of natural resources. There are young women in New York who talk about conservation every evening but aren't quite sure what a natural resource is. Of course the East is very conservation-conscious now, but it is a recent concern. Westerners have been involved in conservation for years, especially the kind which subsidizes farmers, ranchers, miners, and lumber entrepreneurs, which is certainly not what the women in New York have in mind. The typical informed westerner, for instance, may know that Boyd L. Rasmussen is director of the Bureau of Land Management. The typical informed easterner has never heard of the Bureau, though it controls 20 percent of his country's land.

Yet East and West alike are probably ignorant of such names as Dan Poole, Stewart Brandborg, Elvis Stahr, or Paul M. Dunn. These are some of the men who are not in government but who are at the center of the Conservation Establishment, an establishment which has been left behind by its cause. Which is not necessarily bad at this point for both cause and establishment. If some of the young intellectual liberals who have lately embraced conservation found out what some of the leading conservationists thought about the world in general, they might go back to the peace or civil-rights movements.

As an organized movement, conservation still deals in specifics—getting a national park established, preserving a wild river or a species of bird. But the cause, the unorganized but ever more popular movement, has become holistic without quite realizing it. When conservation started in the last century, the basic concept was wise use. Later it was beauty. Now it is ecology, and if you doubt the potency of conservation consider that three years ago you probably didn't know what that word meant; now you surely do. In ecology, by definition, all of a nature is connected, all relates to everything else.

Yet if the North American Wildlife Foundation and the National Audubon Society spent all their time worrying about ecology, fewer woods and rivers would have been saved in the last few years. Sometime soon the New Conservationists must define their beloved ecological conscience and figure out how best to organize to put it to use. But the concept is too new and the organizations are in their infancy. Meanwhile the bulldozers roll on, and someone has to stop them, lest there be no life left to interrelate.

There are really two Conservation Establishments. The first, centered in Washington, is dominated by the "user" groups, or tools of the interests as children of another revolution might call them. It is made up of foresters, fishery managers, and state fish-and-game officials. Its friends in government are in such agencies as the Bureau of Commercial Fisheries or the Bureau of Reclamation. Its friend in Congress is Wayne Aspinall, head of the House Interior Committee, who makes sure that every time some wild land is set aside there remains a way for someone to make money from it. It was Aspinall who included in the Wilderness Bill an amendment allowing all mining until 1984, a loophole which may create in the northern Cascades a pit which can be seen from the moon.

This traditional approach to conservation is the one most often found in the Interior Department, whose task is less to preserve the environment than to subsidize nature's users. Interior's public relations are conservation-oriented—its annual report features colored pictures of natural wonders and inspirational words about saving them—but its budget is not. In fiscal 1968, half of the department's $1,800,000,000 went to "water resources," most of which was for "reclamation," meaning flood-control and irrigation projects which reclaim rivers from running free and reclaim salt marshes from being breeding grounds for fish and nesting spots for birds. Flood control is needed because people decided, before we knew as much as we do today, to live along flood plains. Actually, houses are still being built on flood plains, though everyone knows they will necessitate a new dam somewhere. But then, building homes is often the most profitable use for flood-plain land, and once people need flood control, the government is sure to provide it. Floods also occur downstream because of reckless deforestation upstream. Among their other values, trees hold water. When they are removed, the waters run into the streams in greater quantity than the stream beds can accommodate. The solution to that is to build a dam, upsetting the river basin's ecology, and possibly reducing the number of fish.

The second Conservation Establishment, the one everybody is talking about, is not really headquartered anywhere, and it isn't very established. Nor is it united. It consists of perhaps twenty national organizations, most of them as ineffective as they are unknown, and an uncountable number of local groups, a few of which are very tough indeed. Conservation has all the disadvantages of citizen-oriented politics. Most of the official leaders, especially of the national groups, are part-timers, people who do other tasks, usually well-paid ones, most of the time. For instance, Dr. Edgar Wayburn of the Sierra Club is a successful San Francisco physician; Warren M. Lemmon, the head of the Nature Conservancy, manages extensive California real-estate holdings; Robert Winthrop of the North American Wildlife Foundation is on the board of directors of the First National City Bank. The opening bankroll for the John Muir Institute, the educational and tax-exempt arm of Friends of the Earth, came from Robert O. Anderson, chairman of the board of Atlantic Richfield; and Laurance Rockefeller runs the American Conservation Association. It is not a poor-man's movement. The day-to-day operations are left to small professional staffs made up in large part of unknown men. The citizen leaders like it that way. When David Brower began to act as though he ran the Sierra Club, the paragons of San Francisco society who controlled his executive board got rid of him. And when he challenged them in an election among the club members he had recruited, they beat him badly.

Because the movement is so loosely organized, strong personalities can have an unusually strong effect. Allen Morgan is credited with making the Massachusetts Audubon Society perhaps the most effective conservation organization in the country, and the West Virginia Highlands Conservancy is a force in that little state primarily because of Grover C. Little. Local conservation groups usually start on an ad hoc level, coming into existence to fight one threat to the local environment, but they often stay around to look for more trouble. In Hawaii, a group called Save Diamond Head saved Diamond Head, and it's aiming now to save all of Hawaii. The women of Morris County, New Jersey, did not disband after they had stopped the airline industry from filling in the Great Swamp to make a jetport; now they are fighting power companies and the Army Engineers elsewhere in northern New Jersey. Nearby, the Scenic Hudson Preservation Conference formed to fight Con Ed's Storm King Plant, but when that fight ends there will be more. The Hudson is a big river.

Despite the increasingly political character of the movement, there remain several national conservation organizations which stay out of politics and lobbying in favor of more restricted tasks. The American Conservation Association gives away Laurance Rockefeller's money to select research projects. The Conservation Foundation studies public policy's effects on the environment. The North American Wildlife Foundation and the Wildlife Management Institute, really one outfit supported by the gun industry, have undertaken the research which has brought wildlife management a long way from the days of indiscriminate predator control and un-ecological stocking, though some of that still goes on. Perhaps the organization closest to the heart of the matter is the Nature Conservancy, which with a pittance from private sources does what the government won't do enough of—buy land valuable to nature and about to be lost to it. The Conservancy thus far has been able to save 150,000 acres of the American Earth.

But the Conservation Establishment has been taken over by the militants, some of them so militant they don't even call themselves conservationists, but preservationists. The militant preservationist is a radical. Well, about nature he's a radical; about people he may be quite conservative. This is not a new irony. Since the movement began before the turn of the century, it has been split between those who wanted to save and manage nature for people—all the people— and those who wanted to leave it just as it was for nobody at all, or perhaps for those with the time, money, and culture to appreciate true wilderness. At the beginning, this schism was personalized by Gifford Pinchot, head of the Forest Service under Teddy Roosevelt, and a populist, and John Muir, founder of the Sierra Club, and a mystic. They were friends for a while, camping out together in the Grand Canyon, but they became estranged, first over the fight about sheep grazing on the public lands, then over the Hetch Hetchy Dam, which violated Yosemite National Park but brought low-cost public power to San Francisco. The preservationists fought the dam bitterly, making common cause with the private-utility industry. Then or later, they seemed not at all embarrassed about the bedfellow.

Today, within the militant conservation movement, united opposition to dams can usually be counted on unless the dam will also create a big lake for motorboating and stocked fishing. Which it always will, the power companies and the Army Engineers and the Reclamation Bureau knowing they then have a good chance of splitting the recreationists—the "parks are for people" crowd and the sportsmen—from the preservationists.

Within the Conservation Establishment, these arguments rage within as well as between organizations. There are Sierra Club members who think saving Mineral King Valley not worth the effort, and there are ardent preservationists in the National Wildlife Federation. But in general the recreationist cause is taken up by the hunters, who far outnumber everyone else in organized conservation. Theoretically, they are hunters and fishermen both, but fishermen per se have no clout. Fishing rods are cheap. The only militant and effective sportsmen's group is the National Wildlife Federation, which is run by the state councils of rod-and-gun clubs, thus representing local groups totaling about 2,500,000 people. Many of these members are not really conservationists, and the federation gets most of its money from conservationists who are not members, but who subscribe to *National Wildlife Magazine* or purchase the wildlife stamps the federation sends out without mentioning who controls the beneficiary. Nationally, the federation is not as strong as some other conservation groups, but on the state level its councils are often the only working conservation lobby. Nonsportsman conservationists have only begun to lobby in state legislatures in California, Oregon, Maine, and New York, but the Wildlife Federation has close ties with legislators and state fish-and-game departments. At present, the federation is supporting an anticonservation proposal backed by the western state fish-and-game bureaucracies which would give state departments total control over all wildlife in their states, a move which could open the national parks to hunting and effectively erase federal protection now given eagles and migratory birds.

If the recreationists are most likely to come from the sportsmen's groups, the extreme preservationists are most apt to be found in the Wilderness Society, a single-minded collection of 55,000 persons to whom a well-managed campground is as hideous as an oil refinery on a promontory would be to other conservationists. Wilderness Society members want parks which are not for people other than themselves. They do not seem motivated primarily by ecology, but speak of preserving the pristine for the sake of "our physical and spiritual regeneration." Among other effects, such statements give aid and comfort to the enemy, be they mining interests, the Agricultural Department's Forest Service, which manages the national forests, wherein are most potential wilderness areas, or the power-boat manufacturers who wish every mountain stream to be turned into a huge lake courtesy of the Army Engineers.

Hard-core preservationists are also found in large numbers in the National Parks Association and Defenders of Wildlife. The former spends half its time fighting the National Park Service, which in recent years has suffered the delusion that it is a federation of highway departments commissioned to build roads through all the national parks. The Association's staff head is Anthony Wayne Smith, an abrasive man whose background offers a good defense against charges of elitism. Smith was once conservation director for the C.I.O., where he apparently found a hero. A few years ago, he got angry at the Natural Resources Council of America, a forum for national conservation groups, and, in the manner of John L. Lewis, he disaffiliated.

Defenders of Wildlife began as a group of women who were upset about inhumane trapping and roadside zoos, and expressed their anger in a mimeographed newsletter. As such causes are wont to do, this one attracted the attention of several persons with excess money, and the newsletter became a slick if virtually unedited quarterly which combines valuable facts on conservation with little cutenesses about squirrels. As fierce as any species, Defenders of Wildlife is less nimble than most, hence not very effective.

The bridge between the straight conservationists and the sportsmen is the Izaak Walton League, which is a bit of both. The national Izaak Walton League is a loose collection of chapters which maintain virtual autonomy. In states like Montana, where conservation sentiment is minimal, the Walton League is strictly a sportsmen's group, delving into social issues only to pass a yearly resolution against gun-control laws. In crowded Indiana, the Walton chapter pays no mind to fish and game, concentrating instead on preserving what remains of nature there. At times this local autonomy can be embarrassing. For three consecutive years, the League's national convention was rent by the emotional, and successful, effort to override the California chapter's opposition to the 80,000-acre Redwood National Park, opposed by most sportsmen because hunting is not allowed in national parks. More recently, the refusal of Florida chapter president James Redford—again the importance of personality—actively to oppose the Everglades jetport left the Walton League the only national conservation group outside the anti-jetport coalition. Coalition is the league's hallmark though, and its conservation director, Joe Penfold, until recently headed the Natural Resources Council, essentially a coalition of warring groups.

Actually, they get along rather well, considering basic differences in outlook, because there remain enough specific problems for them to unite on: the lumber industry's raid on the national forests, the jetport that would ruin the Everglades, the dam which would have created in Alaska a lake the size of New Jersey to provide more power than Alaska needs, the possibility that the trans-Alaska oil pipelines will ruin the tundra ecology, the danger that a little-known federal commission will recommend this summer that the public lands be parceled out to the highest bidder. If these fights are won, they will be won by cooperation and old-fashioned lobbying with the conservationist friends in government. Tho Old Conservation has its work cut out for it while the New Conservation figures out just what its work is.

To the New Conservation, rivers, mountains, and wildlife are no more important than cities and suburbs. The New Conservationist's concern is the total environment, and Penfold thinks it's in trouble. The rallying cry of the old preservation was poetry, Thoreau's: "In wilderness is the Preservation of the World." The New Conservationist quotes not poets, but scientists such as Paul Ehrlich, Eugene P. Odum, and Barry Commoner, who say, in effect, that in unfettered technology is the destruction of the world. In place of the whooping crane, the roseate spoonbill, and the California condor, the New Conservation has interposed another endangered species—the two-legged predator, man.

This is not an assumption on which to base moderation. New Conservationists have adopted some of the rhetoric and even a few of the methods of the Left; and the Left, especially the psychedelic Left, has discovered conservation. In Berkeley, something called Ecology Action, which participated in the People's Park campaign and conducts symbolic destruction of automobiles, grew out of a splinter wing of the Peace and Freedom Party. Elsewhere in California, ecological revolutionaries have burned cars as hateful artifacts, lain down in front of trucks carrying what once were redwoods, and pulled out the surveyors' stakes marking the path of a road through Sequoia National Park. The underground press, especially the Los Angeles *Free Press*, devotes considerable space to conservation matters. Despising science, such of the young that meet the turned-on label adore ecology, a science. Logic is not their strong suit.

But militant New Conservation is not solely, even mainly, the province of the young and radical. In Patchogue, Long Island, an outwardly ordinary lawyer named Victor Yannacone has formed the Environmental Defense Fund, which plans to take every polluter to the Supreme Court if need be. In Colorado, the Environmental Protection League threatened to disrupt recent underground nuclear tests. In St. Louis, a group of scientists concerned about nuclear pollution formed the Committee for Environmental Information, now prepared to fight all environmental threats.

Thus the radical and the technical. But political movements succeed by being careful and emotional, and if the New Conservation succeeds, it will be through its mainstream—the Sierra Club, the Audubon Society, and now the Friends of the Earth. The first two are the giants of the movement. It was the Sierra Club which stopped the dams proposed for the Colorado River, dams which would have filled in part of the Grand Canyon, and it is the Audubon Society which is leading the fight against DDT and other hard pesticides. Each has more than 80,000 members, and both have enough knowledge of and connections in media to gain the support of many thousands more whenever needed. Charles Callison, executive vice-president of the Audubon Society, is often on the phone to John Oakes at the *New York Times*, who is never unwilling to rise to any conservation cause. The power of both Audubon and the Sierra Club is acknowledged by the powerful, which is a form of power itself. They complement each other nicely. The Sierra Club, hitting hard and fast, constitutes the shock troops; Audubon, choosing its targets more deliberately, using its well-written, handsome magazine to recruit support, provides the bulwark of the line. The Sierra Club, still West-oriented though half its members now are not from California, leads the fight on saving the public lands and the redwoods, preserving wild rivers, and Alaska. Audubon, strong in the East, concentrates on wetlands and wildlife.

The bitter Sierra Club election which ousted Brower did not weaken the club, other than to deprive it of his services. But neither did it weaken Brower. A committed, even demonic conservationist, Brower was out of a job but not a vocation. Like all conservationists, his emotions may tend him toward the remote and pristine past, but his talents are contemporary. He is an editor, a writer, a public-relations wizard. In 1966, he correctly read the mood of the country by gambling that if only the people knew of it, they would oppose the Colorado River dams. Now he bets the country is ready for an avowedly political conservation group. Friends of the Earth will openly espouse candidates and raise money for them. More, Brower wants conservation to go on the attack, to go back over where men have trod, often unwisely, and reclaim the land in a way the Reclamation Bureau never dreamed. Reclaim shopping centers, not swamps, cities, not mountains, polluted rivers, not free-flowing streams. More open space and less development, more wild animals and fewer people are the political aims of Friends of the Earth, and Brower intends to use money and political muscle to get them. He feels he has to.

For basic to the ecological conscience is the belief—no, the scientific fact—that the earth is finite, and the opinion that we are approaching its limits, that every assault on its nature starts a chain of certainly unknown and possibly cataclysmic events, which could make life for all of us uncomfortable, unsafe, even impossible. No longer is the militant conservationist worried that the whooping cranes might die out, or that the lovely land will disappear, or that the oil will run out. He is worried that the oxygen will run out.

Nor is this a needless panic; the supply of oxygen is not infinite and it is diminishing. Every time a tree is cut down, there is just a touch less, and we cut down a million acres of trees a year. Of course, that's not the source of most oxygen, most of it comes from the phytoplankton in the oceans, oceans now so polluted that the phytoplankton is endangered. Only half-facetiously, Ehrlich has predicted the death of the oceans in 1979, and when the oceans die, we all die. When all the water is salty or polluted we die also, and there are those who say that at current rates we have thirty years of water left. Then there is the weather. Suppose the sun's rays can't get through because the air around the Earth is full of glop. Would the glaciers march south again? Or suppose, once here, the heat could not filter away. Then would the polar ice caps melt, raising the seas and flooding the coasts?

To be more mundane, take southern Florida, and what could be more mundane. By nature, men ought to live only along the coasts there, where the land is high enough and dry enough. What is in the middle is really not land at all, but a unique river which does not flow so much as seep through the saw grass from Lake Okeechobee to Florida Bay. It is no place for men to live, but years ago some pioneers saw it was a good place for men to make money. So, like most pioneers, they went to the government and got an elaborate and expensive system of canals and reservoirs to drain the river of grass, leaving rich black soil, and some roads to cross the newly created farmland. (They also got laws restricting foreign competition and no laws regulating wages and hours, but that is another matter.)

Now the glades produce vegetables in quantity, adding to the national surplus, but the water is not seeping south the way it used to, and the southern Everglades, including the national park, is dryer than it should be. Because the downward flow of fresh water has declined, Florida Bay may be getting too salty and too warm, so that while southern Florida may continue to produce plenty of tomatoes, it may soon cease to produce menhaden and black mullet and spotted sea trout. Tomatoes we can grow in New Jersey, or at least we could until we paved it over. Menhaden and black mullet in such size and numbers come nowhere else. Perhaps the New Conservationists are right. Perhaps nature knows best. Perhaps we should not have messed with it.

As if they don't realize that messing around with nature is both What Made America Great and the basis of Western Civilization. The trouble with society, to a New Conservationist, is not that it is unjust or immoral, but that it is . . . anthropocentric. And it is. We were, after all, given dominion. And now we have established it. We were all brought up to admire the pioneer who cleared the forest and blazed trails through the wilderness. We think Boulder Dam was a triumph of mankind, that swampland filled and built upon is useless land reclaimed, that it is virtuous to build million-dollar ditches to make fallow land fertile. Now who are these people come to tell us different?

They are among the most handsome beneficiaries of dams and irrigation projects and dirty air and water which lie, let's face it, at the foundation of our prosperity. Most of those in the forefront of the fight for clean lakes and rivers belong to country clubs with chlorinated swimming pools. The New Jersey women who saved the Great Swamp had, in addition to fervor, money. Those committed to preserving the Hudson Valley live along it; it is not a low-income neighborhood. When a road is to pass through loveliness, the denizens of the lovely arise to fight it, and if the engineers retreat to the point of rerouting the highway through the ghetto, well, for some, that's victory enough.

Everyone wants to preserve Alaska save the Alaskans, who want to make a passel of money tapping their natural resources. The Sierra Club saved the Red River Gorge from inundation by a proposed dam fought by everyone except the small farmers who live along the river's often-flooded banks. Northern New England is full of impoverished families living in near secrecy off back roads and paying absurd prices for electric power and fuel oil. The prices could come down if the Dickey-Lincoln School Dam were built and an oil-import complex constructed at Machiasport, Maine. And prosperity could come to the hamlets of the North if factories were lured there. But such steps are strongly fought by a lot of $40,000-a-year executives from Boston and New York, who point out that the dam might block free-flowing rivers, the oil pollute the water and deface a lovely harbor, the industry and resultant housing and shopping-center development would dirty the air and spoil the region's character, a character quite irrelevant to many of the region's residents.

The New Conservationists are telling us to stop, and from their perspective, they are quite right. If the power companies are to be prevented from ruining more hills and warming more rivers, we must stop needing more electricity. If we are not to be buried by mountains of bottles and cans, we must use fewer of them, or use them over again. If we are not to pave over all the open land, we must have fewer cars. If we are not to run out of food, or out of open space because we need all the land for farms, we must stop adding to the population. If we are to have clean air and water and decent places to live, perhaps we need less manufacturing. Brower says we must "do more with less." Odum says we must stop being "consumptive" and "learn how to recycle and reuse." Either way, they are saying that this vaunted economy, this sainted Gross National Product, must stop growing.

Stop growing? But growing is the secret of our success. We have mass affluence, to the extent we have it, not because we took from the rich and gave to the poor but because we became—we *grew*—so much richer that even most of the poor live tolerably. They still get the short end of the stick, but the stick is so long now that one can get at least a fingerhold on that end. To stop growing is to stop elongating the stick, and since most people are still clinging to that short end, this presents some problems.

Because the conservationists are not on that end. They are not steelworkers or assembly-line workers or small farmers or hotel clerks. They are Wall Street lawyers and junior faculty and editors and writers and corporate vice-presidents. One does not become a conservationist until one has had the time and learning to care about whether there are eagles or Everglades. Searching for their hundred-fifty-year-old Vermont farmhouses, conservationists wonder how people can actually want to live in a new, $25,000 split-level in the suburbs, apparently never thinking that for most people the alternative is a three-room walk-up in the downtown smog. The suburbs are open to them, as Vermont is to the more affluent, because of technology, because draining swamps and dirtying streams and damming rivers and polluting the air gave them high-paying jobs. Shouting about the environmental catastrophe, urging an end to growth, the conservationists are $20,000-a-year men telling all the $7500-a-year men simply to stay where they are so we can all survive. Ethics aside, there is a serious tactical problem here; there are more $7500-a-year men and they are likely to say no. True, money would go farther in a good environment. True, as Ian McHarg said, ecological planning can give any given area more high-paying jobs and more profits plus good environment. But for the nation as a whole, for the economy, the conservationist's dichotomy remains, and he has not faced up to it: if we do not stop expanding, we ruin the environment; if we do, we condemn the lower middle classes to their present fate.

Unless. Unless of course we did redistribute the profits of affluence by legislative fiat. Unless we planned where industries could locate and how much they could produce and where people ought to live in what numbers, and where, ecologically, no one ought to live, or drive, or even walk. Unless we instituted such extensive public regulation over use of the land, water, air, and people, that hundreds of enterprises, perhaps most of them, could not operate profitably, especially if they couldn't grow, so that perhaps they would have to be operated on a basis other than profit. There is a name for such a system. And can you see Laurance Rockefeller financing a feasibility study on that, and can you see all those $40,000 executives endorsing it?

Well, maybe. Huey Long supposedly said that if fascism came to America it would come from the working class. Now we may have come to the point where if socialism comes to America, it will come from Wall Street lawyers concerned less about the welfare of people than the survival of spoonbills. Maybe. But days after Dave Brower announced formation of Friends of the Earth, he invited to Aspen, Colorado, a select group of scientists and professors and businessmen to discuss "progress in a living environment," and because he is concerned about conservation's upper-class, all-white constituency, he invited also one Ted Watkins, Negro, chairman of the Watts Labor Community Action Committee. For two days, amidst Aspen's beauty, Watkins listened to the learned, concerned men, and then he spoke:

"What are you going to sacrifice to do the kind of conserving we want to do? Which teacher is going to give up his nice two-story home? What doctor, what architect, is going to sacrifice some of his practice to help the cause along? What advertising man is going out and campaign to raise funds without a 25- or 30-percent fee? Who of you in this room is ready to make a sacrifice to do what you say you are going to do?"

There were no takers.

Barry Weisberg

the politics of ecology

The critical importance of ecology as a developing source of political opposition in America stems from the realization that politics in our age has acquired an absolute character. While political decision-making and control is steadily concentrated in the hands of a very few —the arena of control is steadily expanding. Fewer and fewer people control more and more—so that the very conditions which support life on this planet: the land we walk upon, the air we breathe, and the water we drink, are now the subject of political management on a scale beyond normal comprehension. The politics of ecology must start from the premise that present-day reality is increasingly the product of a structure of economic and political power that consolidates and sustains itself through the systematic destruction of man and his physical world. The exploitation of man by man and nature by man are merely two sides of the same coin.

It is then folly to think that the destruction of our global life support systems under advanced industrial capitalism or communism is merely a by-product of progress, a case of bad management, the result of insufficient esthetic sensibilities on the part of business and engineers, or simply a matter of who owns the means of production. In an historical sense, we have reached the point where we can totally violate the processes and structures of the natural world; hence our relationship to nature is no longer determined by the forces of nature but by the rule of political management. The deterioration of the natural environment all around us is therefore clearly a product of the nature of production and consumption, of cultural values and social relationships that today hold sway over industrial technological society —American or Soviet.

Reprinted, by permission of the author, from the January 1970 issue of Liberation Magazine. *Barry Weisberg is a co-director of the Bay Area Institute, San Francisco, and has published widely on the politics of ecology.*

154

In short, our present technical manipulation of the life-support capacity of the planet now threatens the totality of physical conditions which nurture life itself. The oxygen content in the atmosphere, the metabolism of our own bodies, food chains and the relationship between populations and the resources needed to support them, conditions upon which the existence of all plant and animal life today depends, are the products of evolutionary processes extending over billions of years. Our industrial civilization is now destroying them in a matter of decades. We are talking about processes which may well have worked their irrevocable consequences within a decade or two—after which there will be nothing within the human potential to restore their life-giving capacity.

The culture itself is aware of the explosive potential of the imbalances between society and nature. Government and industry through the media have begun to manage these issues on a daily basis. Scientists speak out, reports are called for and committees created. In fact the pattern of action and language emerging around pollution parallels exactly the failures of civil rights and poverty—"a war on pollution," the calling for a "pollution pentagon." Even new bureaucratic offices to replace the Department of Interior are suggested. What such proposals miss is that it is not the control of the land, air and water that is at stake but the control of man.

The obvious question resulting from this brief survey is whether or not these are matters of bad management, dysfunction or the like, as mentioned earlier. The origins of our present destruction of the life-support capacity of this planet are rooted in the very fabric of our civilization, reaching their most insane dimensions in the present corporate America. The Greek rationalism of Aristotle, the Roman Engineering mentality, the biblical anthropomorphic injunctions to "have dominion over the land and subdue every creeping thing," the post-Enlightenment notions of growth and progress, the present technical corporate economic systems motivated by competition—all dominate the Western mentality of man against nature. Where nature works toward harmony, cooperation and interdependence, advanced industrial society works toward growth, competition and independence. The advanced nation-state works in direct opposition to those basic life-giving instincts which have nourished our billion year evolution. To repeat, the domination of man by man and man over nature are two sides of the same coin. The precondition for our survival requires the most basic transformation of the cultural, social, political and economic mentalities and structures which dominate the developed nations and hang as a carrot over the never-to-be developed nations.

In view of the sudden flurry of government-initiated programs (including the spate of officially endorsed campus "teach-ins" planned for next April), it is especially chilling to contemplate the performance of government, industry and their conservationist junior partners. Here's a rundown:

Government

The proportion of the National Budget spent on all natural resource programs has declined steadily since 1959.

1965	2.3%
1966	2.2%
1967	2.0%
1968	1.9%
1969	1.9% est.
1970	1.8% est.

In other words, for fiscal 1969, we spent only 3.6 billion on all natural resource programs, of some 202 billion dollars, spending more (4 billion) to reach outer space than to make the earth habitable. The gap between authorization and appropriation on programs such as air and water pollution has widened every year. This is merely to demonstrate the inability of the Congress to achieve its own stated objectives—not that those objectives would have successfully dealt with any major issue. In fact, there is every reason to believe that more spending would have produced merely more pollution. Add to this a government which at the same time subsidizes the supersonic transport, maintains the depletion allowance for continued off-shore drilling, undermines efforts at consumer protection—and one begins to understand the meaning of federal efforts. While there are more committees, more reports, more research and more attention, less and less is actually done. The frightening conclusion, however, is not that government should do more, for the more it does the worse our ecological systems get.

Industry

What are we to make of the flurry of industrial ads depicting everything from Standard Oil to Dow Chemical to the American Rifle Association as conservation-minded people? Of the recent Business of Pollution Control Technology of the investment of industry in conservation organization? The answer I think is to be found, for instance, in the words of Robert Anderson, chairman of the board of Atlantic Richfield. In a recent address before a State Department-sponsored conference on Man and His Environment, Anderson argued that the costs of pollution control should be passed on to the consumer and that oil should remain the base of energy supply. In short, industry has made of the environmental crisis a commodity. Recent financial reports indicate that the business of pollution control will in fact make a profit out of pollution while at the same time generating more pollution; more growth will be the remedy applied to the perils of growth. In short, that advertising will continue to cost more for business than research, that the consumers will be passed on any costs of "pollution control," and that federal agencies, new or old, will continue to operate as captives of the industry they are to regulate.

Conservation

More than any single element of the present collage of conservation activity, the conservation organizations themselves, to varying degrees, lead the public to believe that the emperor has no clothes when in fact they serve as clothes for the emperor. Such organizations act in the most fragmentary ways, attacking isolated problems and not complex patterns of social and political behavior. They save a nature area and fail to address the entire land use patterns of that region. They save a seashore from development when that seashore is threatened with the biological destruction of its wildlife. As such, their victories are at best stop gaps, always provisional. They foster the existence of centralized forms of authority through the support they lend to present elective procedures—"get the good guys in office." They have virtually no critical understanding of the governments of oil, agri-business, public utilities or chemicals. The conservationists frequently violence-bait the Left or shun it as revolutionary. "The country is tired of SDS and ready to see someone like us come to the forefront," a young conservationist recently noted. Increasingly motivated and supported by various governmental machinations, these people work in total isolation to the civil rights and peace movements, with no relationship to the varied forces of opposition and liberation in the society today—the revolutionary young, women's liberation, labor, and oppressed minorities. They seek private solutions to what more correctly are public issues—picking up litter rather than attacking the production of junk, refusing to use autos rather than struggling against oil and the auto manufacturers, to be merely suggestive.

But most important, the "new breed of young conservationists" fail to see that the crisis of the environment truly is but a reflective of the crisis of this culture itself, of the values, institutions, and procedures which have for some 200 years systematically guided the slaughter of human and all other forms of life at home and abroad. These tendencies were demonstrated too well by a recent selection of "youth" hand-picked by the Department of State to participate in the U.S. Commission for UNESCO Conference on Man and His Environment in

San Francisco last month. Virtually all "program" suggested by these participants lent credence to the status quo by advocating "better" candidates, new ecology colleges, yet additional "research," and more jobs for conservation-minded college kids.

The barrage of petitions and letters to the president was greeted by the conference "adults" with adulation, for the kids turned out to be "reasonable men" just as their parents. The popular press billed their performance as revolutionary—defined as "nonviolent," get-your-man-in-office, and increased student participation. But the role of our benign media goes much further.

By and large, the media has purposely obscured the political and social content of the environmental crisis by confining problems as well as solutions solely to the realm of science and technology. The result is that blind faith in the omnipotence of expertise and technocracy wholly dominates current thinking on ecological issues. Technological innovation and more reasonable methods of resource allocation cannot possibly reverse the present logic of the environment unless the overriding political, social and economic framework which has actually generated that trend is radically rebuilt. Such a transformation cannot reside solely in the realm of culture and values—as most often proposed by the youthful elites of conservation. The critical task today is to raise the issue of pollution/destruction, imperialistic styles of consumption, and of overpopulation to a political status in order to reveal an arena of political opposition in America which the Left has hitherto ignored. That is not to say that the Left can simply absorb the ecological crisis into its own kind of "business as usual" behavior. For the patterns of life in which most of us partake are not much different than those of the ruling class. This is not to say that true solutions reside in private action, but that public transformation without an entirely different style of life is futile. Thus the development of an ecological politics on a practical level may provide the only framework in which the alienated and oppressed can achieve true liberation.

That potential for liberation doesn't lie in the Save the Bay Campaigns, the protection of a redwood grove or planned parenthood. It does not reside alone in the culturally symbolic acts of many ecology action groups around the country. The true origin of what has yet to become an authentic movement is in the People's Park episode, in militant actions against corporate despoilers (including sabotage) and in the private as well as public attempts to create ecologically sound lives.

While the traditional conservationists have made no imaginative attempt to understand what our cities would look like without autos, with decentralized agriculture or power, with neighborhood control and rationed resources, save for few scant efforts, the Left, with few exceptions, has been equally derelict. "Radical" economists still contemplate growth-motivated economies grounded in false notions of affluence and unlimited resources.

The New Left has at this point made little serious effort to understand or relate to the politics of ecology. While the battles in the streets appear more pressing and more direct, it ought to be understood that unless something very basic and very revolutionary is done about the continued destruction of our life support system, there may well be no wind to weather in the near future.

Dismissing overpopulation as simply a matter of genocide, efforts to take back the land as bourgeois or the necessity for clean air and water as a luxury completely fails to grasp what can only properly be understood as a matter of life or death.

The task of ecological radicals is to continually raise those issues which sort those which seek to patch up the status quo from those who struggle for basic transformation. The polarization of the rulers and the ruled is the authentic growth of any true movement for liberation. When conservationists argue that everyone is in the same boat (or on the same raft), that everyone must work together, tempering their actions to suit the imperatives of coalition, they are in fact arguing for the further consolidation of power and profit in the hands of those responsible for the present dilemma.

There is no easy way to summarize exactly how the movement must respond to the growing politics of ecology. Publishing special magazine editions and flimsy attacks on "sewermen" will not do. Few models exist to lend direction to organizing efforts. Already throughout the country people have been organized around industrial accidents and health hazards, consumer boycotts, women's liberation and the nuclear family, the extinction of animal species or the struggle against a new highway. This is just the beginning. This winter and spring we can expect a series of radical ecological actions: the bombing of more corporate headquarters, sabotage to the industrial machinery that pollutes and obstruction at airports and other transportation corridors.

It is safe to suggest that organizing around environment issues that fails immediately to lead to the political causes and implications of that peril is misguided. For too long eco news and reports have begun and ended with nature—without undertsanding that nature itself is today the product of manipulation by man. We should have learned from the People's Park that the road ahead will be perilous and paved with a life and death struggle. If the state of California would defend a parking lot with the life of one person and the shooting of another 150, imagine the cost of taking back a forest, preventing an off-shore drilling rig from being placed, blocking the construction of a nuclear power plant or tampering with the power/communication/food/transport systems which make America grow. But the sooner this happens the better. The sooner the spirit of the People's Park infuses every ecological action, the brighter will be our chances to insure the conditions for our survival and, beyond that, a decent society.

Educating "the people about the impending ecological disaster" without pointing to possible forms of action available is at this point a disservice to the movement. As people engage in direct struggle against the Con Edisons, the Standard Oils, the pollution control agencies, and the United Fruit companies of the world, more and more new insights for strategy will develop. What has been happening to poor whites and blacks for several hundred years, what America has done to the Vietnamese, America is now doing to its own population, en masse. The organizing implications of this single fact may be profound. In a world of total biological slavery, liberation is the very condition of life itself. To fail does not mean growing up absurd, but not growing up at all.

Ecology Action East

the power to destroy,
the power to create

The Power to Destroy

The power of this society to destroy has reached a scale unprecedented in the history of humanity—and this power is being used, almost systematically, to work an insensate havoc upon the entire world
of life and its material bases.

In nearly every region, air is being befouled, waterways polluted, soil
washed away, the land desiccated, and wildlife destroyed. Coastal areas
and even the depths of the sea are not immune to widespread pollution.
More significantly in the long run, basic biological cycles such as the
carbon cycle and nitrogen cycle, upon which all living things (including
humans) depend for the maintenance and renewal of life, are being
distorted to the point of irreversible damage. The wanton introduction
of radioactive wastes, long-lived pesticides, lead residues, and thousands
of toxic or potentially toxic chemicals in food, water, and air; the expansion of cities into vast urban belts, with dense concentrations of
populations comparable in size to entire nations; the rising din of background noise; the stresses created by congestion, mass living, and mass
manipulation; the immense accumulations of garbage, refuse, sewage,
and industrial wastes; the congestion of highways and city streets with
vehicular traffic; the profligate destruction of precious raw materials; the
scarring of the earth by real estate speculators, mining and lumbering
barons, and highway construction bureaucrats—all, have wreaked a
damage in a single generation that exceeds the damage inflicted by
thousands of years of human habitation on this planet. If this tempo of
destruction is borne in mind, it is terrifying to speculate about what
lies ahead in the generation to come.

Reprinted, by permission of Ecology Action East, from the January 1970 issue of
Rat.

The essence of the ecological crisis in our time is that this society—
more than any other in the past—is literally undoing the work of organic evolution. It is a truism to say that humanity is part of the fabric
of life. It is perhaps more important at this late stage to emphasize
that humanity depends critically upon the complexity and variety of life,
that human well-being and survival rest upon a long evolution of organisms into increasingly complex and interdependent forms. The development of life into a complex web, the elaboration of primal animals and plants into highly varied forms, has been the precondition
for the evolution and survival of humanity itself and for a harmonized
relationship between humanity and nature.

Technology and Population

If the past generation has witnessed a despoliation of the planet
that exceeds all the damage inflicted by earlier generations, little more
than a generation may remain before the destruction of the environment
becomes irreversible. For this reason, we must look at the roots of the
ecological crisis with ruthless honesty. Time is running out and the remaining decades of the twentieth century may well be the last opportunity we will have to restore the balance between humanity and nature.

Do the roots of the ecological crisis lie in the development of technology? Technology has become a convient target for bypassing the
deep-seated social conditions that make machines and technical processes harmful.

How convenient it is to forget that technology has served not only
to subvert the environment but also to improve it. The Neolithic Revolution which produced the most harmonious period between nature
and postpaleolithic humanity was above all a technological revolution.
It was this period that brought to humanity the arts of agriculture,
weaving, pottery, the domestication of animals, the discovery of the
wheel, and many other key advances. True there are techniques and
technological attitudes that are entirely destructive of the balance between humanity and nature. Our responsibilities are to separate the
promise of technology—its creative potential—from the capacity of
technology to destroy. Indeed, there is no such word as "technology"
that presides over all social conditions and relations; there are different
technologies and attitudes toward technology, some of which are indispensable to restoring the balance, others of which have contributed
profoundly to its destruction. What humanity needs is not a wholesale
discarding of advanced technologies, but a sifting, indeed a further
development of technology along ecological principles that will contribute to a new harmonization of society and the natural world.

Do the roots of the ecological crisis lie in population growth? This
thesis is the most disquieting, and in many ways the most sinister, to

be advanced by ecology action movements in the United States. Here, an *effect* called "population growth," juggled around on the basis of superficial statistics and projections, is turned into a *cause*. A problem of secondary proportions at the present time is given primacy, thus obscuring the fundamental reasons for the ecological crisis. True, if present economic, political and social conditions prevail, humanity will in time overpopulate the planet and by sheer weight of numbers turn into a pest in its own global habitat. There is something obscene, however, about the fact that an effect, "population growth," is being given primacy in the ecological crisis by a nation which has little more than 7 percent of the world's population, wastefully devours more than 50 percent of the world's resources, and is currently engaged in the depopulation of an Oriental people that has lived for centuries in sensitive balance with its environment.

We must pause to look more carefully into the population problem, touted so widely by the white races of North America and Europe— races that have wantonly exploited the peoples of Asia, Africa, Latin America, and the South Pacific. The exploited have delicately advised their exploiters that, what they need are not contraceptive devices, armed "liberators," and Prof. Paul R. Ehrlich to resolve their population problems; rather, what they need is a fair return on the immense resources that were plundered from their lands by North America and Europe. To balance these accounts is more of a pressing need at the present time than to balance birth rates and death rates. The peoples of Asia, Africa, Latin America, and the South Pacific can justly point out that their American "advisors" have shown the world how to despoil a virgin continent in less than a century and have added the words "built-in obsolescence" to the vocabulary of humanity.

This much is clear: when large labor reserves were needed during the Industrial Revolution of the early nineteenth century to man factories and depress wages, population growth was greeted enthusiastically by the new industrial bourgeoisie. And the growth of population occurred despite the fact that, owing to long working hours and grossly over-crowded cities, tuberculosis, cholera, and other diseases were pandemic in Europe and the United States. If birth rates exceeded death rates at this time, it was not because advances in medical care and sanitation had produced any dramatic decline in human mortality; rather, the excess of birth rates over death rates can be explained by the destruction of preindustrial family forms, village institutions, mutual aid, and stable, traditional patterns of life at the hands of capitalist "enterprise." The decline in social morale ushered in by the horrors of the factory system, the degradation of traditional agrarian peoples into grossly exploited proletarians and urban dwellers, produced a concomittantly irresponsible attitude toward the family and the begetting of children.

Sexuality became a refuge from a life of toil on the same order as the consumption of cheap gin; the new proletariat reproduced children, many of whom were never destined to survive into adulthood, as mindlessly as it drifted into alcoholism. Much the same process occurred when the villages of Asia, Africa, and Latin America were sacrificed on the holy alter of imperialism.

Today, the bourgeoisie "sees" things differently. The roseate years of "free enterprise" and "free labor" are waning before an era of monopoly, cartels, state-controlled economies, institutionalized forms of labor mobilization (trade unions), and automatic or cybernetic machinery. Large reserves of unemployed labor are no longer needed to meet the needs of capital expansion, and wages are largely negotiated rather than left to the free play of the labor market. From a need, idle labor reserves have now turned into a threat to the stability of a managed bourgeois economy. The logic of this new "perspective" found its most terrifying expression in German fascism. To the Nazis, Europe was already "overpopulated" in the thirties and the "population problem" was "solved" in the gas chambers of Auschwitz. The same logic is implicit in many of the new-Malthusian arguments that masquerade as ecology today. Let there be no mistake about this conclusion.

Sooner or later the mindless proliferation of human beings will have to be arrested, but population control will either be initiated by "social controls" (authoritarian or racist methods and eventually be systematic genocide) or by a libertarian, ecologically oriented society (a society that develops a new balance with nature out of a reverence for life). Modern society stands before these mutually exclusive alternatives and a choice must be made without dissimulation. Ecology action is fundamentally social action. Either we will go directly to the social roots of the ecological crisis today or we will be deceived into an era of totalitarianism.

Ecology and Society

The basic conception that humanity must dominate and exploit nature stems from the domination and exploitation of man by man. Indeed, this conception goes back earlier to a time when men began to dominate and exploit women in the patriarchal family. From that point onward, human beings were increasingly regarded as mere resources, as objects instead of subjects. The hierarchies, classes, propertied forms, and statist institutions that emerged with social domination were carried over conceptually into humanity's relationship with nature. Nature too became increasingly regarded as a mere resource, an object, a raw material to be exploited as ruthlessly as slaves on a latifundium. This "world-view" permeated not only the official culture of hierarchical society; it became the way in which slaves, serfs, industrial workers and women of all social classes began to view themselves. As embodied in the "work ethic," in a morality based on denial and renunciation, in a mode of behavior based on the sublimation of erotic desires, and in other worldly outlooks (be they European or Asian), the slaves, serfs, workers, and female half of humanity were taught to police themselves, to fashion their own chains, to close the doors on their own prison cells.

If the world view of hierarchical society is beginning to wane today, this is mainly because the enormous productivity of modern technology has opened a new vision: the possibility of material abundance, an end to scarcity, and an era of free time (so-called "leisure time") with minimal toil. Our society is becoming permeated by a tension between "what-is" and "what-could-be," a tension exacerbated by the irrational, inhuman exploitation and destruction of the earth and its inhabitants. The greatest impediment that obstructs a solution of this tension is the extent to which hierarchical society still fashions our outlook and actions. It is easier to take refuge in critiques of technology and population growth; to deal with an archaic, destructive social system as the premises on which all thinking must rest. Without shedding these premises, all discussions of ecological balance must remain palliative and self-defeating.

The Power to Create

By virtue of its unique cultural baggage, modern society—our profit-oriented bourgeois society—tends to exacerbate humanity's conflict with nature in a more critical fashion than preindustrial societies of the past. In bourgeois society, humans are not only turned into objects; they are turned into commodities; into objects explicitly designed for sale on the market place. Competition between human beings, qua commodities, becomes an end in itself, together with the production of utterly useless goods. Quality is turned into quantity, individual culture into mass culture, personal communication into mass communication. The natural environment is turned into a gigantic factory, the city into an immense market place; everything from a redwood forest to a woman's body has "a price." Everything is equatable in dollars-and-cents, be it a hallowed cathedral or individual honor. Technology ceases to be an extension of humanity; humanity becomes an extension of technology. The machine does not expand the power of the worker; the worker expands the power of the machine, indeed, he becomes a mere part of the machine.

Is it surprising, then, that this exploitative, degrading, quantified society pits humanity against itself and against nature on a more awesome scale than any other in the past?

Yes, we need change, but change so fundamental and far-reaching that even the concept of revolution and freedom must be expanded beyond all earlier horizons. No longer is it enough to speak of new techniques for conserving and fostering the natural environment; we must deal with the earth communally, as a human collectivity, without those trammels of private property that have distorted humanity's vision of life and nature since the breakup of tribal society. We must eliminate not only bourgeois hierarchy, but hierarchy as such; not only the patriarchal family, but *all* modes of sexual and parental domination; not only the bourgeois class and propertied system, but *all* social classes and property; humanity must come into possession of itself, individually and collectively, so that all human beings attain control of their everyday lives. Our cities must be decentralized into communities, or ecocommunities, exquisitely and artfully tailored to the carrying capacity of the ecosystems in which they are located. Our technologies must be readapted and advanced into ecotechnologies, exquisitely and artfully adapted to make use of local energy sources and materials, with minimal or no pollution of the environment. We must recover a new sense of our needs—needs that foster a healthful life and express our individual proclivities, not "needs" dictated by the mass media. We must restore the human scale in our environment and in our social relations, replacing mediated by direct personal relations in the management of society. Finally, all modes of domination—social or personal—must be banished from our conceptions of ourselves, our fellow humans, and nature. The administration of humans must be replaced by the administration of things. The revolution we seek must encompass not only political institutions and economic relations, but consciousness, life style, erotic desires, and our interpretation of the meaning of life.

What is in the balance, here, is the age-long spirit and systems of domination and repression that have not only pitted human against human, but humanity against nature. The conflict between humanity and nature is an extension of the conflict between human and human. Unless the ecology movement encompasses the problem of domination in all its aspects, it will contribute nothing toward eliminating the root causes of the ecological crisis of our time. If the ecology movement stops at mere reforms in pollution and conservation control without dealing radically with the need for an expanded concept of revolution it will merely serve as a safety valve for the existing system of natural and human exploitation.

Goals

In some respects the ecology movement today is waging a delaying action against the rampant destruction of the environment. In other respects its most conscious elements are involved in a creative movement to totally revolutionize the social relations of humans to each other and of humanity to nature.

Although they closely interpenetrate, the two efforts should be distinguished from each other. Ecology Action East supports every effort to conserve the environment: to preserve clean air and water, to limit the use of pesticides and food additives, to reduce vehicular traffic in streets and on highways, to make cities more wholesome physically, to prevent radioactive wastes from seeping into the environment, to guard and expand wilderness areas and domains for wildlife, to defend animal species from human depredation.

But Ecology Action East does not deceive itself that such delaying actions constitute a solution to the fundamental conflict that exists between the present social order and the natural world. Nor can such delaying actions arrest the overwhelming momentum of the existing society for destruction.

This social order plays games with us. It grants long-delayed, piecemeal, and woefully inadequate reforms to deflect our energies and attention from larger acts of destruction. In a sense, we are "offered" a patch of redwood forest in exchange for the Cascades. Viewed in a larger perspective, this attempt to reduce ecology to a barter relationship does not rescue anything; it is a cheap *modus operandi* for trading away the greater part of the planet for a few islands of wilderness, for pocket parks in a devastated world of concrete.

Ecology Action East has two primary aims: one is to increase in the revolutionary movement the awareness that the most destructive and pressing consequences of our alienating, exploitative society is the environmental crisis, and that any truly revolutionary society must be built upon ecological precepts; the other is to create, in the minds of the millions of Americans who are concerned with the destruction of our environment, the consciousness that the principles of ecology, carried to their logical end, demand radical changes in our society and our way of looking at the world.

Ecology Action East takes its stand with the life-style revolution that, at its best, seeks an expanded consciousness of experience and human freedom. We seek the liberation of women, of children, of the gay people, of black people and colonial peoples, and of working people in all occupations as part of a growing social struggle against the age-old traditions and institutions of domination—traditions and institutions that have so destructively shaped humanity's attitude toward the natural world. We support libertarian communities and struggles for freedom wherever they arise; we take our stand with every effort to promote the spontaneous self-development of the young; we oppose every attempt to repress human sexuality, to deny humanity the eroticization of experience in all its forms. We join in all endeavors to foster a joyous artfulness in life and work: the promotion of crafts and quality production, the design of new ecocommunities and ecotechnologies, the right to experience on a daily basis the beauty of the natural world, the open, unmediated, sensuous pleasure that humans can give to each other, the growing reverence for the world of life.

In short, we hope for a revolution which will produce politically independent communities whose boundaries and populations will be defined by a new ecological consciousness; communities whose inhabitants will determine for themselves, within the framework of this new consciousness, the nature and level of their technologies, the forms taken by their social structures, world-views, life styles, expressive arts, and all the other aspects of their daily lives.

But we do not delude ourselves that this life-oriented world can be fully developed or even partially achieved in a death-oriented society. American society, as it is constituted today, is riddled with racism and sits astride the entire world, not only as a consumer of its wealth and resources, but as an obstacle to all attempts at self-determination at home and abroad. Its inherent aims are production for the sake of production, the preservation of hierarchy and toil on a world scale, mass manipulation and control by centralized, statist institutions. This kind of society is unalterably counterposed to a life-oriented world. If the ecology movement does not draw these conclusions from its efforts to conserve the natural environment, then conservation becomes mere obscurantism. If the ecology movement does not direct its main efforts toward a revolution in all areas of life—social as well as natural, political as well as personal, economic as well as cultural—then the movement will gradually become a safety valve of the established order.

It is our hope that groups like our own will spring up throughout the country, organized like ourselves on a humanistic, libertarian basis, engaged in mutual action and a spirit of cooperation based on mutual aid. It is our hope that they will try to foster a new ecological attitude not only toward nature but also toward humans: a conception of spontaneous, variegated relations within groups and between groups, within society and between individuals.

We hope that ecology groups will eschew all appeals to the "heads of government" and to international or national state institutions, the very criminals and political bodies that have materially contributed to the ecological crisis of our time. We believe the appeals must be made to the people and to their capacity for direct action that can get them to take control of their own lives and destinies. For only in this way can a society emerge without hierarchy and domination, a society in which each individual is the master of his or her own fate.

The great splits which divided human from human, humanity from nature, individual from society, town from country, mental from physical activity, reason from emotion, and generation from generation must now be transcended. The fulfillment of the age-old quest for survival and material security in a world of scarcity was once regarded as the precondition for freedom and a fully human life. To live we had to survive. As Brecht put it: "First feed the face, then give the moral."

The situation has now begun to change. The ecological crisis of our time has increasingly reversed this traditional maxim. Today, if we are to survive, we must begin to live. Our solutions must be commensurable with the scope of the problem, or else nature will take a terrifying revenge on humanity.

IV

COSMIC CONSCIOUSNESS: THE METAPHYSICS OF ECOLOGY

The political adjustments demanded by the deterioration of the biosphere will tempt national leaders to utilize the findings of the physical and social sciences (particularly behavioristic psychology and molecular biology) to manipulate and control human behavior. Such techniques would easily fit into the well established modern tradition of perverting the findings of science and technology for inhuman purposes. And in the light of recent history, it would be highly naïve to assume that governments would not use such potent and easily available tools when faced with a major crisis.

Another convenient (and equally dangerous) method for solving environmental problems is simply to maintain the present policies of substituting rhetoric and tokenism for the massive effort required to deal with the predictable catastrophes. By refusing to accept and act upon the implications of ecology, the industrialized nations are directly threatening the existence of the human species.

If, then, the ecological crisis places mankind between a Scylla of physical extinction and a Charybdis of totalitarianism, it also offers unparalleled opportunities for domestic and international cooperation based on the perception of those very threats. Although these may be large claims to make for a movement that as yet has shown few signs of becoming anything more than a middle-class fad, one need only comprehend the dimensions of the problem to realize that it contains the potential to bring forth revolutionary changes in all aspects of human existence.

In addition to the integration of ecological values into social and political systems, these changes must include the development of totally new ways of comprehending man's place in the cosmic order. The function of ecologically oriented philosophy, art, theology, and myth will be to help overcome the sources of national, ethnic, racial,

religious, ideological, and economic conflict. These visions will also pro-
vide transcendent justifications for abandoning ecologically destructive
life styles and practices, thus avoiding the need for coercive government
policies. Finally, these new ways of understanding will work to restore a
sense of communal involvement, to diminish the feelings of alienation
from the nonhuman worlds, and to heal the divisions between thought
and feeling, soul and body, art and craft, religion and theology, that
have plagued Western man for centuries. These are at least a few of
the promises held out by an ecological revolution. As one eco-activist
put it, "a man who masters the intricate art and science of living in
peace with the natural environment . . . can certainly master the prin-
ciples of living in peace with other members of his own species."

The essays in this section show three ways in which the metaphysics
of ecology are beginning to develop. Going far beyond the limitations of
political and social realities, the authors are thematically united in their
agreement that the meaning, order, and purpose of human life cannot
be separated from cosmic order and cosmic "destiny"; nor can the prob-
lem of human discontent be removed from the need to discover man's
true place in the universe.

The ways the authors choose to investigate these themes reflect widely
divergent sensibilities. For R. Buckminster Fuller, designer of the
geodetic dome, high poet/priest of cybernation and technology, the
proper understanding of man's relationship to nature requires the col-
lection, manipulation, and interpretation of vast quantities of computer-
ized data, all shaped, directed and controlled by the evolutionary role of
man's "weightless" thoughts.[1]

Fuller's optimistic faith in salvation through science and technology
has provoked numerous critics to charge that his political and social
views are naïve, if not reactionary, and that his "design solutions" for
all human problems are diverting and dangerous dreams. The critics,
nevertheless, have not shown how man is to master ecological problems
without imaginative applications of technology. Until they do, Fuller's
wild schemes and utopian speculations, as well as the ways in which he
philosophizes about technology, deserve serious consideration.

In the opinion of Zen philosopher Alan Watts, our feelings of
estrangement from nature derive from a number of destructive "mental

----

[1] Fuller's "philosophy is predicated . . . on the assumption that in dynamical
counterbalance of the expanding universe of entropically increasing random dis-
orderliness there must be a universal pattern of omnicontracting, convergent, progressive orderliness and that man is that anti-entropic reordering function of universe. . . ." See his book, *No More Secondhand Gods* (Carbondale, Illinois, 1963)
p. v.

fictions," including the belief that "human consciousness and intelligence" are a collective "fluke in the midst of boundless stupidity." Failing to comprehend "total situations," we drift as "alienated spook[s]" through a dead Newtonian universe.

Meanwhile, we forgo the many benefits of living an ecologically sane life within an ecologically integrated tribe, community or society. By explaining what man lost when in the course of evolution he gave up his ecological consciousness—and with it the "mythological present," the "pure perception of beauty," the "inner song of the self, and of the planet"—eco-poet Gary Snyder simultaneously reveals the values waiting to be reclaimed through spiritual transformation based on ecological awareness.

R. Buckminster Fuller

technology and the
human environment

Your Senate hearing gives me a short but welcome opportunity to talk . . . about all that man has learned fundamentally from his two million years aboard our spaceship earth, wherefor I wish to point out vigorously to you that we are indeed aboard an 8,000-mile-diameter spherical space vehicle. . . .

. . . Earth is a beautifully designed spaceship, equipped and provisioned to support and regenerate life aboard it for hundreds of millions of years, even until the time when so much energy of universe has been collected aboard earth as to qualify it to become a radiant star, shortly before which man will have anticipatorially resituated himself on other planets at nonincineratable distance from the earth nova. . . .

Humans have high destiny, possibly the most important in the universe. And if the human team aboard space vehicle Earth does not make good at this particular occupation of this particular planet there are probably billions times billions of other planets with human crews aboard who will reboard Earth at some time to operate it properly. . . .

Humanity on this North American continent is the beginning of a world man. We are not a nation. Nations are tribes of people who have been isolated for a long time and have, of reproductive necessity, inbred—grandfathers with granddaughters—and have adapted themselves to exclusively local physical conditions.

We are not going to be able to operate our spaceship earth successfully nor for much longer unless we see it as a whole spaceship and our fate as common. It has to be everybody or nobody. . . .

. . . We are going to have to find ways of organizing ourselves cooperatively, sanely, scientifically, harmonically and in regenerative spontaneity with the rest of humanity around earth. . . .

Excerpts from remarks made before the Senate Subcommittee on Intergovernmental Relations, Committee on Government Operations, March 4, 1969.

Considering our present dilemmas aboard our planet and earnestly seeking fundamental clues to both their cause and solution, we may note that we start our children off with a geometry whose lines and planes go (we say) to infinity. The little child says, "Where is that?" The teacher can't answer because she has never experienced infinity. . . .

I have been a visitor at 320 universities and colleges around the world and always have asked those university audiences "How many of you are familiar with the word 'synergy'?" I can say authoritatively that less than 10 percent of university audiences and less than 1 percent of nonuniversity audiences are familiar with the word and meaning of synergy. Synergy is not a popular word. The word synergy is a companion to the word "energy." Energy and synergy. The prefix "syn" of synthesis meaning with, to integrate and the "en" of energy means "separating out." Man is very familiar with energy, he has learned to separate out, or isolate certain behaviors of total nature and thus has become familiar with many of the separate natural behaviors such as optics. But the only partially isolatable behavior is always modifyingly employed by the whole. If humans had to purchase their many separate organs, stomachs, livers, endocrine glands, tongues, eyeballs, and bowels and thereafter to assemble those parts into logical interfunctioning, they would never do so. All those parts had to be preassembled and unitarily skinned in and coordinately operated by multiquadrillions of atoms in the brain which after sixteen years of practical spontaneous coordination becomes so aesthetically acceptable one to the other that as it sings, dances, and smiles one is inclined to procreate with the other.

Synergy is to energy as integration is to differentiation.

The word "synergy" means "Behavior of whole systems unpredicted by behavior of any of the systems parts." Nature is comprehensively synergetic. Since synergy is the only word having that meaning and we have proven experimentally that it is not used by the public, we may conclude that society does not understand nature. . . .

Our school systems are all nonsynergetic. We take the whole child and fractionate the scope of his or her comprehending coordination by putting the children in elementary schools—to become preoccupied with elements or isolated facts only. Thereafter we force them to choose some specialization, forcing them to forget the whole. We start them off with planes and straight lines which run into infinity which no scientist has ever produced experimentally and therefore we defy the child to comprehend, and require that they accept and believe that it is logical to assume "infinity" and therefore to give up the child's innate propensity to learn by experiment and experience, recourse to which exclusively experientially informed reasoning made possible Einstein's epochal reorientation of all scientific theory. We stuff our children's heads with such nonsense as straight, continuous surfaces and solids paying no attention whatever to the fact that science has discovered no solids, nor any continuous surfaces. Science has found only discrete energy packages such as the atoms whose electrons and nucleons are as discreetly remote from one another as is the Earth remote from the Sun. As a consequence of this theoretical mish-mash and our deliberate discard of the child's innate experimental techniques for self-teaching thereby, we find our world society looking askance upon its presently conjured, news-invented concept of its most prominent, inexorably developing fate with none of its predictions coming true and with all of the progenitors of the variously frustrated ideologies becoming progressively vindictive and intransigent. . . .

If the great design of the universe had wished man to be a specialist man would have been designed with one eye and a microscope attached to it which he could not unfasten. All the living species except human beings are specialists. The bird can fly beautifully but cannot take its wings off after landing and therefore can't walk very well. The fish can't walk at all. But man can put on his gills and swim and he can put on his wings and fly and then take them off and not be encumbered with them when he is not using them. He is in the middle of all living species. He is the most generally adaptable but only by virtue of his one unique faculty—his mind. Many creatures have brains. Human minds discover pure abstract generalized principles and employ those principles in the appropriate special cases. Thus has evolution made humans the most universally adaptable, in contradistinction to specialization, by endowing them with these metaphysical, weightless invisible capabilities to employ and realize special case uses of the generalized principles. . . .

We know scientifically that all local physical systems are continually giving off energies. We call this entropy. Due to each of the local systems' unique periodicities, and so forth, the given-off energies are diffuse and randomly released in respect to other systems. Thus the physical universe is continually expanding and increasingly disorderly. Fundamental complementarity requires that there must be some phase of universe where the universe is contracting and increasingly orderly. . . .

All the biologicals are converting chaos to beautiful order. All biology is antientropic. Of all the disorder to order converters, the human mind is by far the most impressive. The human's most powerful metaphysical drive is to understand, to order, to sort out, and rearrange in ever more orderly and understandably constructive ways. You find then that man's true function is metaphysical. Man's physical function is the same as that of all other biological life; to impound and regenerate physical life, which means inherently to produce reconstructive order of every variety. The metaphysical, absolutely weightless function in universe, unique to humans, is that of continually looking for the generalized principles which are operative in all the special case experiences. Thus has humanity discovered that it could move and constructively rearrange multiton rocks that man's individual muscle could not move. He succeeded by his weightless mind's discovery of the generalized principle of leverage. Thus also did mind discover the principles of electron conductivity, whatever that may be, for electromagnetics, though discovered and used by man, is as yet a fundamental enigma. . . .

I find man utterly unaware of what his wealth is or what his fundamental capability is. He says time and again, "We can't afford it." For instance, we are saying now that we can't afford to do anything about pollution, but after the costs of not doing something about pollution have multiplied manifold beyond what it would cost us to correct it now, we will spend manifold what it would cost us now to correct it. That is a geometrical compounding of inevitable expenditures.[1] For this reason I find that in satisfying humanity's vital needs, highest social priority must be assigned to the development of world-around common knowledge of what wealth is. We have no difficulty discovering troubles but we fail to demonstrate intelligent search for the means of coping with the troubles. This is primarily due to our misconditioned reflex which says that "we can't" afford to do the intelligent things. We discover with scientific integrity that wealth is simply the measurable degree to which we have rearranged the physical constituents of the scenery so that they are able to support more lives, for more days, at such-and-such standards of health and nourishment, while specifically decreasing restraints on human thought and action, while also multiplying the per capita means of communication and travel, all accomplished without increased privation of any human. Wealth has nothing to do with yesterday, but only with forward days. How many forward days, for how many lives are we now technically organized to cope? The numerical answer is the present state of our true wealth.

I find that our wealth consists exclusively of two fundamental phenomena: the physical and the metaphysical. The physical in turn consists of two subdivisions. One is the physical/energy associative as matter and the other is energy dissociative as radiation. After science discovered the speed of light, it went on to discover that when energy was lost from one system it was gained by another local system. It is never lost from the universe. Energy is inherently conserved, so the energy component of wealth cannot be depleted.

The other prime constituent of wealth, the metaphysical, is contributed by human intellect. Man's muscle has only a self-starter, button-

---

[1] Originally sidestepped because we believed erroneously that we "couldn't afford" their correction.

pushing function. Man's mind comprehends and masters the energy of
Niagara Falls. His muscle cannot compete with Niagara. Humanity's
unique function is that of his mind's ability to discover generalized
principles and to invent effective ways of employing those principles
in rearranging the physical constituents of the scenery to ever greater
metabolic regeneration advantage and metaphysical freedom of humanity. We discover that every time man makes an experiment, he
always learns more. He cannot learn less. We have learned therefore
that the intellectual or metaphysical half of wealth can only increase.
The physical cannot decrease and the metaphysical can only increase,
wherefore wealth, which results from the synergetic interaction of both
the physical and metaphysical, can only increase. Which is to say—
net—that wealth can only increase with each reemployment, and the
more intelligently and frequently it is reinvested the more rapidly it
increases. This is not disclosed in any books on economics. It is not recognized by the body politic.

So I say to you, man has acquired all the right technology within
only sixty years to amplify from less than 1 percent to 40 percent the
proportion of all humanity who are now economically successful with
the possibility of elevating all of humanity in ever greater degree within
another twenty-five years, all of which enabling technology humanity
said it couldn't possibly afford until the military said, "This is the way
your enemy is going to fight the war. You either acquire an equal or
better technology or die." To which the people responded, "Though
we think we can't afford it and though we don't know how we can
pay for it, if we have the energy resources plus the know-how and
human time to produce that technology we will go ahead and produce
it and find out later how to pay for it," not realizing that in investing
our time and know-how in producing it we were paying all that would
ever be realistically required to pay for it. The constituents belonged
in truth to no one. That physical phenomena which had originally
been commandeered by illiterate sword and gun seizure and had been
deeded thenceforth under guarantee of arms as property and that the
paper equity had been loaned out at interest and compounded arbitrarily as a debt imposed by law on someone did not alter the funda-
mentals of this situation. . . .

These generalized principles were all found to be operating a priori
to man. Man simply finds and employs. He does not put anything into
the universe. We must realize that technology was not put into the universe by man. The universe is the comprehensive system of technology.
Humanity is discovering and beginning to employ it. . . .

I would like to call your attention to a super piece of technology,
the sailing ship. The sailing ship going through the sea is unlike a bulldozer. The sea closes behind the ship. The ship does no damage to the

sea. The sailing ship employs the wind which is swirling ceaselessly around the earth without depleting any of the energy of the universe. This is a very beautiful piece of technology, no damage whatsoever to the environment. It is possible for all humanity to survive at higher standards than any have ever known while employing technologies that do no damage to the ecologically regenerative balance of the environment. It is possible for all humanity to prosper while employing only the natural energy income of wind, tide, sun, gravity as water power and electromagnetics of temperature differentials. We are not justified in using the energy savings account of fossil fuels where the energy-hour investment in their creation and storage would cost us today possibly as much as $1 billion a gallon figured at present kilowatt-hour generating rates. Having discovered that the function of man on earth is to impound and conserve energy, we find him operating antievolutionizarily in using the fossil fuel petroleum and coal for any other than minor self-starter functions when the rate of energy expenditure is negligible as compared to the rate of planet earth's energy storing.

The kind of technology that endangers is that occasioned by the blinders of specialization where each of our various acts are executed without consideration of the others.

So I think we are in an historically critical state of humans aboard space vehicle earth. I think we have been given adequate resources to absorb our many trial and error explorations for knowledge. We have been allowed to make a great mess of things—until now—in order that we might discover our great function. I identify humanity very much with the following analogy—as life is regenerated by the bird. The bird, in order to survive in flight has to take on very small energy increments in order to avoid being too heavy to fly. For reasons of this same flight-maintaining capability, the bird does not gestate the new life inside its womb, because the mother bird would become too heavy to fly to reach the insects to get enough energy to keep both the mother and the new life alive. So the new bird embryo is put in the egg, with all of the chromosomic instructions of how to design the bird's progressive organisms. All of the nutrients are stored inside the shell. The only thing the embryo needs further is energy as heat given off by the mother sitting on the egg in the energy-insulating nest. This design keeps the temperature at exactly the critical level to permit the mother bird's swift, food-gathering sorties from the nested egg.

The little bird develops beautifully inside. The mother is freed to do her flying tasks to gain enough food energy to keep the critical metabolic regeneration balance.

Finally, the little bird develops completely within the shell, having had just enough nutrient to do so.

The new little bird, exhausting the nutriment inside the shell, impulsively pecks at the eggshell, it breaks open, and there is the little bird, suddenly moving about on its own legs, beautifully prepared to operate on an entirely new basis.

I see that all humanity thus far has been guarded by such an innocence-tolerating nutriment which could sustain all the trial-and-error-won ultimate discovery that our muscles are as nothing beside the power of the waterfall and that the power-comprehending and -employing mind which can harness the gravity force of the waterfall to generate electricity and discover how to conduct that power to drive motors to do work anywhere . . . is our unique faculty.

We discover that we are essentially the weightless immortal mind which can comprehend and communicate and invent words and codify them in a dictionary, to implement the integrity of communication by noncontiguously existing humans. I think we are at that critical historical moment in which we have just broken our shell of permitted ignorance and henceforth we can survive only by learning to operate in our universe in a very different way. If we do not comprehend and behave spontaneously with the highest, most unselfish integrity, I think man may readily not make it on this particular planet. . . .

. . . If you are going to be wise . . . you are going to have to look at things in these big ways.

Alan Watts

the world is your body

We have now found out that many things which we felt to be basic realities of nature are social fictions, arising from commonly accepted or traditional ways of thinking about the world. These fictions have included:

1. The notion that the world is made up or composed of separate bits or things.
2. That things are differing forms of some basic stuff.
3. That individual organisms are such things, and that they are inhabited and partially controlled by independent egos.
4. That the opposite poles of relationships, such as light/darkness and solid/space, are in actual conflict which may result in the permanent victory of one of the poles.
5. That death is evil, and that life must be a constant war against it.
6. That man, individually and collectively, should aspire to be top species and put himself in control of nature.

Fictions are useful so long as they are taken as fictions. They are then simply ways of "figuring" the world which we agree to follow so that we can act in cooperation, as we agree about inches and hours, numbers and words, mathematical systems and languages. If we have no agreement about measures of time and space, I would have no way of making a date with you at the corner of Forty-second Street and Fifth Avenue at 3 P.M. on Sunday, April 4.

But the troubles begin when the fictions are taken as facts. Thus in 1752 the British government instituted a calendar reform which required that September 2 of that year be dated September 14, with the result that many people imagined that eleven days had been taken off their lives, and rushed to Westminster screaming, "Give us back our eleven days!" Such confusions of fact and fiction make it all the more difficult to find wider acceptance of common laws, languages, measures, and other useful institutions, and to improve those already employed.

But, as we have seen, the deeper troubles arise when we confuse ourselves and our fundamental relationships to the world with fictions (or figures of thought) which are taken for granted, unexamined, and often self-contradictory. Here, as we have also seen, the "nub" problem is the self-contradictory definition of man himself as a separate and independent being *in* the world, as distinct from a special action *of* the world. Part of our difficulty is that the latter view of man seems to make him no more than a puppet, but this is because, in trying to accept or understand the latter view, we are still in the grip of the former. To say that man is an action of the world is *not* to define him as a "thing" which is helplessly pushed around by all other "things." We have to get beyond Newton's vision of the world as a system of billiard balls in which every individual ball is passively knocked about by all the rest! Remember that Aristotle's and Newton's preoccupation with causal determinism was that they were trying to explain how one thing or event was influenced by others, forgetting that the division of the world into separate things and events was a fiction. To say that certain events are causally connected is only a clumsy way of saying that they are features of the same event, like the head and tail of the cat.

It is essential to understand this point thoroughly: that the thing-in-itself (Kant's *ding an sich*), whether animal, vegetable, or mineral, is not only unknowable—it does not exist. This is important not only for sanity and peace of mind, but also for the most "practical" reasons of economics, politics, and technology. Our practical projects have run into confusion again and again through failure to see that individual people, nations, animals, insects, and plants do not exist in or by themselves. This is not to say only that things exist in relation to one another, but that what we call "things" are no more than glimpses of a unified process. Certainly, this process has distinct features which catch our attention, but we must remember that distinction is not separation. Sharp and clear as the crest of the wave may be, it necessarily "goes with" the smooth and less featured curve of the trough. So also the bright points of the stars "gowith" (if I may now coin a word) the dark background of space.

In the Gestalt theory of perception this is known as the figure/ground relationship. This theory asserts, in brief, that no figure is ever perceived except in relation to a background. If, for example, you come so close to me that the outline of my body lies beyond your field of vision, the "thing" you will see will no longer by my body. Your attention will instead be "captured" by a coat-button or a necktie, for the theory also asserts that, against any given background, our attention is almost automatically "won" by any moving shape (in contrast with the stationary background) or by any enclosed or tightly complex feature (in contrast with the simpler, featureless background).

Thus when I draw the following figure on a blackboard—

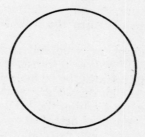

and ask, "What have I drawn?" people will generally identify it as a circle, a ball, a disk, or a ring. Only rarely will someone reply, "A wall with a hole in it."

In other words, we do not easily notice that all features of the world hold their boundaries in common with the areas that surround them— that the outline of the figure is also the inline of the background. Let us suppose that my circle/hole figure were to move through the following series of shapes:

Most people would thereupon ascribe the movement, the act, to the enclosed area as if it were an amoeba. But I might just as well have been drawing the dry patches in a thin film of water spread over a polished table. But the point is that, in either case, the movement of any feature of the world cannot be ascribed to the outside alone or to the inside alone. Both move together.

Our difficulty in noticing both the presence and the action of the background in these simple illustrations is immensely increased when it comes to the behavior of living organisms. When we watch ants scurrying hither and thither over a patch of sand, or people milling around in a public square, it seems absolutely undeniable that the ants and the people are alone responsible for the movement. Yet in fact this is only a highly complex version of the simple problem of the three balls moving in space, in which we had to settle for the solution that the entire configuration (Gestalt) is moving—not the balls alone, not the space alone, not even the balls and the space together in concert, but rather a single field of solid/space of which the balls and the space are, as it were, poles.

The illusion that organisms move entirely on their own is immensely persuasive until we settle down, as scientists do, to describe their behavior carefully. Then the scientist, be he biologist, sociologist, or physicist, finds very rapidly that he cannot say what the organism is doing unless, at the same time, he describes the behavior of its surroundings. Obviously, an organism cannot be described as walking just in terms of leg motion, for the direction and speed of this walking must be described in terms of the ground upon which it moves. Furthermore, this walking is seldom haphazard. It has something to do with food-sources in the area, with the hostile or friendly behavior of other organisms, and countless other factors which we do not immediately consider when attention is first drawn to a prowling ant. The more detailed the description of our ant's behavior becomes, the more it has to include such matters as density, humidity, and temperature of the surrounding atmosphere, the types and sources of its food, the social structure of its own species, and that of neighboring species with which it has some symbiotic or preying relationship.

When at last the whole vast list is compiled, and the scientist calls "Finish!" for lack of further time or interest, he may well have the impression that the ant's behavior is no more than its automatic and involuntary reaction to its environment. It is attracted by this, repelled by that, kept alive by one condition, and destroyed by another. But let us suppose that he turns his attention to some other organism in the ant's neighborhood—perhaps a housewife with a greasy kitchen—he will soon have to include that ant, and all its friends and relations, as something which determines *her* behavior! Wherever he turns his attention, he finds, instead of some positive, causal agent, a merely responsive hollow whose boundaries go this way and that according to outside pressures.

Yet, on second thought, this won't do. What does it *mean*, he asks himself, that a description of what the ant is doing must include what its environment is doing? It means that the thing or entity he is studying and describing has changed. It started out to be the individual ant, but it very quickly became the whole field of activities in which the ant is found. The same thing would happen if one started out to describe a particular organ of the body: it would be utterly unintelligible unless one took into account its relationships with other organs. It is thus that every scientific discipline for the study of living organisms— bacteriology, botany, zoology, biology, anthropology—must, from its own special standpoint, develop a science of ecology—literally, "the logic of the household"—or the study of organism/environment fields. Unfortunately, this science runs afoul of academic politics, being much too interdisciplinary for the jealous guardians of departmental boundaries. But the neglect of ecology is the one most serious weakness of modern technology, and it goes hand-in-hand with our reluctance to be participating members of the whole community of living species.

Man aspires to *govern* nature, but the more one studies ecology, the more absurd it seems to speak of any one feature of an organism, or of an organism/environment field, as governing or ruling others. Once upon a time the mouth, the hands, and the feet said to each other, "We do all this work gathering food and chewing it up, but that lazy fellow, the stomach, does nothing. It's high time he did some work too, so let's go on strike!" Whereupon they went many days without working, but soon found themselves feeling weaker and weaker until at last each of them realized that the stomach was *their* stomach, and that they would have to go back to work to remain alive. But even in physiological textbooks, we speak of the brain, or the nervous system, as "governing" the heart or the digestive tract, smuggling bad politics into science, as if the heart belonged to the brain rather than the brain to the heart or the stomach. Yet it is as true, or false, to say that the brain "feeds itself" through the stomach as that the stomach "evolves" a brain at its upper entrance to get more food.

As soon as one sees that separate things are fictitious, it becomes obvious that nonexistent things cannot "perform" actions. The difficulty is that most languages are arranged so that actions (verbs) have to be set in motion by things (nouns), and we forget that rules of grammar are not necessarily rules, or patterns, of nature. This, which is nothing more than a convention of grammar, is also responsible for (or, better, "goeswith") absurd puzzles as to how spirit governs matter, or mind moves body. How can a noun, which is by definition *not* action, lead to action?

Scientists would be less embarrassed if they used a language, on the model of Amerindian Nootka, consisting of verbs and adverbs, and leaving off nouns and adjectives. If we can speak of a house as housing, a mat as matting, or of a couch as seating, why can't we think of people as "peopling," of brains as "braining," or of an ant as an "anting?" Thus in the Nootka language a church is "housing religiously," a shop is

"housing tradingly," and a home is housing homely." Yet we are habit-
uated to ask, "Who or what is housing? Who peoples? What is it that
ants?" Yet isn't it obvious that when we say, "The lightning flashed,"
the flashing is the same as the lightning, and that it would be enough
to say, "There was lightning"? Everything labeled with a noun is
demonstrably a process or action, but language is full of spooks, like the
"it" in "It is raining," which are the supposed causes of action.

Does it really explain running to say that "A man is running"? On
the contrary, the only explanation would be a description of the field or
situation in which "a manning goeswith running" as distinct from one
in which "a manning goeswith sitting." (I am not recommending this
primitive and clumsy form of verb language for general and normal use.
We should have to contrive something much more elegant.) Furthermore, running is not something other than myself, which I (the organism) *do*. For the organism is sometimes a running process, sometimes
a standing process, sometimes a sleeping process, and so on, and in
each instance the "cause" of the behavior is the situation as a whole,
the organism/environment. Indeed, it would be best to drop the idea
of causality and use instead the idea of relativity.

For it is still inexact to say that an organism "responds" or "reacts"
to a given situation by running or standing, or whatever. This is still
the language of Newtonian billiards. It is easier to think of situations as
moving patterns, like organisms themselves. Thus, to go back to the
cat (or catting), a situation with pointed ears and whiskers at one end
does not have a tail at the other as a response or reaction to the
whiskers, or the claws, or the fur. As the Chinese say, the various features of a situation "arise mutually" or imply one another as back implies front, and as chickens imply eggs—and vice versa. They exist in
relation to each other like the poles of the magnet, only more com-
plexly patterned.

Moreover, as the egg/chicken relation suggests, not all the features
of a total situation have to appear at the same time. The existence of
a man implies parents, even though they may be long since dead, and
the birth of an organism implies its death. Wouldn't it be as farfetched
to call birth the cause of death as to call the cat's head the cause of the
tail? Lifting the neck of a bottle implies lifting the bottom as well, for
the "two parts" come up at the same time. If I pick up an accordion
by one end, the other will follow a little later, but the principle is the
same. Total situations are, therefore, patterns in time as much as patterns in space.

And, right now is the moment to say that I am not trying to smuggle
in the "total situation" as a new disguise for the old "things" which
were supposed to explain behavior or action. The total situation or field
is always open-ended, for

Little fields have big fields
Upon their backs to bite 'em,
And big fields have bigger fields
And so *ad infinitum*.

We can never, never describe *all* the features of the total situation, not only because every situation is infinitely complex, but also because the *total* situation is the universe. Fortunately, we do not have to describe any situation exhaustively, because some of its features appear to be much more important than others for understanding the behavior of the various organisms within it. We never get more than a sketch of the situation, yet this is enough to show that actions (or processes) must be understood, or explained, in terms of situations just as words must be understood in the context of sentences, paragraphs, chapters, books, libraries, and . . . life itself.

To sum up: just as no thing or organism exists on its own, it does not act on its own. Furthermore, every organism is a process: thus the organism is not other than its actions. To put it clumsily: it is what it does. More precisely, the organism, including its behavior, is a process which is to be understood only in relation to the larger and longer process of its environment. For what we mean by "understanding" or "comprehension" is seeing how parts fit into a whole, and then realizing that they don't *compose* the whole, as one assembles a jigsaw puzzle, but that the whole is a pattern, a complex wiggliness, which *has* no separate parts. Parts are fictions of language, of the calculus of looking at the world through a net which *seems* to chop it up into bits. Parts exist only for purposes of figuring and describing, and as we figure the world out we become confused if we do not remember this all the time.

Once this is clear, we have shattered the myth of the Fully Automatic Universe where human consciousness and intelligence are a fluke in the midst of boundless stupidity. For if the behavior of an organism is intelligible only in relation to its environment, intelligent behavior implies an intelligent environment. Obviously, if "parts" do not really exist, it makes no sense to speak of an intelligent part of an unintelligent whole. It is easy enough to see that an intelligent human being implies an intelligent human society, for thinking is a social activity—a mutual interchange of messages and ideas based on such social institutions as languages, sciences, libraries, universities, and museums. But what about the nonhuman environment in which human society flourishes?

Ecologists often speak of the "evolution of environments" over and above the evolution of organisms. For man did not appear on earth until the earth itself, together with all its biological forms, had evolved to a certain degree of balance and complexity. At this point of evolution the earth "implied" man, just as the existence of man implies that sort of a planet at that stage of evolution. The balance of nature, the "harmony of contained conflicts," in which man thrives is a network of mutually interdependent organisms of the most astounding subtlety and complexity. Teilhard de Chardin has called it the "biosphere," the film of living organisms which covers the original "geosphere," the mineral planet. Lack of knowledge about the evolution of the organic from the "inorganic," coupled with misleading myths about life coming "into" this world from somewhere "outside," has made it difficult for us to see that the biosphere arises, or goes with, a certain degree of geological and astronomical evolution. But, as Douglas E. Harding has pointed out, we tend to think of this planet as a life-infested rock, which is as absurd as thinking of the human body as a cell-infested skeleton. Surely all forms of life, including man, must be understood as "symptoms" of the earth, the solar system, and the galaxy—in which case we cannot escape the conclusion that the galaxy is intelligent.

If I first see a tree in the winter, I might assume that it is not a fruit-tree. But when I return in the summer to find it covered with plums, I must exclaim, "Excuse me! You were a fruit-tree after all." Imagine, then, that a billion years ago some beings from another part of the galaxy made a tour through the solar system in their flying saucer and found no life. They would dismiss it as "Just a bunch of old rocks!" But if they returned today, they would have to apologize: "Well —you were peopling rocks after all!" You may, of course, argue that there is no analogy between the two situations. The fruit-tree was at one time a seed inside a plum, but the earth—much less the solar system or the galaxy—was never a seed inside a person. But, oddly enough, you would be wrong.

I have tried to explain that the relation between an organism and its environment is *mutual*, that neither one is the "cause" or determinant of the other since the arrangement between them is polar. If, then, it makes sense to explain the organism and its behavior in terms of the environment, it will also make sense to explain the environment in terms of the organism. (Thus far I have kept this up my sleeve so as not to confuse the first aspect of the picture.) For there is a very real, physical sense in which man, and every other organism, creates his own environment.

Our whole knowledge of the world is, in one sense, self-knowledge. For knowing is a translation of external events into bodily processes, and especially into states of the nervous system and the brain: we know the world *in terms* of the body, and in accordance with its structure. Surgical alterations of the nervous system, or, in all probability, sense-organs of a different structure than ours, give different types of perception—just as the microscope and telescope change the vision of the naked eye. Bees and other insects have, for example, polaroid eyes which enable them to tell the position of the sun by observing any patch of blue sky. In other words, because of the different structure of their eyes, the sky that they see is not the sky that we see. Bats and homing pigeons have sensory equipment analogous to radar, and in this respect see more "reality" than we do without our special instruments.

From the viewpoint of your eyes your own head seems to be an invisible blank, neither dark nor light, standing immediately behind the nearest thing you can see. But in fact the whole field of vision "out there in front" is a sensation in the lower back of your head, where the optical centers of the brain are located. What you see out there is, immediately, how the inside of your head "looks" or "feels." So, too, everything that you hear, touch, taste, and smell is some kind of vibration interacting with your brain, which translates that vibration into what you know as light, color, sound, hardness, roughness, saltiness, heaviness, or pungence. Apart from your brain, all these vibrations would be like the sound of one hand clapping, or of sticks playing on a skinless drum. Apart from your brain, or some brain, the world is devoid of light, heat, weight, solidity, motion, space, time, or any other imaginable feature. All these phenomena are interactions, or transactions, of vibrations with a certain arrangement of neurons. Thus vibrations of light and heat from the sun do not actually become light or heat until they interact with a living organism, just as no light-beams are visible in space unless reflected by particles of atmosphere or dust. In other words, it "takes two" to make anything happen. As we saw, a single ball in space has no motion, whereas two balls give the possibility of linear motion, three balls motion in a plane, and four balls motion in three dimensions.

The same is true for the activation of an electric current. No current will "flow" through a wire until the positive pole is connected with the negative, or, to put it very simply, no current will start unless it has a point of arrival, and a living organism is a "point of arrival" apart from which there can never be the "currents" or phenomena of light, heat, weight, hardness, and so forth. One might almost say that the magic of the brain is to evoke these marvels from the universe, as a harpist evokes melody from the silent strings.

A still more cogent example of existence as relationship is the production of a rainbow.[1] For a rainbow appears only when there is a certain triangular relationship between three components: the sun, moisture in the atmosphere, and an observer. If all three are present, and if the angular relationship between them is correct, then, and then only, will there be the phenomenon "rainbow." Diaphanous as it may be, a rainbow is no subjective hallucination. It can be verified by any number of

---

[1] For this illustration I am indebted to Owen Barfield, *Saving the Appearances* (London: Faber & Faber, 1956).

observers, though each will see it in a slightly different position. As a boy, I once chased the end of a rainbow on my bicycle and was amazed to find that it always receded. It was like trying to catch the reflection of the moon on water. I did not then understand that no rainbow would appear unless the sun, and I, and the invisible center of the bow were on the same straight line, so that I changed the apparent position of the bow as I moved.

The point is, then, that an observer in the proper position is as necessary for the manifestation of a rainbow as the other two components, the sun and the moisture. Of course, one could say that *if* the sun and a body of moisture were in the right relationship, say, over the ocean, any observer on a ship that sailed into line with them *would* see a rainbow. But one could also say that if an observer and the sun were correctly aligned there would be a rainbow *if* there were moisture in the air!

Somehow the first set of conditions seems to preserve the reality of the rainbow apart from an observer. But the second set, by eliminating a good, solid "external reality," seems to make it an indisputable fact that, under such conditions, there is no rainbow. The reason is only that it supports our current mythology to assert that things exist on their own, whether there is an observer or not. It supports the fantasy that man is not really involved in the world, that he makes no real difference to it, and that he can observe reality independently without changing it. For the myth of this solid and sensible physical world which is "there," whether we see it or not, goes hand-in-hand with the myth that every observer is a separate ego, "confronted" with a reality quite other than himself.

Perhaps we can accept this reasoning without too much struggle when it concerns things like rainbows and reflections, whose reality status was never too high. But what if it dawns on us that our perception of rocks, mountains, and stars is a situation of just the same kind? There is nothing in the least unreasonable about this. We have not had to drag in any such spooks as mind, soul, or spirit. We have simply been talking of an interaction between physical vibrations and the brain with its various organs of sense, saying only that creatures with brains are an *integral* feature of the pattern which also includes the solid earth and the stars, and that without this integral feature (or pole of the current) the whole cosmos would be as unmanifested as a rainbow without droplets in the sky, or without an observer. Our resistance to this reasoning is psychological. It makes us feel insecure because it unsettles a familiar image of the world in which rocks, above all, are symbols of hard, unshakable reality, and the Eternal Rock a metaphor for God himself. The mythology of the nineteenth century had reduced man to an utterly unimportant little germ in an unimaginably vast and enduring universe. It is just too much of a shock, too fast a switch, to recognize that this little germ with its fabulous brain is evoking the whole thing, including the nebulae millions of light-years away.

Does this force us to the highly implausible conclusion that before the first living organism came into being equipped with a brain there *was* no universe—that the organic and inorganic phenomena came into existence at the same temporal moment? Is it possible that all geological and astronomical history is a mere extrapolation—that it is talking about what *would* have happened *if* it had been observed? Perhaps. But I will venture a more cautious idea. The fact that every organism evokes its own environment must be corrected with the polar or opposite fact that the total environment evokes the organism. Furthermore, the total environment (or situation) is both spatial and temporal—both larger and longer than the organisms contained in its field. The organism evokes knowledge of a past before it began, and of a future beyond its death. At the other pole, the universe would not have started, or manifested itself, unless it was at some time going to include organisms— just as current will not begin to flow from the positive end of a wire until the negative terminal is secure. The principle is the same, whether it takes the universe billions of years to polarize itself in the organism, or whether it takes the current one second to traverse a wire 186,000 miles long.

I repeat that the difficulty of understanding the organism/environment polarity is psychological. The history and the geographical distribution of the myth are uncertain, but for several thousand years we have been obsessed with a false humility—on the one hand, putting ourselves down as mere "creatures" who came into this world by the whim of God or the fluke of blind forces, and on the other, conceiving ourselves as separate personal egos fighting to control the physical world. We have lacked the real humility of recognizing that we are members of the biosphere, the "harmony of contained conflicts" in which we cannot exist at all without the cooperation of plants, insects, fish, cattle, and bacteria. In the same measure, we have lacked the proper self-respect of recognizing that I, the individual organism, am a structure of such fabulous ingenuity that it calls the whole universe into being. In the act of putting everything at a distance so as to describe and control it, we have orphaned ourselves both from the surrounding world and from our own bodies—leaving "I" as a dis*content*ed and alienated spook, anxious, guilty, unrelated, and alone.

We have attained a view of the world and a type of sanity which is dried-out like a rusty beer-can on the beach. It is a world of *objects*, of nothing-buts as ordinary as a formica table with chromium fittings. We find it immensely reassuring—except that it won't stay put, and must therefore be defended even at the cost of scouring the whole planet back to a nice clean rock. For life is, after all, a rather messy and gooey accident in our basically geological universe. "If a man's son ask for bread, will he give him a stone?" The answer is probably, "Yes."

Yet this is no quarrel with scientific thinking, which, as of this date, has gone far, far beyond Newtonian billiards and the myth of the Fully Automatic, mechanical universe of mere objects. That was where science really got its start, but in accordance with William Blake's principle that "The fool who *persists* in his folly will become wise," the persistent scientist is the first to realize the obsolescence of old models of the world. Open a good, standard textbook on quantum theory:

> . . . the world cannot be analyzed correctly into distinct parts; instead, it must be regarded as an indivisible unit in which separate parts appear as valid approximations only in the classical [i.e., Newtonian] limit. . . . Thus, at the quantum level of accuracy, an object does not have any "intrinsic" properties (for instance, wave or particle) belonging to itself alone; instead, it shares all its properties mutually and indivisibly with the systems with which it interacts. Moreover, because a given object, such as an electron, interacts at different times with different systems that bring out different potentialities, it undergoes . . . continual transformation between the various forms (for instance, wave or particle form) in which it can manifest itself.
>
> Although such fluidity and dependence of form on the environment have not been found, before the advent of quantum theory, at the level of elementary particles in physics, they are not uncommon . . . in fields, such as biology, which deal with complex systems. Thus, under suitable environmental conditions, a bacterium can develop into a spore stage, which is completely different in structure, and vice versa.[2]

Then there is the other, complementary, side of the picture as presented by the eminent biophysicist Erwin Schrödinger:

> It is not possible that this unity of knowledge, feeling and choice which you call *your own* should have sprung into being from nothingness at a given moment not so long ago; rather this knowledge, feeling and choice are essentially eternal and unchangeable and numerically *one* in all men, nay in all sensitive beings. But not in *this* sense—that *you* are a part, a piece, of an eternal, infinite being, an aspect or modification of it, as in Spinoza's pantheism. For we should have the same baffling question: which part, which aspect are *you?* What, objectively, differentiates it from the others? No, but inconceivable as it seems to ordinary reason, you—and all other conscious beings as such—are all in all. Hence this life of yours which you are living is not

---

[2] David Bohm, *Quantum Theory* (Englewood Cliffs, N.J.: Prentice-Hall, Inc., 1958), pp. 161–62.

merely a piece of the entire existence, but is in a certain sense the *whole;* only this whole is not so constituted that it can be surveyed in one single glance.[3]

The universe implies the organism, and each single organism implies the universe—only the "single glance" of our spotlight, narrowed attention, which has been taught to confuse its glimpses with separate "things," must somehow be opened to the full vision, which Schrödinger goes on to suggest:

> Thus you can throw yourself flat on the ground, stretched out upon Mother Earth, with the certain conviction that you are one with her and she with you. You are as firmly established, as invulnerable as she, indeed a thousand times firmer and more invulnerable. As surely as she will engulf you tomorrow, so surely will she bring you forth anew to new striving and suffering. And not merely "some day": now, today, every day she is bringing you forth, not *once* but thousands upon thousands of times, just as every day she engulfs you a thousand times over. For eternally and always there is only *now,* one and the same now; the present is the only thing that has no end.[4]

[3] Erwin Schrödinger, *My View of the World* (Cambridge: Cambridge University Press, 1964), pp. 21–22.

[4] Ibid., p. 22.

Gary Snyder

poetry and the primitive:
notes on poetry as an ecological
survival technique

Bilateral Symmetry

"Poetry" as the skilled and inspired use of the voice and language to embody rare and powerful states of mind that are in immediate origin personal to the singer, but at deep levels common to all who listen. "Primitive" as those societies which have remained nonliterate and nonpolitical while necessarily exploring and developing in directions that civilized societies have tended to ignore. Having fewer tools, no concern with history, a living oral tradition rather than an accumulated library, no overriding social goals, and considerable freedom of sexual and inner life, such people live vastly in the present. Their daily reality is a fabric of friends and family, the field of feeling and energy that one's own body is, the earth they stand on and the wind that wraps around it; and various areas of consciousness.

At this point some might be tempted to say that the primitive's real life is no different from anybody else's. I think this is not so. To live in the "mythological present" in close relation to nature and in basic but disciplined body/mind states suggests a wider-ranging imagination and a closer subjective knowledge of one's own physical properties than is usually available to men living (as they themselves describe it) impotently and inadequately in "history"—their mind-content programmed, and their caressing of nature complicated by the extensions and abstractions which elaborate tools are. A hand pushing a button may

From Gary Snyder, Earth Household. Copyright © 1967 by Gary Snyder. Reprinted by permission of New Directions Publishing Corporation and Jonathan Cape, Ltd.

wield great power, but that hand will never learn what a hand can do. Unused capacities go sour.

Poetry must sing or speak from authentic experience. Of all the streams of civilized tradition with roots in the paleolithic, poetry is one of the few that can realistically claim an unchanged function and a relevance which will outlast most of the activities that surround us today. Poets, as few others, must live close to the world that primitive men are in: the world, in its nakedness, which is fundamental for all of us —birth, love, death; the sheer fact of being alive.

Music, dance, religion, and philosophy of course have archaic roots —a shared origin with poetry. Religion has tended to become the social justifier, a lackey to power, instead of the vehicle of hair-raising liberating and healing realizations. Dance has mostly lost its connection with ritual drama, the miming of animals, or tracing the maze of the spiritual journey. Most music takes too many tools. The poet can make it on his own voice and mother tongue, while steering a course between crystal clouds of utterly incommunicable non-verbal states—and the gleaming daggers and glittering nets of language.

In one school of Mahayana Buddhism, they talk about the "Three Mysteries." These are Body, Voice, and Mind. The things that are what living *is* for us, in life. Poetry is the vehicle of the mystery of voice. The universe, as they sometimes say, is a vast breathing body.

With artists, certain kinds of scientists, yogins, and poets, a kind of mind-sense is not only surviving but modestly flourishing in the twentieth century. Claude Lévi-Strauss (*The Savage Mind*) sees no problem in the continuity:

> . . . it is neither the mind of savages nor that of primitive or archaic humanity, but rather mind in its untamed state as distinct from mind cultivated or domesticated for yielding a return. . . . We are better able to understand today that it is possible for the two to coexist and interpenetrate in the same way that (in theory at least) it is possible for natural species, of which some are in their savage state and others transformed by agriculture and domestication, to coexist and cross . . . whether one deplores or rejoices in the fact, there are still zones in which savage thought, like savage species, is relatively protected. This is the case of art, to which our civilization accords the status of a national park.

Making Love with Animals

By civilized times, hunting was a sport of kings. The early Chinese emperors had vast fenced hunting reserves; peasants were not allowed to shoot deer. Millennia of experience, the proud knowledges of hunting magic—animal habits—and the skills of wild plant and herb gathering were all but scrubbed away. Much has been said about the frontier in American history, but overlooking perhaps some key points: the American confrontation with a vast wild ecology, an earthly paradise of grass, water, and game—was mind-shaking. Americans lived next to vigorous primitives whom they could not help but respect and even envy, for three hundred years. Finally, as ordinary men supporting their families, they often hunted for food. Although marginal peasants in Europe and Asia did remain part-time hunters at the bottom of the social scale, these Americans were the vanguard of an expanding culture. For Americans, "nature" means wilderness, the untamed realm of total freedom—not brutish and nasty, but beautiful and terrible. Something is always eating at the American heart like acid: it is the knowledge of what we have done to our continent, and to the American Indian.

Other civilizations have done the same, but at a pace too slow to be remembered. One finds evidence in T'ang and Sung poetry that the barren hills of central and northern China were once richly forested. The Far Eastern love of nature has become fear of nature: gardens and pine trees are tormented and controlled. Chinese nature poets were too often retired bureaucrats living on two or three acres of trees trimmed by hired gardeners. The professional nature-aesthetes of modern Japan, tea-teachers and flower-arrangers, are amazed to hear that only a century ago dozens of species of birds passed through Kyoto where today only swallows and sparrows can be seen; and the aesthetes can scarcely distinguish those. "Wild" in the Far East means uncontrollable, objectionable, crude, sexually unrestrained, violent; actually ritually polluting. China cast off mythology, which means its own dreams, with hairy cocks and gaping pudenda, millennia ago; and modern Japanese families participating in an "economic miracle" can have daughters in college who are not sure which hole babies come out of. One of the most remarkable intuitions in Western thought was Rousseau's Noble Savage: the idea that perhaps civilization has something to learn from the primitive.

Man is a beautiful animal. We know this because other animals admire us and love us. Almost all animals are beautiful and paleolithic hunters were deeply moved by it. To hunt means to use your body and senses to the fullest: to strain your consciousness to feel what the deer are thinking today, this moment; to sit still and let your self go into the birds and wind while waiting by a game trail. Hunting magic is designed to bring the game to you—the creature who has heard your song, witnessed your sincerity, and out of compassion comes within your range. Hunting magic is not only aimed at bringing beasts to their death, but to assist in their birth—to promote their fertility. Thus the great Iberian cave paintings are not of hunting alone—but of animals mating and giving birth. A Spanish farmer who saw some reproductions from Altamira is reported to have said, "How beautifully this cow gives birth to a calf!" Breuil has said, "The religion of those days did *not* elevate the animal to the position of a god . . . but it was *humbly entreated* to be fertile." A Haida incantation goes:

> The Great One coming up against the current
> begins thinking of it.
> The Great One coming putting gravel in his mouth
> thinks of it
> You look at it with white stone eyes—
> Great Eater begins thinking of it.

People of primitive cultures appreciate animals as other people off on various trips. Snakes move without limbs, and are like free penises. Birds fly, sing, and dance; they gather food for their babies; they disappear for months and then come back. Fish can breathe water and are brilliant colors. Mammals are like us, they fuck and give birth to babies while panting and purring; their young suck their mothers' breasts; they know terror and delight, they play.

Lévi-Strauss quotes Swanton's report on the Chickasaw, the tribe's own amusing game of seeing the different clans as acting out the lives of their totemic emblems:

> The Raccoon people were said to live on fish and wild fruit, those of the Puma lived in the mountains, avoided water of which they were very frightened and lived principally on game. The Wild Cat clan slept in the daytime and hunted at night, for they had keen eyes; they were indifferent to women. Members of the Bird clan were up before daybreak: "They were like real birds in that they would not bother anybody . . . the people of this clan have different sorts of minds, just as there are different species of birds." They were said to live well, to be polygamous, disinclined to work, and prolific . . . the inhabitants of the "bending-post-oak" house group lived in the woods . . . the High Corncrib house people were respected in spite of their arrogance: they were good gardeners, very industrious but poor hunters; they bartered their maize for game. They were said to be truthful and stubborn, and skilled at forecasting the weather. As for the Redskunk house group: they lived in dugouts underground.

We all know what primitive cultures don't have. What they *do* have is this knowledge of connection and responsibility which amounts to a spiritual ascesis for the whole community. Monks of Christianity or

Buddhism, "leaving the world" (which means the games of society) are trying, in a decadent way, to achieve what whole primitive communities —men, women, and children—live by daily; and with more wholeness. The Shaman-poet is simply the man whose mind reaches easily out into all manners of shapes and other lives, and gives song to dreams. Poets have carried this function forward all through civilized times: poets don't sing about society, they sing about nature—even if the closest they ever get to nature is their lady's queynt. Class-structured civilized society is a kind of mass ego. To transcend the ego is to go beyond society as well. "Beyond" there lies, inwardly, the unconscious. Outwardly, the equivalent of the unconscious is the wilderness: both of these terms meet, one step even farther on, as *one*.

One religious tradition of this communion with nature which has survived into historic Western times is what has been called Witchcraft. The . . . antlered and pelted figure painted on the cave wall of Trois Frères, a shaman-dancer-poet, is a prototype of both Shiva and the Devil.

Animal marriages (and supernatural marriages) are a common motif of folklore the world around. A recent article by Lynn White puts the blame for the present ecological crisis on the Judaeo-Christian tradition —animals don't have souls and can't be saved; nature is merely a ground for us to exploit while working out our drama of free will and salvation under the watch of Jehovah. The Devil? "The Deivill apeired vnto her in the liknes of ane prettie boy in grein clothes . . . and at that tyme the Deivil gaive hir his markis; and went away from her in the liknes of ane blak dowg." "He wold haw carnall dealling with ws in the shap of a deir, or in any vther shap, now and then, somtyme he vold be lyk a stirk, a bull, a deir, a rae, or a dowg, etc, and haw dealling with us."

The archaic and primitive ritual dramas, which acknowledged all the sides of human nature, including the destructive, demonic, and ambivalent, were liberating and harmonizing. Freud said *he* didn't discover the unconscious, poets had centuries before. The purpose of California Shamanism was "to heal disease and resist death, with a power acquired from dreams." An Arapaho dancer of the Ghost Dance came back from his trance to sing:

I circle around, I circle around

The boundaries of the earth,
The boundaries of the earth

Wearing the long wing feathers as I fly
Wearing the long wing feathers as I fly.

The Voice as a Girl

"Everything was alive—the trees, grasses, and winds were dancing with me, talking with me; I could understand the songs of the birds." This ancient experience is not so much—in spite of later commentators —"religious" as it is a pure perception of beauty. The phenomenal world experienced at certain pitches is totally living, exciting, mysterious, filling one with a trembling awe, leaving one grateful and humble. The wonder of the mystery returns direct to one's own senses and consciousness: inside and outside; the voice breathes, "Ah!"

Breath is the outer world coming into one's body. With pulse—the two always harmonizing—the source of our inward sense of rhythm. Breath is spirit, "inspiration." Expiration, "voiced," makes the signals by which the species connects. Certain emotions and states occasionally seize the body, one becomes a whole tube of air vibrating; all voice. In mantra chanting, the magic utterances, built of seed-syllables such as OM and AYNG and AH, repeated over and over, fold and curl on the breath until—when most weary and bored—a new voice enters, a voice speaks through you clearer and stronger than what you know of yourself; with a sureness and melody of its own, singing out the inner song of the self, and of the planet.

Poetry, it should not have to be said, is not writing or books. Nonliterate cultures with their traditional training methods of hearing and reciting, carry thousands of poems—death, war, love, dream, work, and spirit-power songs—through time. The voice of inspiration as an "other" has long been known in the West as The Muse. Widely speaking, the muse is anything other that touches you and moves you. Be it a mountain range, a band of people, the morning star, or a diesel generator. Breaks through the ego-barrier. But this touching-deep is as a mirror, and man in his sexual nature has found the clearest mirror to be his human lover. As the West moved into increasing complexities and hierarchies with civilization, Woman as nature, beauty, and The Other came to be an all-dominating symbol; secretly striving through the last three millennia with the Jehovah or Imperator God-figure, a projection of the gathered power of antinature social forces. Thus in the Western tradition the Muse and Romantic Love became part of the same energy, and woman as nature the field for experiencing the universe as sacramental. The lover's bed was the sole place to enact the dances and ritual dramas that link primitive people to their geology and the Milky Way. The contemporary decline of the cult of romance is linked to the rise of the sense of the primitive, and the knowledge of the variety of spiritual practices and paths to beauty that cultural anthropology has brought us. We begin to move away now, in this interesting historical spiral, from monogamy and monotheism.

Yet the muse remains a woman. Poetry is voice, and according to Indian tradition, voice, vāk (vox)—is a Goddess. Vāk is also called Sarasvati, she is the lover of Brahma and his actual creative energy; she rides a peacock, wears white, carries a book-scroll and a vīna. The name Sarasvati means "the flowing one." "She is again the Divine in the aspect of wisdom and learning, for she is the Mother of Veda; that is of all knowledge touching Brahman and the universe. She is the Word of which it was born and She is that which is the issue of her great womb, Mahāyoni. Not therefore idly have men worshipped Vāk, or Sarasvati, as the Supreme Power."

As Vāk is wife to Brahma ("wife" means "wave" means "vibrator" in Indo-European etymology) so the voice, in everyone, is a mirror of his own deepest self. The voice rises to answer an inner need; or as Bus Ton says, "The voice of the Buddha arises, being called forth by the thought of the living beings." In esoteric Buddhism this becomes the basis of a mandala meditation practice: "In their midst is Nayika, the essence of Ali, the vowel series—she possesses the true nature of Vajrasattva, and is Queen of the Vajra-realm. She is known as the Lady, as Suchness, as Void, as Perfection of Wisdom, as limit of Reality, as Absence of Self."

The conch shell is an ancient symbol of the sense of hearing, and of the female; the vulva and the fruitful womb. At Koptos there is a bas-relief of a four-point buck, on the statue of the god Min, licking his tongue out toward two conches. There are many Magdalenian bone and horn engravings of bear, bison, and deer licking abstract penises and vulvas. At this point (and from our most archaic past transmitted) the mystery of voice becomes one with the mystery of body.

How does this work among primitive peoples in practice? James Mooney, discussing the Ghost Dance religion, says

> There is no limit to the number of these [Ghost Dance] songs, as every trance at every dance produces a new one, the trance subject after regaining consciousness embodying his experience in the spirit world in the form of a song, which is sung at the next dance and succeeding performances until superseded by other songs originating in the same way. Thus a single dance may easily result in twenty or thirty new songs. While songs are thus born and die, certain ones which appeal especially to the Indian heart, on account of their mythology, pathos, or peculiar sweetness, live and are perpetuated.

Modern poets in America, Europe, and Japan, are discovering the breath, the voice, and trance. It is also for some a discovery to realize that the universe is not a dead thing but a continual creation, the song of Sarasvati springing from the trance of Brahma. "Reverence to Her who is eternal, Raudrī, Gaurī, Dhātri, reverence and again reverence, to

Her who is the Consciousness in all beings, reverence and again reverence. . . . Candī says."

Hopscotch and Cats Cradles

The clouds are "Shining Heaven" with his
different bird-blankets on

—HAIDA

The human race, as it immediately concerns us, has a vertical axis of about 40,000 years and as of 1900 A.D. a horizontal spread of roughly 3,000 different languages and 1,000 different cultures. Every living culture and language is the result of countless cross-fertilizations—not a "rise and fall" of civilizations, but more like a flowerlike periodic absorbing—blooming—bursting and scattering of seed. Today we are aware as never before of the plurality of human life-styles and possibilities, while at the same time being tied, like in an old silent movie, to a runaway locomotive rushing headlong toward a very singular catastrophe. Science, as far as it is capable of looking "on beauty bare" is on our side. Part of our being modern is the very fact of our awareness that we are one with our beginnings—contemporary with all periods—members of all cultures. The seeds of every social structure or custom are in the mind.

The anthropologist Stanley Diamond has said, "The sickness of civilization consists in its failure to incorporate (and only then) to move beyond the limits of the primitive." Civilization is so to speak a lack of faith, a human laziness, a willingness to accept the perceptions and decisions of others in place of your own—to be less than a full man. Plus, perhaps, a primate inheritance of excessive socializing; and surviving submission/dominance traits (as can be observed in monkey or baboon bands) closely related to exploitative sexuality. If evolution has any meaning at all we must hope to slowly move away from such biological limitations, just at it is within our power to move away from the self-imposed limitations of small-minded social systems. We all live within skin, ego, society, and species boundaries. Consciousness has boundaries of a different order, "the mind is free." College students trying something different because "they do it in New Guinea" is part of the real work of modern man: to uncover the inner structure and actual boundaries of the mind. The third Mystery. The charts and maps of this realm are called mandalas in Sanskrit. (A poem by the Sixth Dalai Lama runs "Drawing diagrams I measured/Movement of the stars/ Though her tender flesh is near/Her mind I cannot measure.") Buddhist and Hindu philosophers have gone deeper into this than almost anyone else but the work is just beginning. We are now gathering all the threads of history together and linking modern science to the primitive and archaic sources.

The stability of certain folklore motifs and themes—evidences of linguistic borrowing—the deeper meaning of linguistic drift—the laws by which styles and structures, art-forms and grammars, songs and ways of courting, relate and reflect each other are all mirrors of the self. Even the uses of the word "nature," as in the seventeenth-century witch Isobel Gowdie's testimony about what it was like to make love to the Devil— "I found his nature cold within me as spring-well-water"—throw light on human nature.

Thus nature leads into nature—the wilderness—and the reciprocities and balances by which man lives on earth. Ecology: "eco" (*oikos*) meaning "house" (cf. "ecumenical"): Housekeeping on Earth. Economics, which is merely the housekeeping of various social orders—taking out more than it puts back—must learn the rules of the greater realm. Ancient and primitive cultures had this knowledge more surely and with almost as much empirical precision (see H. C. Conklin's work on Hanunoo plant-knowledge, for example) as the most concerned biologist today. Inner and outer: the Brihadāranyaka Upanishad says, "Now this Self is the state of being of all contingent beings. In so far as a man pours libations and offers sacrifice, he is in the sphere of the gods; in so far as he recites the Veda he is in the sphere of the seers; in so far as he offers cakes and water to the ancestors, in so far as he gives food and lodging to men, he is of the sphere of men. In so far as he finds grass and water for domestic animals, he is in the sphere of domestic animals; in so far as wild beasts and birds, even down to ants, find something to live on in his house, he is of their sphere."

The primitive world view, far-out scientific knowledge and the poetic imagination are related forces which may help if not to save the world or humanity, at least to save the redwoods. The goal of Revolution is Transformation. Mystical traditions within the great religions of civilized times have taught a doctrine of Great Effort for the achievement of Transcendence. This must have been their necessary compromise with civilization, which needed for its period to turn man's vision away from nature, to nourish the growth of the social energy. The archaic, the esoteric, and the primitive traditions alike all teach that beyond transcendence is Great Play, and Transformation. After the mind-breaking Void, the emptiness of a million universes appearing and disappearing, all created things rushing into Krishna's devouring mouth; beyond the enlightenment that can say "these beings are dead already; go ahead and kill them, Arjuna" is a loving, simple awareness of the absolute beauty and preciousness of mice and weeds.

Tsong-kha-pa tells us of a transformed universe:

1. This is a Buddha-realm of infinite beauty
2. All men are divine, are subjects
3. Whatever we use or own are vehicles of worship
4. All acts are authentic, not escapes.

Such authenticity is at the heart of many a primitive world view. For the Anaguta of the Jos plateau, Northern Nigeria, North is called "up"; South is called "down." East is called "morning" and West is called "evening." Hence (according to Dr. Stanley Diamond in his *Anaguta Cosmography*), "Time flows past the permanent central position . . . they live at a place called noon, at the center of the world, the only place where space and time intersect." The Australian aborigines live in a world of ongoing recurrence—comradeship with the landscape and continual exchanges of being and form and position; every person, animals, forces, all are related via a web of reincarnation—or rather, they are "interborn." It may well be that rebirth (or interbirth, for we are actually mutually creating each other and all things while living) is the objective fact of existence which we have not yet brought into conscious knowledge and practice.

It is clear that the empirically observable interconnectedness of nature is but a corner of the vast "jewelled net" which moves from without to within. The spiral (think of nebulae) and spiral conch (vulva/womb) is a symbol of the Great Goddess. It is charming to note that physical properties of spiral conches approximate the Indian notion of the world-creating dance, "expanding form"—"We see that the successive chambers of a spiral Nautilus or of a straight Orthoceras, each whorl or part of a whorl of a periwinkle or other gastropod, each additional increment of an elephant's tusk, or each new chamber of a spiral foraminifer, has its leading characteristic at once described and its form so far described by the simple statement that it constitutes a *gnomon* to the whole previously existing structure." (D'Arcy Thompson.)

The maze dances, spiral processions, cats cradles, Micronesian string star-charts, mandalas and symbolic journeys of the old wild world are with us still in the universally distributed childrens' game. Let poetry and Bushmen lead the way in a great hop forward:

In the following game of long hopscotch, the part marked H is for Heaven: it is played in the usual way except that when you are finishing the first part, on the way up, you throw your tor into Heaven. Then you hop to 11, pick up your tor, jump to the very spot where your tor landed in Heaven, and say, as fast as you can, the alphabet forwards and backwards,

your name, address and telephone number (if you have one),
your age,
and the name of your boyfriend or girl-friend (if you have
one of those).

Patricia Evans, *Hopscotch*

suggested readings

Anthologies

Cooley, Richard A. and Wandesforde-Smith, eds. *Congress and the Environment*. Seattle: University of Washington Press, 1970.

Darling, F. Fraser and Milton, John P., eds. *Future Environments of North America*. Garden City, N.Y.: Natural History Press, 1966.

Schwartz, William, ed. *Voices for the Wilderness*. New York: Ballantine Books, Inc., 1969.

Shepard, Paul and McKinley, Daniel, eds. *The Subversive Science: Essays Toward an Ecology of Man*. Boston: Houghton Mifflin Co., 1969. The best of the anthologies.

Thomas, William L., Jr., et al., eds. *Man's Role in Changing the Face of the Earth*. Chicago: University of Chicago Press, 1956. A classic study.

Vayda, Andrew P., ed. *Environment and Cultural Behavior*. Garden City, N.Y.: The Natural History Press, 1969.

Books and Articles

Bookchin, Murray. "Toward an Ecological Solution." *Ramparts Magazine* (May, 1970).

Borgstrom, George. *Too Many: A Study of Earth's Biological Limitations*. New York: The Macmillan Co., 1969.

Cloud, Preston. "Realities of Resource Distribution." *The Texas Quarterly* (Summer, 1968).

Dasmann, Raymond. *A Different Kind of Country*. New York: The Macmillan Co., 1968.

Davies, J. Clarence III. *The Politics of Pollution*. New York: Pegasus, 1970.

Dubos, René. *Man Adapting*. New Haven: Yale University Press, 1965.

———. *So Human an Animal*. New York: Charles Scribner's Sons, 1968.

Edberg, Rolf. *On the Shred of a Cloud*. University, Ala.: University of Alabama Press, 1969.

Ehrlich, Paul R. and Ehrlich, Anne H. *Population, Resources, Environ-*

205

ment: Issues in Human Ecology. San Francisco: W. H. Freeman and Company, 1970.

Ellul, Jacques. *The Technological Society.* New York: Alfred A. Knopf, Inc., 1967.

Glacken, Clarence J. *Traces on the Rhodian Shore.* Berkeley: University of California Press, 1967.

Goodman, Paul and Goodman, Percival. *Communitas: Means of Livelihood and Ways of Life.* New York: Vintage, 1960.

Graham, Frank. *Since Silent Spring.* Boston: Houghton Mifflin Co., 1970.

Hersh, Seymour. *Chemical and Biological Warfare.* New York: Bobbs-Merrill Company, 1968.

Jeffers, Robinson. *Not Man Apart.* New York: Sierra Club–Ballantine Books, 1969.

Leopold, Aldo. *A Sand County Almanac.* New York: Oxford University Press, 1949.

McHarg, Ian. *Design with Nature.* Garden City, N.Y.: Natural History Press, 1969.

Marsh, George Perkins. *The Earth as Modified by Human Action: A New Edition of "Man and Nature."* New York: Scribner, Armstrong and Company, 1885.

Nicholson, M. *The Environmental Revolution.* New York: McGraw-Hill Book Company, 1970.

Novick, Sheldon. *The Careless Atom.* Boston: Houghton Mifflin Company, 1969.

Novick, Sheldon, ed. *Environment* (Formerly *Scientist and Citizen*). Best periodical on the subject. Especially strong on specific pollution problems.

Odum, Eugene P. *Ecology.* New York: Holt, Rinehart and Winston, Inc., 1963.

Paradise, Scott. "The Vandal Ideology." *The Nation* (December 29, 1969).

Vogt, William. *Road to Survival.* New York: William Sloane Associates, Inc., 1948.

Whiteside, Thomas. *Defoliation.* New York: Ballantine Books, 1970.